THE SPLENDID GRAIN

ALSO BY REBECCA WOOD

Quinoa: The Supergrain
The Whole Foods Encyclopedia: A Shopper's Guide

THE
SPLENDID
GRAIN

Robust, Inspired Recipes for Grains with
Vegetables, Fish, Poultry, Meat, and Fruit

Rebecca Wood

WILLIAM MORROW AND COMPANY, INC.
NEW YORK

It is the policy of William Morrow and Company, Inc., and its imprints and affiliates,
recognizing the importance of preserving what has been written, to print the books we publish
on acid-free paper, and we exert our best efforts to that end.

Library of Congress Cataloging-in-Publication Data

Wood, Rebecca.
The splendid grain / Rebecca Wood.
p. cm.
Includes bibliographical references and index.
ISBN 0-688-09766-9
1. Cookery (Cereals) I. Title.
TX808.W66 1997
641.6'31—dc20 96-1564
CIP

Printed in the United States of America

First Edition

1 2 3 4 5 6 7 8 9 10

COLOR INSERT DESIGN BY LEAH CARLSON
BOOK DESIGN BY ERIC BAKER DESIGN ASSOCIATES

For my beloved mother and father

For my family, especially Caroline, Karena, Jake, Alan, Judy, and Suzie

To my children, Roanna, Asa, and Elizabeth

And to all my other children, my students, and all those who bring joy to my life and instill in me confidence in the future

Acknowledgments

To THE COUNTLESS PEOPLE who have contributed to this book—both knowingly and unknowingly. First and foremost thanks to Maria Guarnaschelli for her vision of this book. Thanks to Harriet Bell and Gail Kinn for their confidence, enthusiasm, and support and to all the talented staff at William Morrow. To Judith Choate for her invaluable help in shaping the material. To Stephen Pool for his excellent preparation of the manuscript. Special thanks to Susan Derecskey whose careful editing brought my thoughts into focus and showed me at my very best.

For farmers, especially traditional farmers, throughout the world. To my farmer friends for their inspiration: Frank and Marjorie Ford, the Lundberg brothers, Ernie New, Bob and Mack Quinn, Wayne and Elizabeth Carlson, Roger and Patricia Wilkie, Emigdio Ballon, Wendall Berry, Tom and Lillian McCracken, Duane Johnson, O. J. Locheed, Anpetu Oihankesni, Paul Motsinger, and all the Santistevens.

For all the members of our community garden with whom sowing, reaping, and, yes, weeding together are fundamentally satisfying. Thank you Larry and Kathy Howe-Kerr, Sam Hamer, Bernadette Prinster, Kathy Bowman, Judy Diederich, Kevin Betts, Dea Jacobson, Mitch Gosney, Donna Vogel, Caroline Conway, Elizabeth Inskeep, and Deb Piontowski.

For my early teachers who quickened my passion for grain and the energetic properties of food and thus helped provide me with a lifelong direction: Michio and Aveline Kushi, the late Naboru Muramoto, Jack Worsley, Herman and Cornellia Aihara, Lino Stanchich, Wally Gorell, Susan Hillyard, Renée Greemore. And more recently, Paul Pitchford, Bob and Melanie Sachs, and Amadea Morningstar.

To my students who inspire me and who continually challenge me to more deeply understand and appreciate the healing properties of whole foods.

My life is abundantly blessed with monks and social activists who inspire me to walk my talk. Thank you Tich Nhat Hann, Richard Baker Roshi, Gerald and Gisela Weischede, Sogyal Rinpoche, Leslie Towser, Ruben Habito, David Levin, Tessa Beilecki, Pat Lewiter, Kathy Lentsch, Richard Rohr, David Denny, Beth Dadio, Vincentia Rooney, Marie Nord, Mary Vineyard Jordan, Thomas Crutcher, Susan Ryan, Pat and Ceil McGowan, Ross Quigley, Cadmon Whitey, Bev Goodrich, and Dykeman and Avis Vermileye.

For friends who have constantly shared food lore, laughter, and the warmth of their hearths with me, especially Barbara Pilcher and Peggy Markel. For Pam Bertin, Susan Carskadon, Angie Edge, Molly Greacan, Nance Farrar, Betsy Foster, Corinne Holder, TuAnh Holm, Deanna Jenne, Pam Olsen, Christine Palafox, Jane Randolph, Trish Scott, Carole Shane, Susan Sim, and Charlene Weidner, with each of whom a sisterhood was birthed in the kitchen.

Thanks to Chris and Penny Webster who require a paragraph unto themselves.

To the Grand Junction Sangha, Pam and Larry Clark, Paul and Lorraine Cooper, Paul Peterson, Jeanne Shallman, David Koos, Abbie Kay Marschner, Don Neal, and Gene Sacha.

To the children, women, and men at St. Martin's Day Shelter for the Homeless for teaching me about hunger. Confident that common sense food information had universal application, I've learned from these people that other needs take precedence. To St. Martin's staff and to all the disenfranchised.

To the grain malting meister Charlie Papazian and all my friends who sustain me with their laughter and presence: Laurie Walters, Gregory Sams, Buzz Burrell, Jeffrey Markel, Carolyn Ingals, John Clausen, Samuel Basler, David Rickard, Michael Rossoff, Mark and Johni Seagers, Mike Potter, Nancy Potter, Yvette and the late Jacques de Langre, Nina Sprecher, Ken Osborn, Stan Ludmer, Stephan and Kitty Schaffer, Inez Russell, and Bethyla Burns.

Over the years, I've relied upon the camaraderie, assignments, and critiques of fellow food professionals and magazine editors. Special thanks to Lorna Sass, Mark Bittman, Stephen Schmidt, Mark Blumenthal, Dan Seamens, Lenny Jacobs, Mark Mayell, Jan Hammers, Ron Dobrin, Deborah Willoughby, and Kiz Dennit.

Blessing While Cooking

All that I have comes from my Mother.
I give myself over to this pot.
My thoughts are on the good,
The healing properties of this food.
My hands are balanced, I season well!

I give myself over to this pot.
Life is being given to me
I commit to sharing, I feed others.
I feed She Who Feeds Me.

I give myself over to this gift.
I adorn this table with food.
I invite lovers and friends to come share.
I thank you for this gift.
All that I have comes from my Mother.

Luisah Teish
(from *Jambalaya*)

Contents

Introduction

I'VE ALWAYS LOVED GRAINS. As a child I spent hours lolling in meadows and on lawns, plucking blades of grass and nibbling on them—a simple beginning to what has become a lifelong passion. I was raised in Ogden, Utah, but my heart was with my grandparents in Tremonton, a small farming community in northern Utah. Weekends, school holidays, and summer found me in the warm embrace of those loving people. Grandpa had long since turned the family farm over to his son, but every day he would drive out to see how the crops were faring. How I loved those rides! He would drive the big green Buick through section after section of neighboring farmland out to our farm. "Now, look-a-here at the Hansons' barley," he'd say. "Look close and you'll see, compared to ours, theirs isn't up as well. We got ours in before them heavy spring rains." He'd tell me what each crop needed, how to know when to sow and when to reap. He instilled in me a lifelong love of the earth and its riches. When the corn was ripe, Grandpa would drive us out to those fields that had sweet corn planted along the border of the field (livestock) corn. His rheumatism kept him in the car, but he'd send me out carrying a gunny sack with instructions to fill it as best I could. Being alone in a cornfield is a truly awesome experience. It really does get as high as an elephant's eye and is almost as overpowering as the beast itself. Once when I was six or seven, I got lost in the maze of towering cornstalks. Only the sound of Grandpa's forceful honking led me back to the car. The memory still evokes not only awe but a sense of the vital energy of the earth.

Along with the bounty of the farm, our family's table as well as my grandparents' table was laden with the fruits of foraging and hunting. Mushrooms from the meadows, wild asparagus from the roadside, game, birds, and brook trout, and, always, my mother's fresh baked breads and desserts. Our cellar was filled with row upon row of preserves, home-canned fruit, grape juice, and apricot nectar. My parents and grandparents had great respect for our food. It was to be enjoyed and celebrated, abundantly shared, and never, ever to be wasted.

My introduction to grains other than those grown in Utah came in the mid-1960s when, after college graduation, I headed farther west and landed right in the middle of a cultural revolution. I had a job at the University of California Medical Center and my first apartment, on Haight Street in San Francisco, California. Quite unsure of myself, almost petrified in fact, I wandered through the streets of flower children, neatly dressed in my homemade business suit. My fear began to fade when I realized that those hippies seemed to be having more fun than I was. Determined to find out why, I mustered up my courage to ask. A lanky hippie called Howdy, as in "Howdy, my name's Howdy," told me the trick was to get high and stay high. Innocently I asked, "How?" The answer: "Eat brown rice."

I'd never heard of brown rice, but Howdy directed me to a local source. I found the hole-in-the-wall natural foods store and bought a pound of brown rice. I went home and proceeded to burn my first pot.

Soon hooked on brown rice despite that initiation, I moved to Boston, Massachusetts, to study Zen macrobiotic cookery with Michio and Aveline Kushi. Far more important than a knowledge of whole grains and how to cook them was the respect of the whole cooking process and of life itself that I acquired. As Aveline used to say, "A careful cook doesn't spill a single drop of water on the floor."

Over the thirty years since then, I've fed myself and my chosen family of friends and then my own loving family with whole grains. I've made bread once a week, enjoying forming and shaping the loaf, smelling the baking aromas, and, most of all sharing the loaf. Grains, more than any other food, invite this molding of a meal through your own energy and intent with the gift of sharing it with others.

Why do I specify whole grains? The answer is simple. A grain is more delicious when intact, rather than when polished, pearled, degermed, or refined. I subscribe to the late M.F.K. Fisher's observation in *The Art of Eating*, "All of them, whether tender or hard, thick skinned or thin, die when they are peeled . . . even as you and I."

Imagine planting some white rice and some brown rice. The grains that have had the germ and bran removed will rot. The intact grains will flourish. The germ contains the spark of life, and the bran gives shape and form to the kernel. Both germ and bran are concentrated sources of nutrients. When we consume any food, that food becomes us and we become imbued with its properties. That is why whole grains make us feel good and provide us with boundless energy.

Cooking with Whole Foods

Here are three things you'll find only once in this book: triticale, grain blends, and adjustments for high altitude cooking.

Triticale

A laboratory hybrid of wheat and rye, triticale (pronounced trit-uh-KAH-lee) was for many years touted as "science's gift to the world" because of its high protein content. It turned out to be a dud, however, and has all but slipped into oblivion. It does make an aromatic and tasty pancake, but I do not recommend it for bread.

Multiple Grain Blends

I pass on grain blends, be they twelve-grain breakfast cereals, seven-grain breads, or commercial blends of grain mixes. When I prepare a grain, I want its personality to shine so that it's delicious by itself. Occasionally, I'll combine two grains that take similar cooking times and techniques, like Job's tears or wild rice with brown rice, but multiple grain varieties, never. Their cooking times and techniques vary so greatly. To dump a bunch of different grains into one pot or one bread muddies their flavors and challenges the digestive system.

High-Altitude Cookery

Baking with refined flours and sugars requires adjustments for high elevations, especially with cakes and, to a lesser degree, breads. I assume this is because refined ingredients are one-dimensional in character and therefore fragile in performance. Whole-grain cookery is not fussy and does not require minute adjustments for high altitudes. If you bake at a high elevation, slightly reduce the amount of leavening. If the batter seems dry, increase the liquid measure by a few teaspoons. Allow a few extra minutes' baking time or, in the case of yeast bread and pies, increase the initial oven temperature by ten to fifteen degrees for the first ten minutes.

High elevation adjustments for a pot of whole grain are as easy as "use a little extra liquid and cook a little longer." I can't spell this out more precisely than that since cooking time also depends on how heavy the pot is, how much steam escapes during cooking, the temperature of the heat source, and your individual preference for a more—or less—moist grain.

The recipes in this book have been tested in my home kitchens (elevations ranging from 4600 to 7900 feet), by Barbara Pilcher at sea level, and in the homes of many friends and students at varying elevations.

Almost all peoples have revered a particular grain as their sacred mother, kept it at the heart of their diet, and made it central to their rituals. Even today grains remain the primary calorie source for most of the world. Wheat is the daily bread of the West, figuring into countless kitchen staples. Rice, corn, and oats present a most comforting familiarity at mealtime. In our fast-moving, multicultural society, however, other grains are gaining increasing visibility and significance. These enduring and diverse foodstuffs, now widely available in American markets, offer many new taste experiences. They afford the seasoned chef and the home cook alike the opportunity to prepare and enjoy authentic ethnic cuisine. For example, the Ethiopian bread injera is unremarkable when made from any flour but tef. The Bolivian tamale-like humita is unthinkable without quinoa.

The history of cereal grains is endlessly fascinating. Get to know what it is you are going to cook, the history of a food, where it originated, how traditional peoples used it in their daily diet, and how they used it for feasting. By knowing the story of a grain, its anecdotal past and the ancient names by which it is known, you can transpose its place in history into your life.

As members of the grass family, grains are the most complex and highly evolved plant species in that their fruit and seed are one and the same. (An apple, for example, where the fruit encloses the seed, is a more primitive plant.) The grasses are the most widespread plant species on the earth. And the most developed life form of the animal species, humanity, co-evolved with the grains. An examination of the human digestive system and teeth indicates that humanity evolved eating predominantly a grain-based diet.

I could have arranged this book in alphabetical order, starting with amaranth and ending with wild rice, but I chose to start with wild rice for two important reasons. First, because wild rice is the only uncultivated grain with commercial availability. To obtain other uncultivated grains you would have to hand harvest, thresh, and hull wild grass seeds. An inconceivable project—especially if you were hungry—since most wild grass seeds are minuscule. By contrasting an uncultivated grain to cultivated grain we can better appreciate the story of all grains.

The second reason is that wild rice is our only native North American grain. The people living in or having roots in the wild rice bowl bio-region feel a special affinity to this extraordinary grain.

Looking at grains by bio-region also provides added appreciation for grains. For example, I'm of northern European descent, and so rye and oats speak to my most distant roots, but corn is the grain of my bio-region. I certainly don't limit myself to eating or growing only these grains, but they do have special relevance for me.

After wild rice I move south to the other American grains: corn, mesquite, amaranth, and quinoa. Following the sun west to Asia, I go to buckwheat and millet in the north, to rice and

Job's tears in the south. Then to barley and wheat, which were first cultivated in the Near East, to rye and oats from northern Europe. Finally, sorghum and tef, which are from Africa. As it happens, the book opens and closes with one of the most flavorful grains and closes with another, for a tasty beginning and ending.

With the exception of buckwheat, amaranth, mesquite, and quinoa these foods are all members of the grass family. The seeds from these plants, or in the case of mesquite the seeds and pods, however, are commonly used like grains and are thus within the scope of the book.

Sometimes whole grains take a backseat to those that have been processed. In the intense heat of a Grand Junction, Colorado, summer, brown rice is just too warming and heavy, so I cook the lighter and blander white rice. I also sometimes combine white flour for lightness with whole-grain flour for flavor when baking cakes or airy pastries.

For those who have cooked primarily with wheat, discovering more than twenty whole-grain flours is like going from black and white to Technicolor. These whole-grain flours, like the grains from which they are made, carry their own rich flavor profile and unique characteristics. Any of the flours will make a tasty pancake or cracker, most will give you a fine muffin, and some will produce a delicate cake. Baking with whole-grain flours reveals the dramatic range of taste, crumb, and texture these flours can deliver.

Any whole grain can be dressed up for special occasions and be varied enough for satisfying everyday fare. I hope you'll find, too, that grain cooking is time saving, not the contrary as common misconception has it.

Soaking grains speeds up the cooking process. It also lets the flavors blossom and makes the nutrients easier to assimilate. Put the washed whole grain to soak (in the pot in which it will be cooked) in the morning; then when you come in from work all you need to do is turn on the stove and relax while dinner cooks itself. Note, though, that refined grains, such as white rice, bulgur, couscous, and grits, need little or no soaking.

Another way to speed the process, especially for the long-cooking grains, is pressure cooking. As steam loss is minimized in pressure cooking, a pressure-cooked grain needs less water and its flavors and aromas are more concentrated. As food expert Lorna Sass observes in *Recipes from an Ecological Kitchen,* "Since the steam is sealed inside, pressure builds and the internal temperature rises, increasing the boiling point from the standard 212° to 250° Fahrenheit. Under high pressure, the fiber in the food is softened and flavors mingle in record time." I recommend an enamel pressure cooker, such as a Silit available from Natural Lifestyle (see page 377).

With very little planning, you can make grains part of your daily diet. One pot of millet, for example, saw me through this day. My children relished it for breakfast with milk and honey, for lunch we fried it up in croquettes, and the leftover millet added interest to our dinnertime soup.

I never have a problem deciding which grain to cook. If time is short, couscous or quinoa beckon me. If it's freezing outside, my hand automatically reaches for a cold weather grain like buckwheat or oats. If I hanker for an exotic dish, then wild rice or Job's tears suggest themselves. Should we have a guest with wheat allergies, the non-allergen wheats, kamut and spelt, offer a special welcome. If one of my family is headed up the mountain for a rigorous hike, tef is a great endurance aid. Thanks to these splendid grains, it is easy to adapt everyday cooking to my family's specific needs.

In the mid-1980s first oat bran and then rice bran made headlines for their ability to reduce cholesterol. As the bran hoopla subsides, I hope common sense will prevail. We can all include rolled oats, brown rice, whole barley, and other grains in a healthful diet every day, rather than trying to make bran palatable in a variety of less healthful muffins or cereal concoctions. The United States Department of Agriculture's food guide pyramid, released in 1992, aptly depicts the foundation of a healthy diet as being the cereal grains. The pyramid sends the message that Americans should eat, by volume, more grains than any other type of food. A well-balanced diet is easy to attain if we make grains the primary source of nourishment supplemented with fresh produce, beans, and small amounts of animal foods (dairy products, eggs, fish, and meat) as their complementary secondary foods. Although the pyramid is a welcome acknowledgment of the importance of grains in a healthy diet, the USDA does a disservice by picturing highly refined grains, such as white bread and pasta and cold breakfast cereal, instead of high-quality whole grains, which provide the essential fiber, flavor, and the complete nutrition we need.

As a consultant in the natural foods industry, I've been fortunate to be at the ground level in the exploration of the uses for newly introduced (or reintroduced) grains. Some of the more recent discoveries, such as tef, spelt, kamut, quinoa, and sorghum, have been staple foods for centuries. Working with farmers in their fields to bring in a new crop and then seeing how a new grain will perform in the American kitchen is thrilling to me. The more deeply I know a grain and its history, the more appreciation I can bring to it in the kitchen and, I believe, the more pleasure it can provide at the table.

Since the early 1970s, I've taught cooking to people seeking a more healthful diet. At my cooking school, I try to convey to my students respect for the art of cooking and for the ingredients as well as for the land and the farmers from which those ingredients come. Whether in North America or Europe, my students experience how simple foods can offer the most fundamental nourishment. Together, we feel ourselves reflecting the old adage that wholeness is holiness.

Cookware

For best results, I advise cooking grains in lead-free earthenware or ceramic pots. Ceramic gives the most effective and beneficial heat for natural cookery. Beautifully crafted Japanese *nabe* and *donabe* pots come in a variety of sizes and types; they are a pleasure to look at and to handle. Clay bakers, such as Romertopf, are limited to baking; they require presoaking in water and high oven temperatures.

An Oshawa Pot, named after the Macrobiotic founder, George Oshawa, is a covered earthenware insert to place inside of a pressure cooker. I use it for brown rice, whole wheat and rye berries, Job's tears, steamed breads and puddings, and for waterless fruit and vegetable cookery (see page 377).

Glass and enamel are the remaining choices for nonreactive cookware. In this category heavy cast-enamel pots, such as Le Creuset, are superior because they retain and impart more heat than lighter weight pots. With proper care, these heavy pots will last for many decades. Enamel on steel, such as Chantal cookware, is also excellent quality but lighter in weight. The shoddy enamel on mixed metal pots from variety stores are easily chipped. Once chipped, enamel pots have to be discarded, otherwise enamel fragments find their way into your food and the pot's underlying metal core reacts with the food.

Glass tea and coffee pots are available for brewing beverages but are not suited for grain cookery. The popular Corning-Ware and VisionWare pots are a blend of ceramic and synthetic polymers. I do not recommend them.

Reactive Pots and Pans

Heavy-gauge stainless steel is the least reactive metal, but you should still remove cooked food from a metal pot as soon as it is cooked to minimize the metallic taste. Once stainless steel has been scratched through normal scouring, the leaching of flavor is more noticeable.

Cast-iron pots are good for quick breads, pancakes, crepes, and vegetables cooked on the stovetop or in the oven. Do not, however, cook an acid food in cast iron since the acid leaches iron from the pot. Buy cast-iron pots without a graphite coating.

I do not recommend cooking with aluminum or aluminum foil because it enriches your food with aluminum to the detriment of your health. Nor do I recommend cooking with cookware lined with Teflon or any other synthetic coating. These coatings contain toxic substances that react and/or chip off into your food. When dry heated, these polymers emit fumes that are lethal to parakeets. Parakeets or not, who needs noxious fumes in the kitchen?

For all of us seeking ways to help create our whole person, the good news is that the foods that can satiate our deep hunger are as near as our own kitchens. For me, the quest begins in the garden. There grow the grains and vegetables that are the base for most of our meals. I always favor seasonal and regional foods grown from heirloom seed. These ancient varieties have the greatest amount of vitality to impart.

I know that not everyone can have a garden, but what about a community garden? Our half-acre community garden, which would be a burden for just one family, amply provides nourishment for ten households. It's satisfying work, and it builds community ties to weed, sow, harvest, and celebrate the harvest's bounty with others. If gardening isn't your thing, at least put a pot of parsley on the kitchen sill and favor seasonal and local produce. Organically grown products are available in natural foods stores, farmers' markets, through mail order, and increasingly in supermarkets. Get to know what is available to you.

If your local natural foods store is at all like SunDrop Grocery here in Grand Junction, it's a feel-good environment that's filled with friendly customers and an informed and helpful staff. Shelves are laden with organic unrefined oils, juices, seasonings, and other carefully grown and packaged cooking aids. The produce section shines with bright, pesticide-free fruits and vegetables. The bulk bins are filled with high-quality beans, flours, seeds, nuts, dried fruits, and, of course, grains.

Full-service natural foods stores offer a variety of grains and, within a grain, a wide choice of products. Most farmers who produce grains for the natural foods market grow them as a table food rather than for refining or for livestock feed. In addition, many natural foods manufacturers and packagers buy directly from the farmer rather than through a broker or, in many instances, grow the product themselves, thereby ensuring excellent quality.

Back from the garden or home from the store, take a discriminating look at your kitchen. If it needs cleaning, make it shine. Foods cooked in a chaotic kitchen perpetuate chaos. Keep your storage area tidy and well marked. I use clear glass jars filled with the multicolored and textured grains and beans, I find they offer a feast for the eye. The grains I use most, such as kamut, quinoa, brown rice, blue corn, and tef, never make it to jars. I buy them in twenty-five-pound bags and simply open the top, scoop out what I need, then seal and tightly roll the top back down. I strongly recommend bulk buying to people who have a cool dark and dry storage area. The intact germ containing the essential fatty acids of whole grains will become rancid with prolonged exposure to light and heat. By contrast, any grain with the germ removed has a lengthy shelf life.

Although thousands of pounds of grains have moved through my kitchen, I have had

almost no problem with bug infestation. I believe this is because I deal with full-service natural foods stores with good turnover.

I grind all of my own flour as I need it. I wish that all cooks could do the same. The flavor and fresh taste are well worth the effort. A coffee or spice grinder turns out an acceptable flour from almost all grains in small quantities. A blender will reduce such soft grains as oats, buckwheat, quinoa, and barley flakes to a coarse flour. Some whole grain batters may be made by soaking whole grains and then using the blender to process the grains with their soaking liquid. If you become an enthusiast, you can purchase a small flour mill from one of the sources in the back of this book.

In the warmth of your kitchen, remember that in today's world, only a few are blessed with such comfort and abundance. Complete nourishment is made up of more than calories, vitamins, and minerals. It must come from whole, integral foods energized through loving preparation and consumed with appreciation and fellowship at the table. Call in family and friends. Light the candles. Give thanks. Tuck in a fresh linen napkin and share the foods you have reverently prepared.

I love to cook.
I love to eat.
I love to nourish others.
Join me.

NATIVE AMERICAN GRAINS

Wild Rice

Corn

Mesquite

Amaranth

Quinoa

Wild Rice

THIS MORNING I PUT ON a pot of hand-harvested wild rice for breakfast and headed out to the garden for soup ingredients. When I stepped back across the threshold with a basket of thinnings, my kitchen smelled like wild rice country, and for a moment I imagined I was in fragrant wetlands edged by deep green forests. The aroma of this aquatic grass, a complex blend of nutty sweet with a hint of spice, kindles an ancient memory of the movement of water, the change of seasons, the freshness of a breeze through tall grasses, of something wild and free. Wild rice (*Zizania aquatica*) is heady stuff.

Best of all is eating wild rice, which was called manomin, or good berry, by the Chippewa, Ojibwa, Menominee, and other Algonquin tribes. The delicate, complex flavors of manomin harvested from lakes and rivers are as pleasing as its aromas. Almost dry yet meltingly soft, the good berry is energizing. Eat one bowl and deep down you will feel substantially nourished. There's none of that looking for a little something more to nibble on that follows eating highly refined foods.

Our North American rice is stellar when hand harvested, the only truly wild grain that's commercially available. I wish that everyone could enjoy a bowl of the natural wild rice that's sitting in my kitchen right now.

The reason most people haven't tasted real wild rice is that more than 80 percent of all available wild rice is commercially grown, primarily in California. This tamed paddy rice is one of four hybrid varieties selected for responsiveness to petrochemical fertilizers, herbicides, insecticides, and fungicides as well as for ease of mechanical harvesting and factory production.

In contrast, the genetic base of manomin growing wild in the Great Lakes region is awesome. It adapted to this specific eco-niche over thousands of years and is able to endure harsh and varying environmental conditions. In addition, the gene pool of the grain varies from lake to lake and from river to river as a result of natural selection. As with fine wines, wild rice connoisseurs, both native and non-native, have their favorite varieties, which are harvested from a specific lake or river. While humans foraged wild rice, they never cultivated it or selected out those strains that were easiest to harvest. It remains wild.

Knowing the story of natural wild rice makes it easy to understand why it has a greater range of flavors and aromas than cultivated wild rice. Winona La Duke, of the Mukwado daim (black bear clan) of the Anishinabe Ojibwa, who lives on the White Earth reservation in Minnesota, says, "All that is around us is animate. As such it has spirit. I'm very careful when I harvest because I must reckon with that spirit. Because you are respectful when you harvest, this ensures that you are able to continue harvesting. The value of eating and harvesting the same way that our ancestors have done cannot be measured. Both spiritually and culturally it reaffirms those things which are ours and those things which make us strong as a community. We're not a wealthy people in terms of monetary income. We are wealthy in terms of our culture."

Today many native peoples in the wild rice bowl are under- or unemployed and rely upon foraging. Preserved berries, maple sugar, game, and wild rice are household staples. Many families harvest wild rice, reserve a year's supply, and sell the rest. "For my small household, it's myself and my two children," reports Winona La Duke, "I harvest 150 pounds of rice a year."

To appreciate the difference between hand-harvested and commercial wild rice, place a tablespoon or so of one rice in the palm of your hand and hold it a few inches from your mouth. Blow on the grain a couple of times so that your moist, warm breath might quicken it; then, hold the rice even closer to your nose and deeply inhale. Repeat with the second variety. Your nose will unerringly identify the one with the most character.

Comparing the harvest of naturally grown wild rice to commercial processing helps us appreciate the difference between the two. In the past, during the time of manomine-kegisis, the wild rice making moon, in late August and September, many tribes would gather at their harvesting lake for a month. These annual rice camps were like a big reunion or even a county fair. At the Anishinabe camp, the ricing chief would determine a good harvesting day and the birch bark canoes, each with two women, would head out. One would sit in the stern and propel the boat through shallow waters with a forked pole. The other would use two juniper sticks called "knockers" to harvest. She would bend the rice stems over the rim of the canoe and across her lap with one knocker and with the second one knock the grass so that the ripe grains would fall into the bottom of the canoe. On a good day, two women could harvest a canoe full of grain.

Today harvesting is accomplished by both men and women. Licensed non-natives who live on White Earth and Leach Lake reservations may also harvest if there's an abundant crop. Juniper knockers remain the favored hand-harvesting implement because of their light weight.

About four to six days following the first harvest, the patch is gone over a second time to reap the newly ripened grains. One patch may be harvested as many as six or seven times because wild grass seeds on the same stalk ripen over a span of several weeks. This is nature's guarantee for the continuation of the species and protection against a late spring freeze or an early fall frost. During the harvesting some grain falls into the water, thus assuring a crop for the following year.

The harvest of paddy-grown wild rice is radically different. When the greatest number of grains reach maturity the whole plant is cut down. Hybrid grains are selected so that all the grains mature at about the same time.

Traditionally, some of the just harvested rice would be submerged in bags in the lake until spring. As the ice retreated, the cache would be retrieved, the grain air dried, and then parched and eaten. I'm told that rice taken out of the lake in spring is the same color as when it was harvested in fall. In order to germinate, wild rice seed must lie dormant through a winter, under water, at temperatures under 40°F.

Much of the traditional rice, and all paddy rice, is fermented, or cured, immediately following harvest. Just-harvested wild rice has a 25 percent moisture content, which is too high to permit storage. The rice is piled in heaps, and the sun's heat triggers fermentation. The process deepens the grain's flavor, color, and aroma. Due to the lengthy fermentation period, sometimes two weeks, that California paddy wild rice undergoes, it becomes ebony black. The earthy hues of unfermented or lightly fermented wild rice range from an almost blond with a green tint to gray, tan, amber, sorrel, chocolate brown, and black. This demonstrates its wide genetic base and also its varying degree of maturity. The aroma of unfermented rice is similar to green tea; the more fermented it becomes, the more it smells like black tea. Prohibitions of some tribes to harvest each day only as much rice as could be processed the next day effectively limited fermentation.

In the traditional Anishinabe rice camp, after fermentation, the freshly harvested grains were parched by the sun or over low embers. Parching removes the green taste and heightens the grain's sweet and nutty aroma and flavor. In the past, to reach a similar end, freshly scythed wheat and other grains were gathered into sheaves and left in the fields for the sun to finish the ripening and drying process.

Robert Shimek, rice parcher for the Anishinabe clan of the Ojibwa who lives on the White Earth reservation, told me, "The rice from every lake is different, each patch is different." To determine its readiness, Shimek, who has worked rice for fifteen years, looks for "color, hardness, flavor, and the amount of rice beard that's left. I take about a teaspoon of rice out of the parcher, rub it between my hands to see how easy it is to hull. And I smell it. Sunfish, who taught me how to parch, used to say, 'When the lake smell is off of the rice, it's ready.'"

Shimek, who uses two wood-fired parchers and one gas parcher, reports that his native customers prefer the flavor of rice parched over the wood fire. The rice is toasted from two to four hours and brought down to a 7 to 8 percent moisture content, compared to 12 percent moisture for paddy rice. Mert Lego, of the Leach Lake Reservation, points out that at a lower moisture content the consumer is getting more rice, rather than water, for the dollar, and therefore more flavor. Also, the drier grain cooks up to be fluffier and more tender. Or, in Lego's words, "When it's done, it's just a fluff."

Todd Brown, of Fall River Wild Rice, a grower-member cooperative in Fall River Mills, California, tells me that while the big wild rice producers flash-toast their rice, all the co-op rice is slowly parched in the traditional manner. In northern California, Oregon, and northern Idaho some companies are producing organic wild rice that is traditionally parched.

Wild Rice
Selection and Storage

For the most satisfying and complex flavor profile, purchase organic hand-harvested wild rice from the Great Lakes region. Your purchase will also support the way of life of the Native American harvesters. Organic lake rice harvested by airboat would be my second choice. Organic paddy rice ranks next, followed by paddy rice that is traditionally parched. I don't recommend parboiled rice.

The color of wild rice ranges dramatically. The darker the color, the smokier and more fermented it tastes, but these flavors overpower the nutty, woodsy flavors. Once fermented and parched, some of the bran is scarified, or scratched off; this process produces a grain lighter in color, with a shorter cooking time. Try several varieties to determine what degree of color and of scarification you prefer.

There is no national industry standard for wild rice. California commercial rice is graded by length as long (giant), medium (extra-fancy), or short (select). Canadian and paddy rice tends to be longer grained than hand-harvested varieties. The length of the grain alone is not a condition of quality, but when the appearance of a dish matters most, the longer grains are more dramatic.

Because it is parched, wild rice has an excellent shelf life. Store it in a cool, dark, and dry place, preferably in a covered glass container, for one year.

Once parched, the grain needs to be hulled. At the rice camp, parched grain was placed in a shallow pit lined with deerskin. Children would "jig" the rice by dancing on the grains to separate the hulls from the kernels. The jigged rice was winnowed in a large basket until clean and then the feasting began. The first rice was—and among traditional ricers still is—featured in a Megwetch Manomin Feast to celebrate the harvest and to give thanks. Historically the crop was community property, with the harvest divided up according to agreement or social custom. No one, however, was allowed to go hungry for want of rice.

On the reservations, rice is now hulled in converted thirty-gallon drums fitted with paddles to rub off the hull. In commercial operations, the hull is removed by rubber rollers. In both operations, some of the bran will be cut into, or scarified, to shorten the cooking time. To the eye, scarified rice looks scratched, as if it has little nicks taken out of it. As the bran is flavorful, scarifying does reduce flavor.

Another variation of processing is parboiling. Most of California paddy rice is parboiled to create a uniform quick-cooking product that doesn't discolor the cooking water. Parboiling compromises the flavor and nutrients of the grain.

Today each package of rice harvested by the White Earth bands of the Minnesota Chippewa is dated with the year of harvest and the name of the lake or river in which it grew. Dave Reinke, of the White Earth bands, tells me that customers have their favorites and they request the same rice year after year. In a recent cooking class, my students sampled four different varieties of hand-harvested wild rice from four different lakes; they were amazed that such a range of subtle flavor differences could exist from lake to lake. Most of them favored rice from Tamarack lake, but naming a favorite wasn't easy.

In 1972 a non-shattering strain of wild rice was found by Harold Kosbau. It enabled paddy cultivation of what had been a truly wild grain. Commercial wild rice paddies flourished and, by 1977, paddy rice accounted for more than three quarters of all the wild rice sold. The Native American rice economy was devastated. The harvesting of this grain had been a major source of income to many Native Americans and others living in the Great Lakes region. In Minnesota, it became necessary for state law to regulate every aspect of the wild rice harvest in an attempt to safeguard the interests of the tribes against agribusiness, fluctuating water levels, and pollutants.

Unfortunately, there are no labeling laws and commercial wild rice continues to be marketed with brand names and art that suggest it is hand harvested. For example, the largest Canadian producer, Grey Owl, owned and operated by the Cree in northern Saskatchewan, correctly label their product organic and Indian harvested. Wild rice is neither traditional to these peoples nor to the area. The lakes are seeded with hybrid seed and harvested by airboat. While this rice is a superior commercial product, it is not hand-harvested wild rice.

It is odd that a basic food source of hunters and gatherers is considered epicurean. Rarity makes it so. Whether harvested by hand or machine, it takes about three pounds of seed to get one pound of marketable rice, a ratio reflected by its retail price. Its high nutritional worth, unique flavor, and generous volume when cooked more than make up for the high cost. Wild rice is a low-calorie, low-fat, fiber-rich carbohydrate, higher in protein, iron, niacin, and riboflavin than brown rice, corn, and hard red winter wheat. It triples in volume when cooked, and it takes only a small amount to give a distinctive character to a pilaf, stuffing, salad, or soup.

In fact, because it has so much flavor many people haven't tasted the real thing. According to Todd Brown, 70 percent of all wild rice consumed is blended with less costly rice. In the popular wild rice soups, pilafs, and mixes, the flavorful namesake is a token ingredient. Because this grain has such dramatic flavor, even a little bit flavors a blend enough so that you know you're not eating just rice. If you've never tasted wild rice, try a bowl of it the way the Native Americans still eat manomin in the Great Lakes region, cooked unto itself in water or corn silk tea.

Steamed Wild Rice

❧

Wild rice recipes usually suggest cooking with extra water and then draining off the excess. This is because liquid needs and cooking times vary widely, depending on the source of the grain and how it was processed. But draining off cooking liquid drains off flavor and nutrients.

Rather, use the box on page 23 to estimate the amount of water and time that's appropriate for your particular rice. This chart cannot be more precise because the width of the grain, its moisture content, and the degree of scarifying also determine cooking time. I recommend buying wild rice in quantity. Figure out the water to time ratio with the first pot, record it, and then refer to it for that supply of rice.

The grain is done when it is tender but not mushy and some of the grains have butterflied, or burst open. At this point, the liquid should be totally absorbed. If a lot of liquid remains, drain and reserve it for stock or just drink it all up. If only a little remains, cook the rice, uncovered, for several minutes, or until the extra liquid is evaporated. Then cover the pot, remove from the heat, and let the rice steam for five to ten minutes.

If, on the other hand, the rice is still hard and the liquid is already absorbed, sprinkle on a tablespoon or so of water and continue to cook until done.

I do not recommend presoaking wild rice as this step results in a curious and undesirable mix of some mushy and some crunchy grains.

Makes about 3 cups

1 cup wild rice

Water or stock

1 tablespoon unsalted butter or unrefined sesame oil

Pinch of sea salt

Put the wild rice in a bowl of cold water, scrub lightly between the palms of your hands for about 5 seconds, and pour the rice and water into a strainer to drain.

Combine the water, butter, and salt in a heavy saucepan over high heat and bring to a boil. Add the rice and return to a boil. Lower the heat and simmer, covered, until some kernels have puffed and split open with the pale inner core visible and most of the liquid has been absorbed. Remove from the heat and let steam, covered, for 10 minutes.

Fluff with a fork and serve. If not using immediately, put in a glass bowl, cover with a cotton cloth, and leave out at room temperature for up to 24 hours. Within 4 hours of cooking, use the wild rice in a salad. After that, use it in a soup, pie, stuffing, stir-fry, griddle cake, or tortilla.

VARIATIONS: Sauté ½ cup minced onion, ¼ cup chopped celery, and the rice in 1 tablespoon unsalted butter or extra virgin olive oil. Add boiling liquid and salt.

Add ¼ teaspoon ground spice of choice.

Add ½ cup chopped toasted nuts or seeds to cooked rice.

Replace ¼ cup water with an equal amount of white wine.

When the rice is about 10 minutes from being done, add whole kernels from one ear of sweet corn and continue to cook.

In place of stock or water use infused corn silk tea. For the tea, bring 1 quart of water to a boil, remove from the heat, and add ½ cup fresh corn silk or ¼ cup dried corn silk. Let steep for 10 minutes, then strain. Dried corn silk is available in the herb section of natural foods stores.

Autumn Soup of Wild Rice, White Beans, and Olives

❦

Stellar colors and flavors make this soup a standout. The flavors are from the mountains of central Greece and are a fantastic play of sweet, sour, salty, and pungent with a hint of bitter. Giant La Sal beans are an heirloom crop in my region, but any other large white bean will do. Prepare the peppers a day in advance to give them time to marinate.

Cut the peppers into a fine dice. Combine with the vinegar, 2 tablespoons of the olive oil, salt, and pepper. Cover and refrigerate for 8 hours.

Heat the remaining oil in a medium saucepan over medium heat. Add the leek, carrot, and celery and sauté for 5 minutes, or until soft. Add the rice, beans, stock, oregano, 1 tablespoon of the savory, salt, and pepper and bring to a boil. Lower the heat and simmer, covered, for 15 minutes. Drain the peppers and add to the soup. Stir in the olives. Taste and adjust the seasoning. Garnish with the remaining savory. Serve hot.

Serves 4

1 red bell pepper, roasted (see page 353), peeled, and seeded

1 yellow bell pepper, roasted (see page 353), peeled, and seeded

1 tablespoon red wine vinegar

4 tablespoons extra virgin Greek olive oil

1 leek, well washed and chopped

1 carrot, thinly sliced

1 stalk celery, diced

2 cups Steamed Wild Rice (page 9)

1 cup cooked La Sal or other white beans

6 cups rich Vegetable Stock (page 364) or Chicken Stock (page 366)

2 tablespoons minced fresh oregano

2 tablespoons minced fresh savory, thyme, or rosemary

Sea salt and freshly ground black pepper, to taste

12 Greek Amphissa olives, pitted

Note: Greek Amphissa olives are large, purplish black olives with a very sweet taste. They are available in Greek, Middle Eastern, and some specialty food markets. If not available, substitute kalamata olives.

Wild Rice and Sauerkraut Soup

Serves 4 to 6

1 tablespoon chili-flavored
  sesame oil

1 leek, well washed and chopped

1 clove garlic, minced

1 stalk celery with leaves, chopped

1 cup Steamed Wild Rice
  (page 9)

6 cups Vegetable Stock (page 364)

1 cup chopped sauerkraut, drained,
  storebought or homemade
  (see page 362)

2 tablespoons Sucanat or light brown
  sugar

Soy sauce, to taste

Sea salt and freshly ground
  black pepper, to taste

1 large organic egg

2 tablespoons minced fresh dill

When I learned that wild rice is cultivated in Hungary, I could almost taste sauerkraut soup enhanced with the ebony grain. I went to the kitchen, tried it, and found it as good as I'd imagined. I serve this in the spring and summer; the sour flavor is cooling and refreshing.

Heat the oil in a medium saucepan over medium heat. Add the leek and garlic and sauté for 5 minutes. Add the celery and sauté for about 3 minutes, or until it softens. Do not brown. Add the rice and sauté for 2 minutes. Add the stock, sauerkraut, Sucanat, soy sauce, salt, and pepper and simmer for 15 minutes. Remove from the heat.

Break the egg into a small bowl. Using half of the egg shell as a measuring unit, fill it with water and mix with the egg. While stirring constantly, slowly stir the egg mixture into the hot soup. Taste and adjust seasonings. Garnish with dill and serve hot.

Mango and Wild Rice Salad

❦

Mango's sweet perfume and lush flavor enhance the wildness of the rice; dill somehow seals this union. This salad makes a filling one-dish lunch. Or serve it as a side dish with any white fish or crab. Organic mango vinegar is available in most natural foods stores.

Cut the tofu into 1-inch slices. Bring the water to a boil over high heat and add the tofu. As soon as the water returns to a boil, remove from heat and drain well.

Put the tofu, vinegar, and miso in a food processor or blender and process until smooth.

If the cucumber is not organic peel it. Cut it lengthwise in half, remove the seeds, and chop it fine. Combine the cucumber with the rice, mango, walnuts, parsley, and dill in a large bowl. Stir in the tofu dressing. Taste and adjust the seasoning. Let stand for 10 minutes before serving. Arrange on bed of mâche or lettuce.

Serves 4

6 ounces firm tofu, packed in water

2 cups water

¼ cup mango vinegar

¼ cup white miso (see page 220)

1 cucumber

3 cups Steamed Wild Rice (page 9)

1½ cups diced mango

1 cup toasted walnuts, chopped

¼ cup chopped fresh parsley

¼ cup chopped fresh dill

Mâche or dark green leaf lettuce

Deborah Madison's
Wild Rice and Asparagus Salad

❧

Serves 6

1 pound asparagus

3 cups Steamed Wild Rice (page 9)

2 tablespoons chopped fresh chervil

2 tablespoons chopped fresh parsley

1 tablespoon black sesame seeds, toasted (see Note)

2 tablespoons sesame seeds, toasted

6 tablespoons fresh orange juice

3 tablespoons unrefined sesame oil

2 tablespoons unrefined roasted sesame oil

2 tablespoons tamari soy sauce

1 tablespoon rice wine vinegar

1 tablespoon freshly grated orange zest

1 tablespoon grated ginger

2 scallions, minced

2 cloves garlic, minced

4 cups mesclun, washed and dried

Note: Black sesame seeds are available in Asian markets and some natural foods stores and specialty food shops. If not available, substitute untoasted hulled sesame seeds.

When asparagus is in season, I splurge with this salad inspired by Deborah Madison, the innovative vegetarian cook and author. At other times, I substitute boiled daikon or artichoke hearts. This salad is great warm, at room temperature, or chilled. If you want to serve it warm, start with just cooked and still warm rice; make a little extra dressing as a warm grain absorbs more dressing than cold.

Snap off the tough ends of the asparagus and set aside for another use. Slice the stalks on the diagonal into thin pieces. Drop them into boiling salted water and cook for 1 minute, or until bright green and tender but still a bit firm. Rinse under cold water and drain well.

Combine the asparagus, wild rice, chervil, parsley, and both black and tan sesame seeds in a large bowl. Whisk together the orange juice, sesame oils, tamari, vinegar, orange zest, ginger, scallions, and garlic. Pour over the rice mixture and toss to combine. Line a serving platter with mesclun and put the rice on top.

Salmon, Wild Rice, and Huckleberry Pot Pie Topped with Biscuits

❦

Here in Colorado we regard huckleberries as a treasure because they grow above ten thousand feet, sparsely. One summer my children and I bought huckleberries for five dollars a pound on the shore of Montana's Flathead Lake. Unimaginable abundance! Nearby in Idaho's panhandle we saw organic wild rice growing in the lakes, and recalling salmon fishing in Idaho as a child, I imagined this pie. Once home I admit I substituted the more readily available supermarket blueberries, but in my mind's eye huckleberries they are.

Combine the stock, vermouth, and arrowroot in a small bowl. Set aside. Melt 1 tablespoon of the butter in a 10-inch cast-iron skillet and sauté the leek until soft, about 3 minutes. Add 2 teaspoons of the tarragon and sauté for 1 minute more. Scrape half of the leek mixture into a small bowl and set aside.

Add the garlic, mushrooms and ginger to the remaining leek and sauté for 5 minutes. Add the corn and sauté for about 3 minutes, or until almost cooked. Stir the arrowroot mixture and stir it in. Cook, stirring constantly, until thickened. Stir in the wild rice, hazelnuts, salt, and pepper. Mix well and remove from the heat. Gently fold in the huckleberries, salmon, parsley, and remaining tarragon. Evenly distribute the filling in the skillet and set aside.

Preheat the oven to 425°F.

Cut the remaining 4 tablespoons butter into ½-inch cubes. Mix the flour, baking soda, and salt in a large bowl. With 2 knives, a pastry blender, or your fingertips cut in the butter until the mixture is the texture of coarse crumbs. Add the leek and tarragon mixture, using a fork to work it in thoroughly. Pour in the buttermilk and stir just until a soft dough forms.

Drop the dough by the heaping tablespoonful onto the salmon pie, to decoratively cover its surface. Bake until just golden in color, 12 to 15 minutes. Set the skillet on a trivet on the table and serve hot.

Serves 4

1 cup Vegetable Stock (page 364) or Fish Stock (page 367)

½ cup vermouth

2 tablespoons arrowroot

5 tablespoons unsalted butter, chilled

1 small leek, washed and finely chopped

3 tablespoons chopped fresh tarragon

2 cloves garlic, minced

1 cup chopped portobello mushrooms

1 tablespoon minced fresh ginger

1 cup whole fresh corn kernels (see page 27)

2 cups Steamed Wild Rice (page 9)

½ cup hazelnuts, toasted

Sea salt and freshly ground black pepper, to taste

1 cup huckleberries or blueberries, fresh or frozen

2 cups cooked salmon

¼ cup chopped fresh parsley

2 cups whole wheat pastry flour

½ teaspoon baking soda

½ teaspoon sea salt

1 cup buttermilk or Clabbered Soy Milk (page 371)

Whitefish Stuffed with Wild Rice

Serves 4

1 fresh whitefish (about 3 pounds)

2 tablespoons unsalted butter

1 cup minced mushrooms
 (3 ounces)

2 shallots, minced

¼ cup diced red bell pepper

¼ cup walnuts

2 tablespoons sherry wine

2 cups Steamed Wild Rice
 (page 9)

1 cup fresh peas

2 tablespoons minced fresh chives

Sea salt and freshly ground black
 pepper, to taste

1 tablespoon fresh lemon juice

2 tablespoons chopped fresh parsley

Fresh, sweet whitefish from the clear lakes of northern Minnesota and Wisconsin is the logical choice of fish to accompany the native wild rice. If you can't find fresh whitefish, use sea trout, bass, or any local whitefish.

Clean the fish, leaving the head on if desired. Or have your fishmonger prepare a whole fish for stuffing. Wash and dry well.

Preheat the oven to 350°F. Grease a shallow baking dish.

Heat 1 tablespoon of the butter in a medium sauté pan. When warm, add the mushrooms, shallots, red pepper, and walnuts and sauté for 5 minutes, or until the mushrooms soften. Add the sherry and cook for 3 minutes. Stir in the wild rice, peas, and chives. Season with salt and pepper.

Sprinkle the fish, inside and out, with salt and lemon juice. Place in the baking dish. Spoon enough of the wild rice mixture into the cavity to generously fill but not overstuff it. Pat down to flatten slightly. Brush the fish with the remaining butter. Cover with aluminum foil. Place the remaining stuffing in a greased 1-quart casserole. Cover and bake with the fish but remove the stuffing 5 to 10 minutes before the fish is done. Bake for 30 minutes, or until the fish is cooked through and the stuffing is hot. Remove from the oven and let rest, uncovered, for 5 minutes. Carefully lift the fish from the dish and place on serving platter. Spoon remaining stuffing around the edge. Garnish with chopped parsley and serve hot.

VARIATION: Roll fresh whitefish fillets around the stuffing.

Mom's Wild Rice Stuffing

❧

This is the stuffing I've always had—and still have—at holidays. It will always mean home to me. Mom uses her home-dried "cherry raisins" from the garden and piñon which during my childhood we foraged. At times I have tried new flavors or different vegetables, but then I miss the familiar tastes and regret my experimentation. If it ain't broke, don't fix it. Thanks, Mom.

Cook the wild rice in the chicken stock as directed on page 366. Melt the butter in a large sauté pan. Add the onion and sauté for 2 minutes. Add and sauté the mushrooms, celery, parsley, sage, thyme, and celery seeds for about 3 minutes, or until the mushrooms soften slightly. Add the piñon, cherries, and water and simmer for about 4 minutes, or until the cherries are softened. Combine the sautéed vegetables with the cooked rice. Season with salt and pepper. When well combined, use to stuff poultry or game or as a bed for roasted pork or ham.

VARIATION: For an extra-rich stuffing, add the giblets to the cooking vegetables: Peel and discard the membrane surrounding the gizzard. Chop the gizzard, heart, and liver if organic. Add to the onion and sauté for 2 minutes.

Makes about 7 cups

2 cups wild rice

About 3 cups Chicken Stock (page 366)

1 tablespoon unsalted butter

1 onion, diced

1 ½ cups diced mushrooms

1 stalk celery, diced

2 tablespoons chopped fresh parsley

1 tablespoon minced fresh sage

1 teaspoon minced fresh thyme

½ teaspoon celery seeds

¼ cup piñon (pine nuts)

½ cup dried sweet cherries

½ cup water

Sea salt and freshly ground black pepper, to taste

Wild Rice and
Yellow Summer Squash

❦

Serves 4

*1 tablespoon unsalted butter or Ghee
 (page 359)*

1 teaspoon minced fresh ginger

1 teaspoon cumin seeds

1 teaspoon ground coriander

¼ teaspoon turmeric

1 clove garlic, minced

½ cup chopped shiitake mushrooms

*1 small yellow summer squash,
 scrubbed and chopped*

2 leaves kale, finely sliced

*2 cups Steamed Wild Rice
 (page 9)*

½ cup pumpkin seeds, toasted

*Sea salt and freshly ground black
 pepper, to taste*

Anpetu Oihankesni, a longtime friend of mine, told me about hand-harvesting wild rice in some sloughs off the Connecticut River north of Hatfield, Massachusetts. He went in with hip waders as the plants grew in a mucky bog. With each step he'd sink several feet into the mud. Slow going. The wild rice plants grew ten to twelve feet high and had, in Anpetu's words, "a strong presence about them." He'd grasp several stalks, place their bowing heads, heavy with grain, in a paper bag and shake. He harvested a quart or so, cured and parched it, and cooked some up. He called in a few friends, and they feasted on his harvest. Anpetu's favorite way of preparing wild rice is to cook it in a stock made of corn silk tea which makes it particularly sweet (see page 10). I too like corn-silk wild rice, especially in this spicy and multitextured dish.

Heat the butter in a small sauté pan. Add the ginger, cumin, coriander, and turmeric and sauté for about 3 minutes, or until the spices release their aroma. Add the garlic and shiitakes and sauté until limp, about 4 minutes. Add and sauté the squash for about 3 minutes, or until it starts to soften. Sauté the kale for about 5 minutes, or just until cooked. Add the wild rice and pumpkin seeds and sauté until heated through. Season with salt and pepper and serve.

Elderberry Blossom and Wild Rice Griddle Cakes with Hot Apple Syrup

❧

You won't find elderberry blossoms at your nearest convenience store, but these tart berries were an important food for Native Americans and a popular ingredient in homemade wines and jellies. Wild or cultivated, the elder bush is commonplace throughout North America (and in Asia and Europe), so I do hope you can try this recipe. One or two umbrella-like flower clusters will provide ample blossoms for this recipe. Here in western Colorado, the elderberry blossoms in early July; the bushes are found in woodlands, mountains, and yards with old-fashioned landscaping. I planted elderberry in the hedge around my garden because it provides food for birds—and because these pancakes are such a great pleasure to eat. Raw, the flowers and buds are unremarkable in flavor, but when cooked, they make these pancakes satisfyingly sweet without the addition of another sweetener; they give off an aroma like muscat grape.

S nip the larger stems from the blossoms and discard. Set aside ³/₄ cup blossoms.

Sift together the whole wheat and all-purpose flours, baking powder, salt, and nutmeg. Combine the egg yolk with the milk. Combine the wet and dry ingredients, stirring only until the batter is well blended. Beat the egg white until stiff. Fold in the egg white, wild rice, and elder blossoms into the batter.

Heat a griddle over medium heat and brush with butter. Pour ¹/₃ cup batter onto the griddle for each pancake. Cook until 1 side is nicely browned, turn, and cook the other side until browned. Continue cooking until all the batter is used, keeping cooked cakes warm. Serve hot with Hot Apple Syrup.

Serves 4

2 clusters of elder blossoms

¹/₂ cup whole wheat pastry flour

¹/₂ cup unbleached all-purpose flour

1 teaspoon baking powder

¹/₄ teaspoon sea salt

¹/₂ teaspoon freshly grated nutmeg

1 large egg, separated

1 cup milk or soy milk

¹/₂ cup Steamed Wild Rice (page 9)

Melted butter

Hot Apple Syrup (recipe follows)

Hot Apple Syrup

Makes 1 cup

1 cup natural apple juice

¹/₂ cup maple syrup

¹/₄ cup apple brandy

1 cinnamon stick (3 inches)

Combine all the ingredients in a medium saucepan over medium-high heat and bring to a boil. Boil, uncovered, for 15 minutes, or until slightly thickened. Remove from heat and serve hot. (The syrup will keep, tightly covered, in the refrigerator, for about 1 month.)

Wild Rice Tortillas with Poached Huevos Rancheros and Ginger-Peach Salsa

❦

Blending masa and wild rice was inevitable in my kitchen. These tortillas can be made with yellow or white masa, but for poached eggs I favor the blue. The blue-black tortillas with the white and gold egg on top and peach salsa on the side are spectacular. On school mornings, I make extra tortillas for my children's packed lunches.

Combine the wild rice, masa, chili, and cilantro and season with salt. Divide in six. With moistened hands, shape into flat pliable cakes. If the rice is moist, increase the masa by 1 tablespoon; if it is dry, add a tablespoon or so of water. Press with a tortilla press or roll between 2 sheets of wax paper (see page 59), and cook on a heated griddle for about 3 minutes on each side or until nicely browned. Or press and cook on an electric tortilla cooker. Wrap in a fresh towel to keep warm.

Pour 1½ inches of lightly salted water into a large skillet and bring to a boil. Reduce the heat to a simmer. Break an egg into a cup and gently slide the egg into the water. Do this with each egg. Cover and simmer the eggs for 4 minutes, or until the whites are set and the yolks appear cooked. Remove eggs, one at a time, with a slotted spoon and drain on a towel.

Arrange 2 tortillas on each serving plate. Place a poached egg on top and a dollop of salsa on the side. Garnish with a cilantro sprig. Serve hot.

Serves 4

1 ½ cups Steamed Wild Rice (page 9)

½ cup masa harina, preferably blue

1 tablespoon New Mexican chili pepper, roasted (see page 353), peeled, seeded, and diced

2 tablespoons chopped fresh cilantro

Sea salt to taste

4 large eggs

Ginger-Peach Salsa (recipe follows)

4 sprigs of cilantro

Ginger-Peach Salsa

Makes about 1 cup

2 ripe peaches

2 tablespoons minced scallions

2 tablespoons minced fresh cilantro

1 tablespoon finely minced fresh ginger

3 tablespoons fresh lime juice

2 tablespoons Sucanat or light brown sugar

$1/2$ teaspoon Tabasco Sauce, or to taste

Blanch the peaches in boiling water for 1 minute. Drain and refresh in cool water. Slip off the skins. Cut in half and remove pits. Cut into fine dice and combine with the remaining ingredients. Let stand for 1 to 24 hours before using. The longer the salsa stands, the mellower the flavors will become. Store, covered, in the refrigerator for up to 4 days. The salsa may also be frozen or home canned.

Wild Rice	Water or Stock	Time
1 cup		
$\frac{1}{2}$ inch long, variegated dark hues	1 $\frac{3}{4}$ to 2 cups	30 to 40 minutes
$\frac{1}{2}$ inch long, black	2 $\frac{1}{2}$ cups	45 to 55 minutes
1 inch long, variegated dark hues	2 $\frac{1}{2}$ cups	45 to 55 minutes
1 inch long, black	3 to 3 $\frac{1}{4}$ cups	60 to 70 minutes

Corn

ONE JUNE I WAS INVITED to the Zuni pueblo in remote western New Mexico for their summer rain dance. It was incredible to join these people in their ages-old ceremonies and to experience directly how central corn is to their lives. At sunset we walked to the outskirts of the pueblo to watch the men and boys of the Deer Lodge clan and the Mudheads return from their daylong pilgrimage. Since dawn they'd walked, most of them barefoot, to a sacred salt mine to obtain salt for the ceremony. Upon returning to the village, they would dance through the night and until noon the next day. At noon a food giveaway would end the festivities.

The men of the Deer Lodge clan were bedecked with eagle feathers, fox pelts, evergreen ruffs, tortoiseshell rattles, and elaborate turquoise rings, bracelets, belts, and necklaces. The unadorned Mudheads were in plain brown garb with their heads enclosed in extraterrestrial-looking brown masks. Chanting prayers and walking gingerly on blistered and sore feet, the men and boys entered the village single file, dust covered, sweat streaked, and bone weary. The villagers, lined up along both sides of the road, silently blessed them for their sacrifice by placing a pinch of blue cornmeal on the shoulders of each passing pilgrim.

A guest of the Deer Lodge clan matriarch, I was privileged not only to feast with them but also to help prepare posole, a traditional corn dish, for the second day's feast. On a starlit evening, we cooked the posole in the outdoor *horno*, an adobe and stone oven. As the men danced in the lodges, we clustered around the oven waiting for the juniper fire to heat the interior stones to white-hot. Then with a rake and shovel we scraped out the embers, slid in three five-gallon pots of posole, and sealed the door with mud. A wizened old granny in a cotton print bib apron oversaw the operation. At her side was her six-year-old great-great-grand-daughter, wearing a brightly colored embroidered apron.

The role of corn in Native Americans rites, prayers, and meals acknowledges the importance of what was their staple food. Long before the first white men came to the Americas, corn (*Zea mays*) was known to and grown by all of the Indian tribes between the St. Lawrence River and Lake Titicaca. Each tribe had its own name for it, but whether spoken by Inca, Aztec, Creek, Sioux, Crow, Mohawk, Iroquois, or Algonquin, the name for maize translated to "She Who Sustains Us," "Our Mother," "Our Life." For thousands of years, in hundreds of guises and in thousands of dishes, maize has endured.

Maize, the name by which corn is known almost everywhere except the United States, has been identified in fossil pollen dated from at least eighty thousand years ago. It is the only commonly used grain that is native to the western hemisphere. It is unlike other grains in that with its cob structure it has multiple grains enclosed in the husk rather than each grain, individually, contained in a husk. This unique structure makes corn dependent upon human cultivators for its propagation since corn kernels, unlike the other grains, cannot fall from the stalk and reseed themselves.

As with many other foods, you may assume that the darker and richer the color of a corn kernel, the more flavor it has. What is more, high flavor is an apt indicator of nutrient density. White corn has the blandest flavor, yellow corn has a corny, butter flavor, and blue corn has the widest range of flavor components. In commercial corn products, I favor blue corn. In my garden patch I favor multicolored corn. Blue and multicolored corn are typically open pollinated varieties that contain more protein and manganese than hybrid corn. Besides, an advantage of purchasing a colored corn is that you are getting an heirloom corn bred for culinary, not feedlot use.

Classified by the type of starch found in their kernels, there are five types (races) of corn, which may be any color of the rainbow. The three types of field or grain corn are dent, flint, and flour corn. While field corn is still in its soft, juicy "milk" stage, it is available throughout Latin American and in Southwestern pueblos roasted on the cob, in soup (see page 223), and in green corn tamales. Otherwise dent, flint, and flour corn varieties (and popcorn) are allowed to mature fully and dry on the stalk, a process that converts their sugar into starch. It is in the mature, dry form that field corn is ground or processed into our common corn products.

- Dent corn takes its name from the indentation that forms on the top of each kernel as it dries. It is the corn variety grown in the American corn belt, with 90 percent grown for livestock feed and the rest used primarily in commercial corn products, from corn sweeteners to breakfast cereal.

- Flint corn has a hard shell and starch that make it, as its name suggests, difficult to grind. Flint kernels are rounded and, like popcorn, the color is translucent rather than opaque and permeates the whole kernel. Dried colored corn used decoratively is usually flint corn. Otherwise flint corn's commercial availability is limited to a yellow flint corn brought to Europe in the 1500s. Polenta, a coarse flint corn meal, cooks up into a firm mush called *polenta* in Italy, *mamaliga* in Romania, and *puliszka* in Hungary. Polenta has such an extraordinarily high beta-carotene content that its color is a vivid yellow-orange. Although you may make cornmeal mush from dent or flour cornmeal, it is flint corn that gives authentic polenta its soft but never mushy texture.

  Posole, also known as hominy, nixtamal, and samp, is made of either flint or dent corn kernels. Traditionally dried corn is cooked in a bath of ashes or slaked lime long enough to loosen the hull. Today's commercial posole is boiled in a solution of water and sodium hydroxide to achieve the same result. The hulls and germ are then washed from the plumped kernels. This wet posole may be canned, frozen, ground into fresh masa, or dried for later reconstitution or grinding. Whole posole is traditionally used in soups, stews, or as a side dish; I also enjoy it in a salad.

  Masa is dough ground from just cooked posole. Although the Spanish word *masa* literally means "dough," when applied to Mexican, Southwestern, and Native American cooking it means dough made from slaked corn. Masa harina is dried posole meal. Tortillas and tamales are made from either dried or fresh masa.

- Flour corn has a smooth rounded crown (like flint and popcorn) and a soft starch which makes it easy to grind into flour. Unlike flint or dent corn, a kernel of flour corn can be easily sliced in half with a kitchen knife. Although the exterior of the kernels may, as in other types of corn, be variously colored, the interior is almost always white. Flour corn, as its name suggests, is used exclusively for corn flour, cornmeal, and pinole. Pinole is a fine whole corn flour made of an especially soft flour corn variety; it is used in corn beverages and atole.

- Popcorn is the original corn "pod" in which each seed was enclosed in its own husk. In fact, popped corn, carbon dated from 2300 B.C., has been found in a cave in New Mexico. Modern popcorn has a husk that envelops the whole ear and is typified by a hard hull and endosperm that seals in the moisture content. Popcorn kernels are small, pointy, and translucent. About 14 percent of the kernel is water, which turns to steam when the corn is heated and causes the explosion, or popping, into a white flower.

- Sweet corn is consumed as a vegetable in its immature, or green, stage rather than as a

Corn
Selection and Storage

If your use of corn products has been limited, possibly it's because you've not had the pleasure of flavorful whole-corn products. Even more than with wheat, degerminated corn is a vapid, flat product with little flavor. (The germ of wheat is 2 percent of its volume, whereas the germ of corn is 11.5 percent of its volume.)

Whole Field Corn
(Flint, Flour, and Dent)

If you have a flour mill or want to make posole, then you'll be in the market for whole-grain corn, and the only place to find it is a well-stocked natural foods store or by mail order. Favor a flour corn for cornmeal, corn flour, or a corn beverage (dent and flint corn may be substituted). Use only dent or flint corn to make posole from scratch. Select flint corn for making the meal for polenta or Rhode Island cornmeal mush.

Stored tightly wrapped in a cool, dark, and dry place, whole corn keeps well for several years.

Corn Flour, Cornmeal, and
Corn Grits

These are different only in particle size and may be ground from whole or from degerminated corn. Always favor freshly ground (preferably stoneground) whole-grain cornmeal and flour for their sweet full-flavor corn taste. Stoneground meals absorb liquid more slowly and so require longer cooking. If the taste is flat or bitter, the whole-corn product is old and should be discarded. If low in flavor—and therefore nutrients—it is made from hulled degerminated corn.

Corn flour is almost as fine as white wheat flour and best used in corn beverages, cakes, and cookies. Corn flour is not to be confused with cornstarch, a highly processed thickening agent, which is called corn flour in the United Kingdom.

Cornmeal is coarsely ground and yields a granular crumb. It may be coarse or fine; preferences for texture depend on regional tastes.

High-lysine cornmeal, a new hybrid dent corn, improves corn's amino acid balance to make a more complete protein. Available through Arrowhead Mills (see page 377), high-lysine cornmeal has a nutty, sweet flavor and a longer shelf life than other whole-grain cornmeals.

Corn grits, also called hominy grits even though they're not made from hominy, are the coarsest grind of whole or degerminated corn; they are used for porridge. While refined grits are available in quick-cooking and instant-cooking forms, the most flavorful are coarse stoneground grits, speckled with bits of germ and bran.

To store whole-grain corn flour, cornmeal, and grits, wrap tightly and place in the freezer for up to 6 months. According to Linda Glenn, consumer specialist of Arrowhead Mills, corn flour and cornmeal are best frozen. When refrigerated, condensation occurs in the package, and this may lead to the formation of mold. Grits made from whole corn may be refrigerated or frozen. Flour, meal, or grits from degerminated corn may be stored, tightly wrapped, on a pantry shelf indefinitely.

Corn is one of the harder and more difficult grains to grind. A stone flour mill is preferred, though for small quantities you may use a spice or coffee grinder.

Posole

Also called hominy, posole is widely available. You'll find dried posole in supermarkets, variety stores such as WalMart and Kmart, natural foods stores, and Latino food stores. Store dried posole, airtight, in a cool, dark, and dry area for several years. Frozen posole is available in supermarkets and Latino food stores. Canned posole, which I do not recommend because the flavor of the can masks the posole's flavor, is widely available.

Freshly Ground Masa

This product is found frozen in some supermarkets and Latino food stores. It is available in two grades, fine (masa para tortillas) and coarse (masa para tamales). Keep frozen until ready to use for up to 3 months.

Masa Harina

This is flour ground from dried posole. Organic masa is available from Col. Sanchez Foods (see page 376) in both blue and yellow. The supermarket brands, Maseca, Ricamasa, and Quaker, come in only white. Store masa harina in a closed container in a cool, dark, and dry area for up to 1 year.

Pinole

A fine corn flour, pinole is available in Latino markets, natural foods stores, and some specialty markets. It comes packaged in small (2 to 3 ounces) quantities. When made from the whole grain, it tastes fresh and sweet, has a finite shelf life, and should be refrigerated or frozen until use. If it has a flat, stale taste, it is rancid and should be discarded.

Polenta

Made of ground flint corn and imported from Italy, polenta meal is available in grades coarse and fine. The coarse grind makes a firmer, more tasty polenta. Both have been hulled and degermed and so have a long shelf life. Store, tightly wrapped, in a cool, dark cupboard. Domestic cornmeal or grits available in natural foods stores are sometimes mistakenly labeled polenta, but are not made of flint corn and yield a mushy polenta. A bright yellow color indicates an authentic polenta. If you have flint corn and a grain mill, you may grind your own polenta.

Popcorn

Organic popcorn from the bulk bin of your natural foods store is the best. While yellow popcorn is the most commonly available popcorn, you may sometimes find red, white, or blue. Once popped, this corn is mostly air and so the flavor nuances between popcorn colors are elusive. The blue, however, has a delicate bluish tint. Store popcorn airtight in a cool, dark, and dry place. For dehydrated popcorn with a high percentage of kernels that don't pop, add 1 teaspoon of water for every 2 cups of unpopped corn and seal the jar. Within a few days the corn will be rehydrated.

cereal grain. It is what most of us think of as corn. Once the corn is picked, its sugar begins to convert to starch, and the kernels become tough, dry, and less sweet. An ear of traditional sweet corn contains 14 percent sucrose, comparable to an apple. The recently developed supersweet corn varieties contain a whopping 36 percent sucrose. They are bred with a recessive gene that blocks the normal sugar-to-starch transformation. This means that supersweets grown in Mexico and Florida can provide year-round availability of fresh corn throughout the United States. Although the supersweets are indeed sweet, I find their flavor thin and lacking the robust, almost buttery, real corn flavor of traditional sweet corn.

Dried sweet corn kernels, also known as chicos and shaker dried corn, are a tasty vegetable. Drying intensifies the sweetness and gives the rehydrated kernels a deep, caramel taste with a chewy texture. Traditionally the corn is dried in the sun or in *hornos*, the adobe ovens of the Southwest.

Fresh Corn on the Cob

We anxiously wait for our sweet corn to ripen and then—how could we not?—we stage a corn feast in which ears upon ears of corn are the first and second courses. Favorite condiments include sweet butter, Tabasco, salt, lime juice, and umeboshi (Japanese plum paste). My two favorite methods of cooking fresh corn on the cob are steeping, which produces the most tender kernels, and grilling, which gives a great smoky flavor.

TO STEEP CORN, fill your largest pot with water. Add 1 teaspoon of salt for each gallon of water and while it comes to a boil, husk as many ears as will easily fit into the pot. Put the ears in the boiling water. When the water returns to a boil, immediately cover the pot and turn off the heat. After 10 minutes, remove the lid and, using tongs, remove the corn.

TO GRILL CORN, remove the silk and soak the ears in their husks in cold water to cover for 30 minutes. Place the soaked ears on a preheated grill and roast, turning frequently, for about 20 minutes, or until tender. Remove and husk the corn.

Sweet Corn
Selection and Storage

For real corn flavor, rather than just sweetness, I grow a traditional corn variety, and that's what I recommend. During the peak of corn season, ask your greengrocer about the availability of a traditional corn and plan to purchase it the day it reaches the market. The supersweets, on the other hand, have a ten-day shelf life, which makes them commercial favorites.

The corn silk strands emerging from husk at the top of the ear accurately indicate how fresh corn is. Each individual silk should be, in a word, silky. At harvest, the silk immediately begins to dehydrate and within a few days mats together and turns brown. The dry silk of corn that is more than several days old is usually removed for cosmetic reasons.

To store corn, refrigerate it in the husk wrapped in plastic for several days.

Fresh Corn Off the Cob

There are several methods, besides teeth, that you may use to remove corn from the cob. All techniques invite the wearing of a bib apron as some of the milk-packed kernels will squirt when sliced or grated. Depending on the texture I want in the finished dish, I remove corn from the cob in one of the following ways:

Grate and Scrape

This technique yields lush, smooth, and hull-free corn puree. Rubbing against the large holes of a standard box grater, grate the corn into a bowl. With the back of a butter knife, firmly and carefully scrape the cob to extract the remaining pulp. Don't scrape too hard, or the hulls will also be pulled from the cob. Grated corn enhances soufflés, soups, chowders, fritters, puddings, corn oysters, and other delicate dishes. If you prefer, slice through each row of kernels and scrape the pulp from the cob. This takes twice as long as grating, is more cumbersome and equally messy, but will produce the same textured puree.

Double-Cut

This technique yields halved corn kernels. With a sharp knife, slice down the side of an ear of corn, slicing halfway through the kernels. Rotate the cob and continue until all the kernels are sliced in half. Repeat the slicing a second time to remove the bottom halves of the kernels.

Single Cut

Using a sharp knife, slice the whole kernels from the cob. Some corn pulp will remain on the cob. Scrape this pulp off for seasoning soups or stews or use the cob, as is, in stock. Whole kernels are used in relishes, pickles, and chowchow where a whole-grain texture is desired.

Traditional Grits

❦

Unless you live in the South, where regular grits are available, you'll probably find only chemically enriched instant grits in the supermarket. If you can't grind your own grits, I recommend buying stoneground grits by mail order (see page 376).

Bring the water and salt to a boil in a heavy saucepan over high heat. Slowly whisk in the grits. Lower the heat to medium-low and continue to cook, stirring frequently, for about 20 minutes, or until thick. Stir in the butter and pepper and serve immediately.

VARIATIONS: Add 6 cloves roasted garlic, chopped, with the butter.
Add 3 tablespoons chopped green chilies with the butter.
Add a small sautéed onion and/or ½ cup toasted sunflower seeds.

Makes about 4 cups

4 cups water

½ teaspoon sea salt, or to taste

1 cup coarse stoneground grits

3 tablespoons unsalted butter, or to taste

Freshly ground white pepper, to taste

Cornmeal Mush

❧

Makes about 4 cups

4 cups water

½ teaspoon sea salt, or to taste

1 cup stoneground cornmeal

*2 tablespoons unsalted butter
(optional)*

From colonial times to the early part of this century, cornmeal mush was almost daily breakfast fare throughout the United States. I believe that a reason for its demise is the cornmeal itself. Degermed enriched cornmeal doesn't make good mush. Fresh stoneground cornmeal does. It is a nutritious time-saver since cornmeal mush can be eaten immediately with a sweetener and warm milk or cream, or with butter, salt, and pepper, and then the leftover mush can be molded into a loaf and refrigerated for later use. Similar to polenta (but with softer texture), the molded mush can be sliced and fried, broiled, or grilled and served with sweet or savory accompaniments.

Bring the water and salt to a boil in a heavy saucepan over high heat. Slowly stir in the cornmeal. If necessary, use a whisk to break up lumps. Reduce heat to low and cook, stirring frequently, for about 15 minutes, or until the mush pulls away from the sides of the pan. Remove from the heat and stir in the butter. Serve hot.

Polenta

❧

In Italy, polenta is made in an unlined copper kettle called the paiolo *and is always cut with a string. I use an enameled cast-iron pot and my old kitchen knife and I think the result is quite all right. Whether making polenta the Italian way or my way, you do need a strong arm. Serve it plain or topped with melted butter and grated Parmesan cheese, extra virgin olive oil, and cracked black pepper or a sauce.*

Makes about 4 cups

3 cups water

1 teaspoon sea salt, or to taste

1 cup imported Italian cornmeal

1 tablespoon extra virgin olive oil

Bring the water and salt to a boil in a heavy saucepan over high heat. Very slowly whisk in the cornmeal. Do not let the water stop boiling. When all of the cornmeal is in the pot, lower the heat to medium and begin stirring with a wooden spoon. Cook, stirring frequently, for about 30 minutes, or until the polenta is quite thick and pulls away from the sides of the pan. Stir in the olive oil. Scrape the polenta from the pot into a bowl. Let rest for about 7 minutes. Turn the polenta out from the bowl onto a serving platter. Serve hot.

VARIATION: For grilled or fried polenta, scrape the cooked polenta out onto a baking sheet, wooden board, or into a 9-inch square pan. Using a spatula, push it out to about ½ inch thick. Cover and allow to cool for about 3 hours. When ready to cook, cut into desired slices, trimming off any dry crust.

For grilling, preheat the grill, rub the slices with olive oil, sea salt, and pepper and chopped fresh herbs if desired. Place polenta slices on the grill and cook for about 7 minutes, or until the bottom is browned. Turn and brown the other side. Polenta may also be broiled about 6 inches from the heat for 7 minutes, or until the tops are bubbly and beginning to brown. Turn and broil the other side. (The polenta should be crunchy on the outside and soft in the middle.) Serve at once.

For frying, heat extra virgin olive oil or butter in a sauté pan and, when hot, fry slices for about 4 minutes on each side, or until crisp.

Posole from Scratch

Makes 4 cups

*2 cups whole dried blue, white,
or yellow dent or flint corn
(see page 28)*

4 cups water

*$^1/_4$ cup unadulterated wood ash or
2 tablespoons food-grade pickling
lime or baking soda (see Note)*

Note: Pickling lime is a seasonal offering
available at your supermarket in the home
canning section. One nationally distributed
brand is Mrs. Wage Pickling Lime.

*Posole is not a dish to make when you are hungry. But if you're in the mood
to have your kitchen filled with a heavenly aroma for several hours, I recommend it. Limed corn requires long cooking, but the hands-on time is relatively short, not laborious, and well worth the effort.*

*Corn was traditionally slaked with wood ash. Today, a commonly used
alkalinizing agent is pickling lime (calcium hydroxide, available from a phar-
macy or builders' supply outfit); baking soda also works. I've made posole
using wood ash and baking soda and have found that wood ash yields the best
flavor.*

Put the corn in a nonreactive pot. Add the water and soak
overnight. Add the wood ash, place over high heat, and bring
to a boil. Lower the heat and simmer for about 2 hours, covered, or until the hulls loosen from the grain. Or pressure cook for $1^1/_2$
hours. Drain the corn and rinse several times to remove the alkaline
taste. Working with a handful at a time, rub the hulls and germ off
between your palms. Rinse off the hulls.

You may grind freshly cooked posole into masa for tortillas or
use it as you would rice in such dishes as stuffings, stews, soups, salads, and casseroles. Freshly cooked posole may be frozen, tightly
wrapped, for up to 9 months, or dried in the sun or oven. Store dried
posole, tightly wrapped, in a cool dark place for up to 1 year.

Creole Corn Oysters

These irresistible little cakes are meltingly soft, like an oyster. They brown like a pancake yet surprise the palate with a creamy, pudding-like center. I learned about this dish from the 1885 book Creole Cooking *by Lafcadio Hearn, one of my favorite writers. The pancakes are equally good for breakfast with syrup or molasses or as a main course with a spicy sauce.*

Husk the corn and prepare the kernels using the grate and scrape method (see page 32). Combine the kernels, milk, and ghee in a mixing bowl. Combine the dry ingredients. When blended, stir into the corn mixture to make a thick batter.

Heat a griddle over medium-high heat. Grease the griddle. Drop batter by the tablespoonful onto the griddle. Cook for about 2 minutes, or until the bottom has browned and the top starts to dry. Turn and brown other side. Remove from the griddle and keep warm while cooking remaining batter.

When all the corn oysters are cooked, divide among 4 warm plates. Place a dollop of sour cream on top of each corn oyster. Garnish with caviar and a bit of chopped chives. Serve immediately.

Serves 4

4 ears fresh corn in the husk

¹/₂ cup milk or soy milk

1 teaspoon Ghee (page 359) or unsalted butter, melted

¹/₂ cup unbleached all-purpose flour

¹/₄ teaspoon sea salt

¹/₂ teaspoon baking powder

¹/₈ teaspoon freshly grated nutmeg

¹/₂ cup sour cream, or to taste

3 tablespoons American sturgeon caviar, or to taste

1 tablespoon minced fresh chives

Grilled Gorgonzola Polenta with Portobello Ragout and Fried Sage

❦

Serves 4

1 recipe Polenta (page 35)

¼ cup crumbled gorgonzola

3 tablespoons extra virgin olive oil

1 tablespoon minced fresh sage

¼ teaspoon sea salt, or to taste

Cracked black pepper, to taste

Portobello Ragout (recipe follows)

2 tablespoons grated Parmesan

16 fried sage leaves (see Note)

Note: Fried herb leaves are a simple but elegant garnish. Wash the sage leaves and dry them well. Fry them quickly in hot oil and drain on paper towels.

The meatiness of mushroom, the crisp-fried sage, and the melt-in-your-mouth polenta—grains don't get much better than this. It's so easy to prepare, I usually make a double batch of polenta and use half for breakfast and the other half for this delectable side or as a hearty and satisfying main dish. At dinnertime, while the grill is heating, I make the ragout and fry the sage.

When the polenta is cooked and still hot, stir in the gorgonzola. Scrape from the pan into a 9-inch square pan. Let cool for at least 4 hours. Cut into 3-inch squares. Preheat the grill or broiler.

Combine the olive oil, sage, salt, and pepper. Generously coat the polenta slices on both sides with seasoned oil. Grill for about 2 minutes on each side, or until heated through and seared. Place 2 squares on each of 4 plates. Place a mound of Portobello Ragout in the center and sprinkle with grated Parmesan. Garnish with fried sage leaves and serve immediately.

Portobello Ragout

Put the porcini mushrooms in a small heatproof bowl and cover with the boiling water. Let steep for 30 minutes, or until the mushrooms are softened. Drain through a fine sieve, reserving both the mushrooms and liquid. Strain again if the liquid seems dirty. Chop the mushrooms and set aside.

Clean the portobello mushroom. Remove and chop the stem. Set aside. Thinly slice the cap and set aside. Trim the fennel bulb. Cut crosswise into fine slices. Set aside.

Heat $1/2$ tablespoon of the olive oil in a large nonreactive sauté pan over medium heat. Stir in the leek and garlic. Sauté for 7 minutes, or until the vegetables begin to soften. Add the porcini, chives, thyme, chervil, and chopped portobello stems. Sauté for about 7 minutes more, or until the vegetables begin to caramelize. Stir in the vinegar and deglaze the pan. Add the reserved porcini liquid, salt, and pepper and bring to a boil. Lower the heat and simmer, uncovered, for 15 minutes, or until reduced to about 1 cup.

Meanwhile, heat the remaining oil in a sauté pan over medium heat. Add and sauté the sliced portobello cap for about 5 minutes, or until just softened. Add and sauté the fennel for about 5 minutes, or until tender. Remove from the heat and keep warm.

Stir the porcini mixture into the portobello and fennel. Keep warm until ready to serve. Just before serving, stir in the parsley.

Makes about 2$1/2$ cups

$1/2$ cup dried porcini mushrooms

2 cups boiling water

1 large portobello mushroom

1 small fennel bulb

2$1/2$ tablespoons extra virgin olive oil

1 medium leek, well washed and chopped

4 cloves garlic, minced

1 tablespoon minced fresh chives

1 tablespoon minced fresh thyme

1 tablespoon minced fresh chervil

2 tablespoons balsamic vinegar

Sea salt, to taste

Cracked black pepper, to taste

2 tablespoons chopped fresh parsley

Corn and Clam
Chowder with Roasted Parsnips

❧

Serves 4 to 6

5 ears fresh corn in the husk

2 large parsnips, scrubbed and trimmed

2 pounds littleneck clams

4 cups water

2 tablespoons unsalted butter

1 medium chopped onion

Sea salt and freshly ground black pepper, to taste

¼ cup minced fresh cilantro

I love creating bold flavors with just a few ingredients. The inspiration for this recipe came when I was making corn and clam chowder and happened to have a roasted parsnip on hand. It made all the difference in flavor.

Soak the corn in cold water for 30 minutes. Place the parsnips in the top rack of a steamer basket over boiling water. Cover and steam for 5 minutes. Remove from the basket.

Preheat the grill.

Place the corn and parsnips on the grill. Cover and roast, turning often, until parsnip skins and outer corn husks brown, 5 to 10 minutes for the parsnips, about 20 minutes for the corn. Remove from the heat and let cool slightly. When cool enough to handle, shuck the corn and remove the kernels, using the double-cut method (see page 32). Cut the parsnips into a fine dice. Set aside the corn and parsnips.

Wash the clams in cold running water, scrubbing the shells to remove any loose particles and sand. Place the clams and 1 cup of the water in a heavy saucepan over medium-high heat. Cover and cook for about 5 minutes, or until clams just open. Discard any clams that do not open. Drain and set aside the clams and cooking liquid separately. Remove the clams from the shells. Discard the shells. Coarsely chop the clams and set aside. Strain the clam liquid through a fine coffee filter or a double thickness of cheesecloth. Set aside the liquor.

Melt the butter in a large saucepan over medium heat. Add the onions and sauté for 5 minutes, or until soft. Stir in the corn, parsnips, clam liquor, the remaining 3 cups water, salt, and pepper, and bring to a boil. Reduce the heat and simmer for 5 minutes. Add the chopped clams and simmer, covered, for 3 minutes more. Taste and adjust the seasoning. Just before serving, stir in the cilantro.

Curried Corn and Coconut Soup

✣

Corn and curry—though not native to Africa—have been enthusiastically adopted there. This African-inspired soup can be served either hot or cold. For family fare, I often substitute soy milk for the coconut milk for a lighter but still highly flavored soup.

Remove the kernels from the corn using the double-cut method (see page 32) and put in a food processor. Process until smooth. Set aside.

Melt the butter in a large saucepan over medium heat. Stir in the coriander, cumin, turmeric, cardamom, and cayenne. Sauté for about 3 minutes, or until the spices are quite aromatic. Add the coconut milk, corn puree, stock, salt, and pepper and bring to a simmer. Do not boil. Reduce the heat and simmer, covered, for 25 minutes. Taste and adjust seasoning. Pour into warmed soup bowls and garnish with toasted coconut and a sprinkling of parsley.

Serves 4

3 ears fresh corn, husked

1 tablespoon unsalted butter

2 teaspoons ground coriander

1 teaspoon ground cumin

¹⁄₂ teaspoon turmeric

¹⁄₂ teaspoon ground cardamom

¹⁄₄ teaspoon cayenne

3 cups Coconut Milk (page 354)

1 cup Vegetable Stock (page 364)
  or Chicken Stock (page 366)

Sea salt and freshly ground black
  pepper, to taste

¹⁄₄ cup unsweetened shredded coconut,
  toasted

2 tablespoons minced fresh parsley

Herbed Posole Salad
with Dried Cranberries

❧

1 ¹/₂ cups dried white posole

¹/₂ teaspoon cumin seeds

2 cups water

¹/₄ teaspoon sea salt

Freshly ground black pepper,
  to taste

1 cup diced red bell pepper

¹/₂ cup chopped fresh chives

¹/₂ cup minced fresh cilantro

¹/₄ cup dried cranberries

2 tablespoons brown rice vinegar

¹/₄ cup extra virgin olive oil

1 head leaf lettuce

The dazzling colors and tangy flavors make this salad welcome anytime of the year. As a luncheon entree, it stands alone. For dinner, include soup and bread or serve it as a side dish. The salad also packs well for sack lunches. For convenience, the posole may be cooked ahead of time and the salad may be made one or two days in advance.

Combine the posole, cumin, and water in a large pot over high heat, cover, and bring to a boil. Lower the heat and simmer for 1 hour, or until the kernels are soft and start to burst. Add salt and pepper and cook for 5 minutes more. (To shorten cooking time, you may presoak the posole for 4 hours or overnight or pressure cook it for 45 minutes.) When the posole is soft, drain well, reserving liquid for another use, if desired. Let the posole cool to room temperature.

Combine the posole, bell pepper, chives, cilantro, cranberries, vinegar, and olive oil in a large bowl. Taste and adjust seasonings. Let stand for 15 minutes.

Separate the lettuce. Wash and dry well. Arrange lettuce leaves on a serving platter. Mound salad in the center and serve immediately.

Stir-Fried Dried Scallops
with Baby Corn and Bean Sprouts

❧

I concocted this recipe when I discovered fresh baby corn at a farmers' market. Baby corn is just what its name implies—tiny, immature ears with the kernels barely formed and without silk. You can also buy canned baby corn in the Asian foods section of the supermarket. This dish is also delicious served with polenta, rice, or pasta, but my favorite is quinoa.

Place the dried scallops in warm water to cover. Let soak for 2 hours. (If using fresh scallops, omit this step.) Drain and place on a heatproof plate on the rack of a steamer over boiling water. Cover and steam for about 20 minutes (about 5 minutes for fresh scallops), or until tender. Remove from the steamer and let cool. Blot dry using a paper towel. When cool enough to handle, pull into shreds and blot dry a second time.

Heat the corn oil in a wok over medium-high heat until hot. Add half the shredded scallops and fry, stirring frequently, for about 3 minutes, or until the shreds are golden. Using a slotted spoon, remove the shreds and drain on a paper towel. Cook the remaining scallop shreds. When well drained, transfer to a clean paper towel and sprinkle with salt.

Cut any baby corn ears that are over 3 inches long in half. Set aside. Cut the white part of the scallions lengthwise in half, then cut the entire scallions into 3-inch lengths. Set aside.

Discard the cooking oil. Add the sesame oil to the wok or to a nonreactive skillet and place it back on medium heat. When hot, add and sauté the corn, snow peas, beansprouts, and scallions for 6 minutes, or until they slightly soften and the color changes. Add the sugar, vinegar, and soy sauce. Stir-fry for about 2 minutes, or until the vegetables are hot but still crisp. Scrape onto a serving plate. Sprinkle with the scallop shreds. Serve immediately with quinoa.

Serves 4

8 dried scallops or 8 fresh scallops

½ cup peanut oil

¼ teaspoon sea salt

½ pound fresh baby corn, husked, or 1 can, rinsed and drained

1 tablespoon unrefined sesame oil

2 cups snow peas

6 ounces fresh bean sprouts

4 scallions

1 teaspoon Sucanat or light brown sugar

1 teaspoon brown rice vinegar

1 tablespoon soy sauce, or to taste

1 recipe just-cooked white quinoa (see page 83)

Masa Linguine with Lobster, Fresh Corn, and Tomato Sauce

✤

2 ears fresh corn in the husk

6 very ripe tomatoes, peeled, cored, and seeded (see page 370)

1 cup chopped fresh basil

$^1/_2$ small red onion, minced

2 cloves garlic, minced

1 $^1/_2$ teaspoons sea salt

Cracked black pepper, to taste

2 cups kamut, semolina, or unbleached all-purpose flour

1 cup masa harina

5 large eggs

Cold water

$^1/_4$ cup extra virgin olive oil

1 pound cooked lobster meat, diced

2 tablespoons grated pecorino romano

Masa adds its own flavor and also lets you squander the olive oil. This is because corn, considered a medicinal food for the heart, has an amazing ability to soak up oils and fats and to moderate their impact.

Preheat the grill or preheat the oven to 400°F.

Soak the corn in cold water for 30 minutes.

Place the corn on the grill or on a rack on a baking sheet. Grill or roast for about 20 minutes, or until the husk is brown and the corn is cooked. Let cool slightly. When cool enough to handle, remove husks. Cut off whole kernels (see page 32) and set aside.

Dice the tomatoes over a small bowl to catch the juices. Add the corn, basil, onion, and garlic to the tomatoes. Season with $^1/_2$ teaspoon sea salt and pepper. Let marinate at room temperature for at least 2 hours.

Combine the flour, masa harina, and 1 teaspoon salt in a large mixing bowl. When well blended, make a well in the center and break in the eggs. Mix egg into the flour using a fork and then your fingers until the dough forms a ball. Add water, 1 tablespoon at a time, if the dough requires more liquid. Place the ball on a lightly floured surface and knead for about 10 minutes, or until the dough is smooth. Cover and refrigerate for 1 hour.

Prepare pasta by hand or with a pasta machine as directed on page 246. Cut into linguine-size ribbons by hand or using an attachment.

Heat 1 tablespoon of the olive oil in a sauté pan over medium heat. Add the lobster and sauté for 2 minutes, or until just warmed. Remove from the heat and keep warm.

Bring a large pot of water to a boil over high heat. Add salt to taste. Add the linguine and cook for about 1 minute, or until al dente. Drain well. Return to the pot and combine with the corn and tomato sauce and remaining olive oil. When well mixed, turn out onto a serving platter. Top with lobster and sprinkle with grated cheese. Serve immediately.

Rio Grande Stew of Chicos, Posole, and Pinquitos

❦

In New Mexico, a dish of posole means a fatty and salty mutton or pork broth with posole served with a side dish of green chili. This high-flavored posole soup, however, is zero cholesterol. Chicos are nuggets of horno-dried sweet corn. If you don't have them on hand, don't let that stop you from preparing this dish. With or without chicos, Rio Grande Stew is substantial; I frequently serve it in cold weather with tortillas or corn bread. Epazote is a Mexican herb that is traditionally cooked with beans both to reduce the flatus level and to add flavor. Fresh epazote leaves are not readily available, but dried epazote can be found in the herb section of natural foods stores, in herb shops, and in the Latino section of many supermarkets.

Soak the beans in water to cover for 4 to 8 hours. Soak the posole and chicos in 2 cups water for 4 to 8 hours. Drain the beans and discard their soaking water. Place the posole, chicos, their soaking water, and the drained beans in a large soup pot. Add the kombu, half of the garlic, bay leaves, and water. Cover and bring to a boil. Reduce the heat and simmer for 1 hour.

Heat the olive oil in a saucepan and lightly sauté first the cumin seeds for 1 minute, or until aromatic. Add and sauté the remaining garlic and onion for 5 minutes, or until softened. Add and sauté the squash for 5 minutes, or until softened. Add and sauté the celery and chilies for 3 minutes, or until softened. Transfer the onion mixture and the chilies to the soup pot and cook for 1 hour more, or until the beans are thoroughly soft and many of the posole kernels are opened. Season with salt, pepper, and epazote and simmer for 10 minutes. Garnish with the cilantro or oregano and serve.

Serves 4 to 6

¾ cup pinquito or other chili-type beans

¾ cup posole

¼ cup chicos

½-inch strip kombu

4 cloves garlic, minced

2 bay leaves

4 cups water

2 tablespoons extra virgin olive oil

1 large onion, chopped

1 cup cubed butternut squash

2 stalks celery, chopped

1 to 3 New Mexican chilies, roasted (see page 353), peeled, seeded, and diced

Sea salt and freshly ground black pepper, to taste

1 tablespoon dried epazote or oregano

2 tablespoons chopped fresh cilantro or oregano

Onion Tart in Fresh Corn Crust

❦

This unusual tart makes a splendid brunch or lunch entree.

Serves 4 to 6

4 large yellow onions

2 tablespoons extra virgin olive oil

Sea salt to taste

1 tablespoon balsamic vinegar

White pepper, to taste

4 ears fresh corn, husked

1 cup chopped fresh cilantro

½ cup whole wheat pastry flour

1 large egg

1 tablespoon unsalted butter, melted

Peel and thinly slice the onions. Heat the olive oil in a large skillet over medium heat. Add the onions and sauté for about 10 minutes. Stir in the salt and continue to sauté for 20 minutes more, or until almost caramelized. Stir in the vinegar and season with pepper. Sauté for 5 minutes more.

Preheat the oven to 350°F.

Remove the corn kernels using the grate and scrape method (see page 32). Combine with the cilantro, flour, egg, and butter. Season with salt and pepper. Press into a 9-inch tart pan and bake for 30 minutes.

Scrape the onions into the corn crust, pressing in and smoothing the top. Bake for an additional 20 minutes, or until the crust is golden. Let stand for 5 minutes before cutting into wedges. Serve hot.

Southwestern Cheese Sandwiches with Sweet and Hot Pepper Sauce

✺

I often make this rather upscale sandwich for a supper dish to be served with a tossed green salad and a tall cold drink.

Cut the queso blanco into 8 equal pieces. Press each piece flat with your fingertips. Or slice Monterey Jack cheese into 8 pieces about 2½ inches in diameter. Set aside.

Combine the corn, eggs, chili, garlic, flour, and salt in a food processor and process, using quick on and off pulses, for about 1 minute, or until well blended.

Heat a griddle over medium-high heat until hot. Lightly brush with corn oil. Using a fourth of the batter, drop it by the tablespoonful to make 4 round cakes. Smooth the tops with the back of a spoon. Place a circle of queso blanco in the center of each cake. Sprinkle cilantro on top. Spoon another tablespoon of corn batter on top of each cake. Allow to cook for 3 minutes more, or until the bottom has browned. Turn and cook for 3 minutes more, or until well browned on both sides and the center has cooked around the melting cheese. Remove from the griddle and keep warm while preparing 4 more sandwiches with the remaining ingredients. When all the sandwiches are cooked, spoon a circle of Sweet and Hot Pepper Sauce in the center of each of 4 plates. Place 2 sandwiches, overlapping each other, on the edge of the circle. Garnish with a sprig of cilantro and serve immediately.

Serves 4

2 ounces queso blanco or Monterey Jack

2 cups fresh whole corn kernels (see page 32)

2 large eggs

1 New Mexican green chili, roasted (see page 353), peeled, seeded, and chopped, or to taste

2 cloves garlic, roasted

2 tablespoons unbleached all-purpose flour

½ teaspoon sea salt, or to taste

1 tablespoon unrefined corn oil

2 tablespoons minced fresh cilantro

Sweet and Hot Pepper Sauce (recipe follows)

4 sprigs of cilantro

Sweet and Hot Pepper Sauce

Makes about 3 cups

1 pound very ripe tomatoes

2 large red bell peppers

15 large cloves garlic, unpeeled

2 tablespoons extra virgin olive oil

*3 poblano chilies, roasted (see
  page 353), peeled, seeded, and chopped*

*1 teaspoon crushed red pepper
  flakes, or to taste*

1 teaspoon minced fresh oregano

1 teaspoon minced fresh cilantro

¹/₂ teaspoon sea salt, or to taste

Freshly ground black pepper, to taste

Preheat the oven to 400°F.

Wash the tomatoes and bell peppers. Cut crosswise in half, core, and seed. Place the tomatoes and bell peppers, cut side down, and the garlic on a jelly-roll pan. Drizzle with olive oil. Roast for 10 minutes. Reduce the heat to 350°F. and roast for 20 minutes more, or until the vegetables are soft and their skins have browned. Remove from the oven and cool slightly. When cool enough to handle, peel the garlic. Place the garlic, tomatoes, peppers, chilies, red pepper flakes, oregano, cilantro, salt, and pepper in a blender. Process until smooth. Scrape into a medium saucepan. Place over medium heat and cook, stirring frequently, for about 15 minutes, or until the flavors have blended.

Greens and Herbed Cornmeal Dumplings with Roasted Red Pepper Sauce

In five minutes flat you can have succulent greens and fresh bread—two sure winners. I've updated this classic of the American South by lightly cooking the greens and by cutting way back on the fat. I top the dish with a smoky sweet Roasted Red Pepper Sauce.

Trim and wash the greens but do not dry. If using lamb's-quarters, coarsely chop. If using turnip greens, collards, or kale, cut into fine strands. Set aside.

Combine the cornmeal, flour, baking soda, ¼ teaspoon salt, and ¼ teaspoon pepper in a small mixing bowl. In another bowl, beat the egg. Stir in the milk, melted butter, thyme, and orange zest. Combine with the flour mixture to form a batter.

Put the greens, stock, and remaining salt and pepper in a large saucepan over high heat and bring to a boil. Drop in dumplings by the heaping tablespoonful to form 8 dumplings. Cover the pot, reduce the heat to medium, and simmer for about 5 minutes, or until greens are tender and dumplings are cooked. Test by piercing one with a fork. Arrange on a platter with lemon wedges. Top with the pepper sauce and serve while hot.

VARIATION: Substitute ¼ cup mesquite flour for ¼ cup of the wheat or barley flour.

Serves 4

2 bunches fresh lamb's-quarters, young turnip greens, collards, or kale

½ cup stoneground blue or yellow cornmeal

½ cup whole wheat pastry or barley flour (see page 212)

½ teaspoon baking soda

½ teaspoon sea salt, or to taste

½ teaspoon white pepper, or to taste

1 large egg

½ cup buttermilk or Clabbered Soy Milk (page 371)

1 tablespoon unsalted butter, melted

1 tablespoon minced fresh thyme

1 teaspoon freshly grated orange zest

½ cup Vegetable Stock (page 364)

Lemon wedges

Roasted Red Pepper Sauce (recipe follows)

Roasted Red Pepper Sauce

Makes 1 ¼ cups

*2 red bell peppers, roasted (page 353),
  peeled, seeded, and chopped*

3 cloves garlic, roasted and peeled

3 tablespoons extra virgin olive oil

1 tablespoon balsamic vinegar

2 tablespoons pine nuts, toasted

¼ teaspoon sea salt

Pinch of ground cumin

1 to 2 tablespoons chopped fresh basil

Puree all of the ingredients until smooth in a blender or food processor. Serve warm or at room temperature. (Store any remaining sauce,
airtight, in the refrigerator for up to 48 hours.)

Thumbprint Molletes

✿

In Mexican bakeries you pick up a tray and tongs at the door to select your own bread and pastries. Of the cookies, molletes have long been my favorite. I appreciate the pleasant sandy texture, sweet aroma, and taste that corn brings to the cookies. For this recipe I use white sugar rather than Sucanat so that the cookies stay light to contrast dramatically with the dark jam filling.

Preheat the oven to 350°F. Lightly grease a baking sheet and set aside.

Put the cornmeal in a skillet over medium heat. Toast, stirring constantly, for 3 minutes, or until lightly browned.

Cream together the sugar and butter. Beat in the egg yolk and vanilla. Sift together the flour, toasted cornmeal, baking powder, cinnamon, and salt and stir into the creamed mixture. Let stand for 5 minutes. If the dough seems too soft to shape with your hands, stir in a few more tablespoons of flour, being careful not to add too much as the dough will continue to stiffen and dry out slightly as the cornmeal absorbs moisture.

Pull off small portions of the dough and roll between your palms to form 1-inch balls. Slightly beat the egg white. Dip each ball into egg white and roll in pecans. Place on cookie sheets about 1 1/2 inches apart. Press your thumb deeply in center of each cookie. Bake for 15 minutes, or until pale gold on top and lightly browned at the edge. Let stand for several minutes, or until partially cool. Transfer the cookies to wire racks and let cool completely. Fill the thumbprints with jelly.

Makes 15 cookies

1/4 cup yellow stoneground cornmeal

1/4 cup granulated sugar

8 tablespoons (1 stick) unsalted butter

1 large egg, separated

1/2 teaspoon pure vanilla extract

3/4 cup unbleached all-purpose flour

1/2 teaspoon baking powder

1/2 teaspoon ground cinnamon

1/4 teaspoon sea salt

3/4 cup finely chopped pecans

About 1/2 cup jelly or jam

Honey Caramel Corn
with Roasted Almonds

❦

Makes 4 quarts

1 cup honey

1 tablespoon butter (optional)

4 quarts popped corn

1 cup almonds, toasted

For those times when you're hungry for a quick and satisfying snack, here's a fantastic one. It's guaranteed to bring out the kid in anyone. I've made this countless times, and sometimes the caramel corn easily forms into balls (butter your hands and work fast) and sometimes it doesn't. I asked the National Honey Board—who had never heard of a 100 percent honey "caramel"—why that might be. All they could think of was that it might be because honey's nutrient content varies according to the bees' food source.

Put the honey in a medium saucepan over medium-high heat and bring to a boil. Lower the heat and simmer, without stirring, for about 7 minutes, or until the honey reaches 265°F. on a candy thermometer. Initially the honey will be frothy; when the froth disappears and the honey becomes thicker and denser and turns a shade darker, it is ready. Remove from the heat. Add the butter, if using, and stir to melt. Handle with care to prevent burns. Pour the hot honey over the popped corn. Add almonds and stir to coat, using a long-handled wooden spoon.

Sage and Blue Corn
Skillet Bread with Fresh Corn

❦

On a hot summer day, I "bake" this great-tasting cornbread on top of the stove so I don't have to heat up the kitchen. Use a cast-iron skillet and a Flame Tamer to moderate and evenly disperse the heat. You can also bake the bread, uncovered, in a preheated 425°F. oven for 25 minutes.

Combine the cornmeal, flour, baking powder, sage, and salt. In a separate bowl, beat the eggs. Add the butter, milk, and lemon zest and mix in. Combine the wet and dry ingredients, being careful not to overmix. Add the corn kernels, stirring just enough to combine. Heat an 8½-inch cast-iron skillet over high heat and grease generously. Pour the batter into the pan and cover with a tight-fitting lid. Lower the heat to medium-low and cook for 25 minutes, or until the bread pulls away from the sides of the skillet and a toothpick inserted into the center comes out clean. Remove the lid and cook an additional 3 minutes or until the top dries slightly. Remove from the heat. Turn out onto a rack and let cool for about 5 minutes before serving.

VARIATION: Substitute ¼ cup mesquite flour for ¼ cup of the cornmeal.

Makes 1 round loaf

2 cups stoneground cornmeal, preferably blue

½ cup rye flour

1 ½ teaspoons baking powder

1 teaspoon rubbed sage

½ teaspoon sea salt

2 large eggs

2 tablespoons unsalted butter, melted

1 ½ cups milk or soy milk

½ teaspoon freshly grated lemon zest

2 cups fresh double-cut corn kernels (see page 32)

Santa Fe–Flavored but Otherwise Authentic Spoon Bread

Authentic spoon bread made with grits is one of the South's most elegant corn preparations. I think that the flavors of the Southwest make it even better.

Serves 4

$^1/_4$ cup white stoneground cornmeal

1 teaspoon ground cumin

$^1/_2$ teaspoon baking soda

1 teaspoon sea salt

Freshly ground pepper, to taste

3 scallions

1 cup water

$^1/_4$ cup grits, preferably stoneground (do not use instant)

1 tablespoon unsalted butter

$^3/_4$ cup milk or soy milk

2 large eggs, separated

1 New Mexican green chili, roasted (page 353), peeled, seeded, and chopped

$^1/_4$ cup minced fresh cilantro

2 tablespoons grated Romano

Preheat the oven to 375°F. Generously butter a 9-inch square baking dish.

Stir together the cornmeal, cumin, baking soda, salt, and pepper. Set aside. Trim the scallions. Cut crosswise into $^1/_4$-inch slices. Set aside.

Pour the water into a medium saucepan over high heat and bring to a boil. Slowly whisk in the grits, stirring constantly. Reduce the heat and cook, stirring frequently, for 25 minutes. Stir in the butter and milk and return to a boil. Remove from the heat and quickly stir in the cornmeal mixture. Let cool to lukewarm. Beat in the egg yolks.

Beat the egg whites until stiff. Fold the chili, scallions, and cilantro into the egg whites. Fold the egg white mixture into the batter. Pour into the baking dish, sprinkle the cheese on top, and bake for about 20 minutes, or until puffed and just brown. Serve immediately.

Griddle-Cooked Turnip and Masa Harina Flatbread

Makes six 5-inch flatbreads

2 medium turnips or 1 plump 12-inch daikon, washed and trimmed

1 cup white masa harina

¹/₂ teaspoon sea salt

3 teaspoons Ghee (see page 359) or melted unsalted butter

Here's a bold bread with the sweet taste of turnips. It looks like a flecked tortilla but is more pliant, moister, and lighter. The Punjabi Sikhs make an tasty corn-daikon bread but the delicate dough makes it too fussy a recipe for me. By substituting masa harina for the cornmeal I double the flavor and have an easy-to-handle dough. Although cooking mellows the pungent bite of turnip, it's a wide-awake taste compared to the subtle flavor of cooked daikon. My children prefer the daikon. This is the only recipe in which I favor yellow or white masa harina over the blue, this because the blue masa obscures the vegetable shreds. An electric tortilla press expedites the process. If fresh young turnips are not available, substitute a plump daikon or even a carrot.

Finely grate the turnips. Measure out 1 cup by gently pressing into a 1 cup measure. Combine the turnips, masa harina, and sea salt in a small mixing bowl. Using your fingertips, blend together. The liquid from the turnips will moisten the flour enough to make a soft dough that is wet to the touch. Divide the dough into 6 equal portions. Cover with plastic wrap and let rest for 5 minutes.

Place each piece of dough on the counter and cover with wax paper. Using a rolling pin, roll into a round ¹/₈ inch thick.

Heat a griddle, cast-iron skillet, or heavy frypan over medium heat. Add ¹/₂ teaspoon ghee. Place bread on the griddle. Cook for 3 minutes, or until the underside is flecked with brown. Turn and cook the second side for 2 minutes. Transfer to a platter. Cover and place in a warm oven while cooking the remaining breads. Serve warm or at room temperature.

VARIATION: These may be made in an electric tortilla press. Cook according to the manufacturer's directions.

Corn Tortillas with Marjoram

❧

Makes 12

2 cups masa harina

About 1¼ cups warm water

1 tablespoon minced fresh marjoram or other fresh herb such as cilantro, basil, oregano, or savory (optional)

I have a Guatemalan friend, Feliciano Merida, who needs both hands to eat every meal of the day. In his right hand, the utensil, his left, a neatly folded tortilla. A meal without a tortilla—inconceivable. Thanks to Feliciano's influence, I often place a stack of warm tortillas wrapped in a linen napkin on the table. Whether it's Szechwan soup or a breakfast omelet, I've watched my family and guests eat with both hands.

The dying art of hand patting tortillas is replaced by two gadgets, the hand tortilla press and the electric tortilla press, which also cooks the tortilla. With the wide availability of the presses and with masa available nationally, making tortillas is a snap.

Mexicans and Central Americans usually keep the tortilla about 6 inches in diameter and under ⅛ inch thick. They traditionally use the comal, *a thin unglazed tile, to bake the tortillas over an open fire; it can also be used over a gas flame. Hopis and Navahos favor a smaller, thicker disk.*

Deviating from convention, I oftentimes embellish the basic recipe with an herb or spice. Marjoram has a gentle flavor, and the flecks of green decorate the finished bread.

Put the masa harina in a mixing bowl and stir in the water and marjoram. Knead thoroughly for about 3 minutes, or until the dough forms a smooth, silky mass that does not stick to your hands. It should be moist and pliable enough that a pinch of dough will easily press flat when pushed between your fingertips. Cover the dough and let it rest for at least 5 minutes or refrigerate it for up to 24 hours.

With moistened hands, divide the dough into 12 balls. Roll each ball between your palms until smooth. Cover the balls with plastic wrap to keep them from drying out.

Heat an electric tortilla press and prepare according to the manufacturer's directions. If using a hand press, cover the surfaces with plastic wrap to prevent the dough from sticking. Press each ball into a disk shape with your hands, and then flatten with the tortilla press. Open the press; turn the tortilla 180°. Press down a second time to create a round disk of uniform thickness. Remove the tortilla from the press and toss it back and forth a few times to aerate it. When all the tortillas are made, cover them with plastic wrap to keep them moist. (Tortillas may also be shaped with a rolling pin. Place a flattened disk on the counter, cover with a piece of wax paper, and gently roll out.)

Heat a heavy ungreased skillet or griddle over medium-high heat until hot. Bake the tortillas, one at a time, for 30 seconds. Turn and bake for 1 minute more, or until lightly browned in spots. Turn and bake for another 30 seconds. If the temperature is exactly right, the tortilla will puff up slightly and then deflate. Remove tortilla from griddle and keep warm, tightly wrapped in a cloth, while you bake the remaining tortillas. Stack the finished tortillas and keep the stack tightly wrapped. When finished baking, let tortillas rest, wrapped, for about 15 minutes to finish their cooking and become soft and pliable. Tortillas are best used immediately. However, they will keep, tightly wrapped and refrigerated, for up to 5 days.

VARIATION: For an easier to handle but less flavorful tortilla, substitute up to ¼ cup wheat tortilla or all-purpose flour for the same amount of masa.

Blue corn tortillas are more fragile than white. When making them, divide the dough into 11 instead of 12 balls so that they are not quite as thin as usual. Also, let the pressed tortilla rest for a minute before cooking to increase its resiliency.

Chili-Flavored Tortilla Chips

❧

Makes 36 chips

2 tablespoons water

¹/₂ teaspoon sea salt

¹/₄ teaspoon chili powder

1 dozen corn tortillas, purchased or homemade

My homemade no-fuss chips have more flavor than packaged chips, and they certainly are fresher. Plus, making them fills the house with a great corn aroma. It's hard to imagine any left over, but if there are, return them to the oven to briefly crisp before serving.

Preheat the oven to 350°F.

Combine the water, salt, and chili powder in a spray bottle. Shake to dissolve the salt. Lightly mist both sides of each tortilla. Stack 3 tortillas at a time on a cutting board. As if you were cutting a pinwheel, cut into quarters, leaving the centerpoint uncut. Repeat stacking and cutting until all the tortillas are cut. Place in a single layer on ungreased baking sheets and bake for 10 minutes, or until each tortilla is well crisped. Cool. Break into wedges.

Note: Thicker homemade tortillas will require several additional minutes' crisping time.

Corn and Quinoa
Raspberry Muffins

When it's raspberry harvest time, this is my favorite way to show off the red jewels in a sunny-yellow muffin. If fresh raspberries are not available, you can substitute frozen berries. I use quinoa flour for a corn muffin with a superior moist crumb and piquant flavor, but unbleached white flour, or even barley flour, also works.

Preheat the oven to 350°F. Line the cups of a 12-cup muffin tin with paper liners.

Combine the quinoa flour, cornmeal, baking soda, and salt. In a separate bowl, combine the butter, honey, eggs, and buttermilk. Stir the wet ingredients into the dry, being careful not to overmix. Gently fold in the lemon zest and raspberries. Spoon into muffin cups and bake for 25 minutes, or until the muffins start to brown and a toothpick inserted into the center comes out clean.

VARIATIONS: Substitute cranberries, blackberries, or blueberries for the raspberries.

Substitute blue cornmeal for the yellow.

Makes 12 muffins

1 ½ cups quinoa flour or unbleached all-purpose flour

1 ½ cups yellow cornmeal, preferably stoneground

1 ½ teaspoons baking soda

¾ teaspoon sea salt

4 tablespoons (½ stick) unsalted butter, melted

½ cup honey or maple syrup

2 large eggs, lightly beaten

1 ¼ cups buttermilk or Clabbered Soy Milk (page 371)

½ teaspoon freshly grated lemon zest

1 cup red raspberries

Hominy Breakfast Cakes

❧

Serves 4

2 cups cooked hominy

½ cup diced cooked ham, smoked
  turkey breast, or seasoned tempeh

2 tablespoons unbleached all-purpose
  flour

2 tablespoons chopped fresh chives

1 large egg

Sea salt and freshly ground black
  pepper, to taste

1 teaspoon unsalted butter

Warm maple syrup (optional)

*This is a fast all-in-one breakfast: corn, ham, and eggs. When I prepare this
dish for my two vegetarian daughters, I substitute tempeh for the ham. They
love it.*

Combine the hominy, ham, flour, chives, egg, salt, and pepper.
Form into flat patties. Brush a griddle with butter and heat
over medium-high heat. Add the patties and cook, turning
once, for about 3 minutes on each side, or until well browned. Serve
hot, either as is or with warm maple syrup.

Strawberry and Blue Corn Waffles

These magenta waffles have an earthy sweet and pleasingly tart flavor that works equally well as breakfast or as a dessert when topped with ice cream or frozen yogurt. For breakfast, serve the waffles with butter and strawberry preserves or maple syrup. I sometimes substitute blueberries for the strawberries for a dramatic indigo color and a sweeter flavor. If you use the one-pound supermarket package of frozen unsweetened strawberries, there will be enough berries left over for a garnish. Do not make the batter in advance.

Puree the strawberries in a food processor until smooth and soupy. Add the remaining ingredients and process to just mix.

Preheat a waffle iron and cook the waffles according to manufacturer's directions. This waffle browns quickly, so watch carefully not to overcook. Serve hot.

VARIATION: For a wheat-free waffle, substitute rye or barley flour for the wheat.

Serves 3

2 cups sliced fresh or frozen unsweetened strawberries

1 cup blue cornmeal

¼ cup whole wheat pastry flour

1 tablespoon Sucanat or light brown sugar

½ teaspoon baking soda

½ teaspoon sea salt

3 tablespoons unsalted butter, melted

1 large egg

Pinole

❧

This popular Mexican and Native American drink aids digestion and lifts the spirits. My former neighbor, Lorraine Fox Davis, of the Blackfoot tribe, served this to me upon the completion of a purification sweat in her lodge. In winter, I substitute one teaspoon of ginger juice for the cinnamon; ginger increases blood circulation and makes the drink even more warming. It's far more sustaining than hot cocoa in a thermos for winter sports.

Serves 4 cups

¹/₂ cup pinole flour or finely ground blue or white stoneground corn flour (see Note)

1 tablespoon Vanilla Sugar or Instant Vanilla Sugar (page 269), or to taste

¹/₂ teaspoon ground cinnamon

4 cups hot milk or soy milk

Note: If using corn flour, sift and remove any coarse particles. If pinole or corn flour is not available, use sifted cornmeal.

Put the pinole flour in a saucepan or wok over medium-high heat. Toast, stirring constantly, for 2 to 3 minutes, or until aromatic and a shade darker.

Combine the corn flour, Vanilla Sugar, and cinnamon in a 1¹/₂-quart saucepan. Add 1 cup of the milk and stir to blend. Stir in the remaining milk. Place over medium heat and bring to a boil, watching carefully to prevent boiling over. Stir as necessary and simmer for 15 minutes. Serve hot.

Atole

I remember the first time I had atole, lunching at an atolería in the open-air Indian market in Uruapan, Mexico. I didn't know whether it was a soup or a drink, but I'd never tasted anything so wonderful. I determined then to duplicate atole at home and to serve it daily. This was fifteen years ago. Well, my determination has wavered, but atole remains a frequent treat. Whenever my busy teenage children think they don't have time for breakfast, the aroma of atole wafting through the house tempts them into the kitchen. It may also be served at lunch or dinner or any time you need a pick-me-up.

Combine the almonds, pinole flour, sugar, and anise in a 2-quart saucepan. Stir in about ³/₄ cup milk, or enough to make a gruel. Whisk in the remaining milk and bring to a simmer over high heat, stirring constantly. Reduce the heat to low and cook for 5 minutes, stirring occasionally to prevent burning. Pour into mugs. Serve hot with a grating of Mexican chocolate on top, if desired.

Serves 2

¹/₂ cup finely ground blanched almonds

¹/₂ cup pinole flour or finely ground blue or white stoneground corn flour (see Note)

4 teaspoons Mexican sugar (piloncillo), grated, Sucanat, or light brown sugar

¹/₄ teaspoon ground anise

4 cups milk or soy milk

Grated Mexican chocolate (optional)

Note: If using corn flour, sift and remove any coarse corn particles. If pinole or corn flour is not available, use sifted cornmeal.

Mesquite

MOST PEOPLE KNOW mesquite as a novelty charcoal for grilling or as honey with a desert bouquet. Mesquite is much more. It has been perhaps the single most important wild plant food of native Southwestern peoples and is used for a wide variety of medicinal and utilitarian purposes. The pods and seeds of this leguminous drought-resistant small tree (*Prosopis veluntina*) are ground for bread, cake, cereal, and beverages by desert-dwelling native peoples throughout the Americas. This mesquite meal has a pleasant malty sweetness and bold character.

Mesquite wood is highly valued for furniture, wood crafts, and charcoal making. Consequently, the fragile desert ecosystem throughout the Southwest and northern Mexico is being threatened as mesquite is stripped from it. In an effort to counter this destructive trend, ProNatura, the Mexican Association for Conservation of Nature in Tucson, Arizona, makes mesquite meal available. As foraging mesquite pods for meal becomes more financially lucrative than cutting down the trees, it is hoped the desert will be stabilized. A purchase of mesquite meal, currently imported from Mexico and Peru, from ProNatura supports this important work.

Mesquite is high in lysine and rich in calcium, magnesium, potassium, iron, and zinc; it also provides carbohydrates. Mesquite's natural sweetness makes it unnecessary to add a sweetener in many recipes. Lacking gluten, though, the meal is best combined with wheat flour in baked goods. It can be added to dishes to enhance flavor and as a nutritional supplement, much as one would add wheat germ, in breads and quick breads.

Mesquite
Selection and Storage

If you're near the desert in Mexico, southern California, Arizona, New Mexico, Texas, Oklahoma, Arkansas, even Kansas, collect mesquite pods from the trees or from the ground soon after they fall, let them dry, and store them in a closed container in a cool, dark, dry place for up to several years. When ready to use, grind the pods, the numerous seeds, and the sweet yellowish mealy substance surrounding the seeds in a blender and sift out any coarse material. For 1 cup mesquite meal, grind $1^1/_2$ cups of pods. Store purchased mesquite meal, tightly wrapped, in the freezer for up to 1 year. It can be ordered from ProNatura (see page 376).

My favorite use of mesquite after pinole is in cornbread. I sometimes substitute up to 20 percent of the corn with mesquite in Greens and Herbed Cornmeal Dumplings (page 51) or Sage and Blue Corn Skillet Bread with Fresh Corn (page 55). I sprinkle some of the meal on the counter when shaping a loaf of bread—it makes a glossy, sweet, aromatic crust—but I don't recommend mesquite as a waffle ingredient as it tends to stick.

Tarahumara Pinole Mix

❧

The best way to use mesquite is in pinole, a dietary staple of the indigenous American peoples. Pinole in a corn mixture that traditionally included other local ingredients and was eaten dry in pinches or cooked with water into a cereal or beverage. This particular mix uses energizing foods from northwestern Mexico, home to the world-famous Tarahumara runners, who ate pinole to sustain them in their legendary hundred-mile mountain marathons. I recommend this mix to mountaineers and others engaged in endurance sports. It is also available ready-made from Sourcepoint Organic Seeds (see page 377).

Heat a wok or saucepan over medium-high heat and toast the corn flour for 2 to 3 minutes, or until it becomes aromatic and a shade darker. Scrape into a bowl. Toast the mesquite meal for 1 to 2 minutes, or until it becomes aromatic and a shade darker. Add to the corn. Toast the sunflower seeds for 2 to 3 minutes, or until they become aromatic and a shade darker. Grind the seeds in a spice mill or coffee grinder and add to the mixture. Add the chia seeds and salt and stir to blend. When thoroughly cool, store in an airtight container. Eat in pinches.

VARIATIONS: For breakfast cereal, mix 1 cup pinole mix in 3 cups water and simmer for 30 minutes, stirring from time to time.

For a beverage, dissolve 1 to 2 tablespoons pinole mix in 1 cup water, milk, or soy milk and simmer for 15 to 20 minutes.

Makes 1^1/$_2$ cups

1 cup blue corn flour or cornmeal

^{1}/$_4$ cup mesquite meal (see page 68)

^{1}/$_4$ cup sunflower seeds

2 tablespoons chia seeds (see Note)

^{1}/$_4$ teaspoon sea salt

Note: Chia seeds are almost as small as poppy seeds and almost as black. They have a mild flavor, similar to sesame seeds. Prized by Native Americans of the Southwest as an endurance food, they are available in natural foods stores.

Amaranth

WHAT WAS ONCE the sacred food of the Aztecs has recently begun to appear on the shelves of American natural foods stores. Amaranth (*Amaranthus*) was domesticated about seven thousand years ago in Mexico. By the time of Cortez's arrival in the New World, amaranth was as important a crop as maize. Although we'll probably never know whether the conquistadors actually forbade the cultivation of amaranth or simply discouraged its use in so-called pagan ritual, one thing is certain: A grain that had been the staple food of thousands of people throughout the Americas virtually disappeared within decades.

Amaranth is truly an untamed grain. Its biggest culinary drawback is that its tiny seeds leave an unfamiliar mouth feel and require attentive chewing. On the plus side is that amaranth is filling, warming, and energizing. It has a pleasant fresh cornlike aroma and a woodsy flavor.

Amaranth is not a cereal grass. Rather, this broad-leafed annual is a member of the order Caryophyllales, which also includes leafy greens like spinach and chard. It is a tall, stately plant with a vibrant maroon color and shaggy heads that each contain thousands of tiny seeds. The small patch of amaranth in my garden provides ample grain as well as leaves, and it always reseeds itself.

Today amaranth is cultivated primarily for the food value of the grain; the leaves are used as a vegetable, for food coloring, and for ornament. The entire plant has been used traditionally for medicinal, magical, and religious purposes.

Amaranth Selection and Storage	Amaranth Flour
Odds are that your natural foods store stocks only one variety of amaranth because of its low volume of sales. Store amaranth in a cool, dark, and dry place, preferably in a covered glass jar. Amaranth will keep for up to 1 year, but if it is old or if it is stored in a warm place or exposed to the light, it will develop a bitter taste.	Buff in color, amaranth flour has a slightly grassy taste. You can increase the flavor and nutrient profile of bread and other baked goods by adding up to 10 percent amaranth flour. Because the seeds are so tiny, amaranth is difficult to grind at home unless you have a stone flour mill, but amaranth flour is available in natural foods markets. Store amaranth flour tightly covered in the freezer or refrigerator for up to six months.

The pinhead-size seeds have an unusually high protein content, 18 percent, with the protein carrying high levels of lysine, one of the most vital amino acids. It is also higher in both iron and calcium than conventional grains; it contains slightly higher levels of oil and has twice as much fiber as wheat. The germ and seedcoat of amaranth contain high concentrations of vitamins, particularly vitamin E, minerals, protein, oil, and fiber, with the germ holding almost all of the protein. For impoverished countries, where the population often lives on marginal lands, those tiny amaranth seeds could hold the key to healthy survival. Scientists looking for new ways to feed the modern world's hungry have recently rediscovered amaranth's potential, with its protein balance better than that of cow's milk and its ability to thrive in adverse agricultural conditions.

In the past few years production in the United States has increased significantly to about five thousand acres, mostly in Nebraska, Colorado, and Minnesota. Generally though, wherever grain amaranth appears in cultivation today it is a secondary or marginal crop. In Asia, amaranth is largely cultivated by scattered hill peoples, and in Central and South America and Africa it is cultivated by rural subsistence farmers. The yield of grain amaranth is greater than corn but the seeds are tiny and difficult to process.

Most of the amaranth consumed around the world is prepared as a gruel or thick soup flavored with a bit of fat or chilies. The high starch content creates a thick sauce when the grain is cooked, making it more suitable to porridge-type dishes than to dry pilafs. I sometimes add just a tablespoonful of amaranth to other grains for its texture and wild flavor.

Steamed Amaranth

❦

Over the years, I've tried countless methods of cooking amaranth and was always put off by its gooey texture. I finally devised a method that works, and I now prepare this grain fairly often, especially when I want to eat something fast and filling. It is critical to toast the grain first and to add it to boiling water. Since the seeds are so tiny, they are impossible to rinse before cooking, but I have found that organically grown amaranth is clean when packaged.

Makes 1 ¹⁄₂ cups

1 cup amaranth seeds

1 cup water

1 teaspoon unrefined vegetable oil

Gomasio (page 361)

Toast the amaranth in a saucepan or wok over medium heat, stirring constantly, for 4 minutes, or until it starts to pop and emits a toasty aroma.

Bring the water and oil to a boil over high heat. Add the amaranth, cover, lower the heat, and simmer for 7 minutes, or until all the liquid has been absorbed. Remove from the heat and let steam, covered, for 5 to 10 minutes. Serve with Gomasio.

VARIATIONS: For a soft breakfast cereal, double the water and cooking time.

Add 1 teaspoon grated fresh ginger and/or 1 clove garlic, minced, and/or ¹⁄₄ cup minced onion.

Popped Amaranth
Cold Breakfast Cereal

❦

**Makes 1 serving or 1¹/₂ cups
popped amaranth**

¹/₂ cup amaranth seeds

1 cup cold milk or soy milk

3 fresh strawberries, sliced

Maple syrup, to taste

Popped amaranth is earthy sweet and crunchy dry, but unlike popcorn, substantial. A decidedly new taste experience. The aroma of popping amaranth quickly draws people into the kitchen from afar. I pop amaranth to use as a cold breakfast cereal, a condiment, or a sprinkle for other dishes and to make into the traditional Mexican candy, Alegría (page 77).

Heat a wok or large saucepan, not a cast-iron pot or a pan with low sides, over high heat. Add ¹/₄ cup of the amaranth and stir constantly until most of the grains have popped and those that do not pop are a shade or two darker. Remove from the pan. Repeat with the remaining amaranth. Put in a cereal bowl, pour milk over, add the strawberry slices, and sweeten to taste with maple syrup. To store popped amaranth, cool thoroughly and store in a tightly covered container for several weeks. The flavor and aroma, however, are best when fresh.

Pink Potato Soup

✦

Amaranth leaves tint this soup a delicate pink, which has great eye appeal, and add a mild flavor. I've made this soup with red potatoes, blue potatoes, and yellow Finns. My choice is blue potatoes, which turn a soft violet that is right at home in the pink broth. I use amaranth leaves from my garden, but they're also available from Asian markets.

Heat the oil in a large saucepan over medium heat until warm. Add the onion and garlic and sauté for 4 minutes. Add the potatoes, stock, and bay leaves. Bring to a boil, reduce the heat, and simmer for 10 minutes, or until the potatoes are tender. Add the amaranth leaves and marjoram and season with salt and pepper. Simmer for 5 minutes, or until the amaranth leaves are tender. Correct the seasoning. Ladle the soup into large bowls.

Serves 4

1 ¹/₂ tablespoons extra virgin olive oil

1 onion, finely chopped

3 cloves garlic, minced

4 small potatoes, preferably blue, peeled and finely diced

6 cups Vegetable Stock (page 364)

2 bay leaves

3 cups amaranth leaves, chopped (see Note)

2 tablespoons chopped fresh marjoram

Sea salt and freshly ground black pepper, to taste

Note: Amaranth leaves are a striking magenta in color. The leaves are lance shaped to egg shaped. At first glance they look like a very large purple basil, but there are no serrations on the leaves. They are available in Asian markets. They are mild with a spinachlike flavor, and like beets, they will color a whole dish. If you're harvesting your own amaranth leaves, pick them before the seed heads develop, while they are still young and succulent. For the same flavor, substitute the green leaves of the common weed pigweed (*Amaranthus graecizans*), which grows throughout the western United States.

Piñon Crackers

❧

Before corn became a staple in the Southwest, amaranth, piñon, and other wild seeds were used to make bread. The untamed flavors of amaranth and piñon inspired these crackers. Tender yet crisp, these little flatbreads take minutes to prepare. They are irresistible hot or cold, and they upgrade any bowl of soup. I especially like them with Quinoa and Winter Squash Potage (page 90) and Autumn Soup of Wild Rice, White Beans, and Olives (page 11).

Makes fifty 1½-inch crackers

½ cup amaranth flour
  (see page 72)

½ cup piñon (pine nuts)

1 cup whole wheat pastry flour

1 teaspoon baking powder

½ teaspoon sea salt

2 tablespoons unsalted butter, chilled

⅓ cup cold water

1 teaspoon cumin seeds, lightly toasted

Preheat the oven to 350°F.

Toast the amaranth flour in a saucepan or wok over medium heat for 2 minutes, or until it gives off a fragrance and darkens slightly. Set aside.

Put the piñon in a food processor and process to a coarse meal. Add the amaranth flour, whole wheat flour, baking powder, and salt and pulse once or twice to mix. Cut the butter into chunks. Add to the flour mixture and pulse to form a crumbly meal. Add enough water to make a pliable dough, similar in touch to pie crust dough. Remove the dough from the processor and pat into an oblong shape.

Turn an 18 × 12-inch jelly-roll pan upside down and grease the bottom. Center the dough on the pan. Cover with wax paper and roll the dough nearly to the edge of the pan, to a thickness of ⅛ inch. With a pastry wheel or butter knife, cut the dough into 1½-inch vertical strips. Cut 1½-inch strips on the diagonal to form diamond shapes. Bake for about 12 minutes, or until golden brown. Cool on a wire rack until set and serve while still warm. Or cool thoroughly on a rack, place in an airtight container, and store in a cool place for up to 1 week. To recrisp the crackers, place in a hot oven for 3 to 4 minutes.

VARIATIONS: Substitute sunflower seeds for the piñon.
Substitute 1¼ cups barley flour for the whole wheat pastry flour.

Alegría

In Mexico and India, cakes or large bars of popped amaranth seeds bound with a sweetener are sold by street vendors. Known as Alegría in Mexico and ladoos in India, these sweet treats are rather like sesame candy in appearance. I use rice syrup, which gives a deep and mellow sweetness that is not at all cloying. Maple syrup is a good second choice. Honey also works but has a more intense sweetness. The candy stays fresh for weeks.

Lightly grease an 8-inch square cake pan and set aside. Put the rice syrup in a medium saucepan over medium-high heat and bring to a soft boil. Boil for about 10 minutes, or until the syrup reaches 244°F. on a candy thermometer. Remove from heat. Stir in the sunflower seeds and cinnamon. When well combined, stir in the amaranth, stirring just enough to coat. Press into the pan and let cool somewhat. Cut into 2-inch squares. Wrap any that are not eaten immediately airtight and store in a cool, dry place. These will keep for a month or more.

Makes twenty-four 1-inch square candies

¹/₃ cup rice syrup (see page 374), maple syrup, or honey

¹/₄ cup toasted sunflower seeds

¹/₄ teaspoon ground cinnamon

1 ¹/₂ cups popped amaranth (page 74)

Quinoa

WHEN I TOOK my first bite of quinoa I was hooked, so much so that five years later I traveled to Peru and Bolivia to research my book *Quinoa: The Supergrain*. There I fell in love with the stark and dramatic altiplano country, its people, and their foods, especially quinoa (*Chenopodium quinoa willdenow*). Chances are that the mellow taste of quinoa (pronounced KEEN-wah) will hook you too. Its subtly sweet yet nutty flavor delivers an almost piquant aftertaste. Eating it is nothing short of a revelation, and quinoa boasts the highest nutrition profile of all grains and is the quickest cooking.

A careful look at a single grain of quinoa quickly reveals its nutritional superiority to other grains. The germ, equivalent to the yolk of an egg, is the most power-packed part of any seed. In most grains it is little more than a speck, but quinoa's germ completely surrounds the rest of the seed. This helps explain why quinoa contains up to 20 percent high-quality protein. Hard spring wheat, the next highest common grain in protein, contains only 14 percent by comparison. The United Nations World Health Organization observes that quinoa is closer to the ideal protein balance than any other grain, being at least equal to milk in protein quality. This dynamic grain is high in B vitamins, iron, zinc, potassium, calcium, and vitamin E.

When quinoa is cooked, the thin germ circlet falls from the seed and remains almost crunchy; the grain itself, pearly and translucent, melts in your mouth. This dual texture makes it very interesting to eat. It is the lightest of grains, and since it is relatively soft, it is easily milled into flour, further extending its usefulness. Unlike rice, wheat, corn, and the other common grains, which are members of the grass family (*Gramineae*), quinoa is a member of the goosefoot family (*Chenopodiaceae*). The goosefoots are so named because their three-lobed leaf is shaped like the foot of a goose. Lamb's-quarter, a near relative of quinoa, is the most common wild goosefoot in the United States; it is highly valued by foragers.

Quinoa was first cultivated in South America eight thousand years ago. The people of the altiplano, the highlands of the Andes, gathered seeds from the wild plant and began to domesticate it at about the same time farmers began to plant rice in eastern Asia and wheat in the Near East. The choice was an obvious one since quinoa grows readily and in a wide variety of poor conditions.

Quinoa does best in a cool and lofty environment. Though some varieties grow at sea level, most grow in high mountain valley deserts at elevations above ten thousand feet. Some varieties thrive even above fourteen thousand feet, where no other foods grow. At these high altitudes rain falls only in the spring, the soil is poor and rocky, and the thin oxygen provides little buffer to the frigid temperatures and the intensely powerful solar radiation that stresses all living things. Quinoa leaves contain minute vessels that hold calcium oxalate crystals that provide protection from the high levels of radiation. The calcium oxalate crystals also retain moisture, making quinoa far more tolerant of drought than other crops.

Quinoa has been successfully grown outside the Andean region since 1982. The fact that it matures and sets seed despite drought, frost, and radiation has significant agricultural implications. Throughout the world more and more farmers work marginal lands, where neither rainfall nor irrigation are sufficient to support the growth of the common grains. Quinoa can be grown easily in many of these often barren areas. Unfortunately, the cultivation of quinoa is currently limited even in its South American homeland, for reasons that have nothing to do with nutrition, flavor, or hardiness but everything to do with the subversion of the Inca culture. For thousands of years, quinoa was a staple throughout the Andes region. The Incas not only relied upon quinoa, they revered it, calling it their sacred mother grain. In an annual highly symbolic ritual, their ruler, the Inca, ceremonially planted the first quinoa seed with his symbol of state, a golden spade.

While Inca civilization is remembered for its archaeological sites, such as Machu Picchu—which was an agricultural testing station—what strikes me is that hunger was unknown. An extensive storage and road system linked the vast Inca empire. Public storehouses held quinoa and other foods, such as dried potatoes and chilies, for distribution during times of shortage. When the Spanish conquered the Incas in the sixteenth century, they virtually destroyed this ancient civilization in just one year. They prohibited the cultivation of the sacred mother grain, and barley soon flourished in former quinoa terraces so that foreign thirsts might be quenched with Spanish-style beer. Only in remote mountain areas where barley could not possibly grow and where the Spanish rarely ventured did quinoa continue to thrive.

Quinoa
Selection and Storage

The major U.S. quinoa distributors currently import the grain from South America. This imported variety is large, about the size of millet, and uniformly buff or cream colored. It has been well processed so that most of the bitter saponin coating is removed.

Domestic quinoa is smaller, with a richer, deeper flavor. The seeds vary in color from off-white to dark tan with even a few black seeds thrown in. This type of quinoa requires an extra washing and cooks up less dry and fluffy even though it requires less liquid (2 cups liquid to $1^1/_3$ cups domestic quinoa as opposed to 2 cups liquid to 1 cup imported quinoa). I recommend the full-flavored domestic quinoa over the imported.

Watch for black quinoa, which currently has some market availability. The Quechua Indians of Bolivia consider black quinoa especially strengthening to the kidneys.

Quinoa is available in most natural and specialty food stores, either packaged or in bulk bins, and in supermarkets. Store it in a cool dark place, preferably in a covered glass jar, for 1 year or more.

Washing Quinoa

Quinoa is coated with saponin, a bitter naturally occurring substance that acts as a pesticide. Although quinoa has been processed to remove the saponin, it still needs to be thoroughly washed before cooking.

To wash quinoa, put it in a deep bowl and cover with cold water. Gently rub it between your palms for about 6 seconds or so to wash off the saponin. Drain the quinoa in a fine-mesh strainer. Repeat. If using domestic quinoa, wash a third time. Place the strainer under cold running water and rinse the quinoa until the water runs almost clear.

Quinoa Flour

Quinoa flour is available in natural foods stores. Since quinoa is a soft grain, you can easily make your own in a grain mill, spice or coffee mill, or blender.

To make quinoa flour, use imported quinoa, which has had most of the saponin removed. (Domestic quinoa must be washed and thoroughly dried before grinding.) Grind $^2/_3$ cup quinoa to make 1 cup flour. Store quinoa flour, tightly wrapped, in the refrigerator or freezer and use within 4 months.

From the seventeenth century onward, barley and wheat became the grain of the upper classes, and quinoa came to be associated with poverty, illiteracy, and chicken feed. Today the Aymara and Quechua peoples, descendants of the once proud Incas, are unaware that quinoa was once revered. These poor people depend upon costly imported noodles and rice that are nutritionally inferior to quinoa, because they believe that if they feed quinoa to their children, it will make them stupid, a belief that can be traced to the conquistadors.

In 1982, when my friends Steve Gorad and Don McKinley began marketing Bolivian quinoa in the United States, I was putting quinoa into everything from soup to cake. They asked me to develop recipes for them. Gorad and McKinley didn't know of the failed attempts of the U.S. Academy of Science, Rodale Organic Farms, and others to grow quinoa north of the equator and east of the Rocky Mountains. The late David Cussack, a Colorado University professor, joined forces with them. Raised on a high-elevation Colorado potato farm, he thought of the obvious. He would plant quinoa in the nation's highest irrigated mountain valley, the San Luis Valley of southern Colorado and northern New Mexico. Cussack drove to the valley to find a farmer willing to gamble a field on an untested grain. He pulled into Ernie New's Mosca Pit Stop for gasoline. When snow blankets New's potato fields he pumps gas at the only store in Mosca, Colorado. Ernie New sold the professor a tank of gas and Cussack sold New a dream—the dream of a new cash crop that would grow on marginal land—plus the thrill of being the first in this agricultural adventure. New's billed cap advertises Valley Feed Co., his turquoise belt buckle proclaims Jesus, and his fields, at seventy-five hundred feet, offer drama as they nestle between the Sangre de Cristo Mountains and the massive San Juan mountain range. Today New and his wife, Virginia, host "Introducing Quinoa" suppers for their potato-farming neighbors. The menu features quinoa in everything from chile con carne to orange Jell-O with mini marshmallows.

I've worked with New and other farmers in the San Luis Valley, weeding, harvesting, and threshing quinoa. I also grow it in my garden. The leafy five-foot-high plant looks something like sorghum when green but at harvest it is a flamboyant fuchsia. The heavily laden seed heads are a dazzling color display—orange, red, ivory, purple, yellow, green, ocher, rose, lavender, and black. The quinoa commercially available in the United States is buff yellow in color, but I've seen hundreds of other varieties, some with typical grain colors and some with such colors as ebony, brown, peach, or white with a single red eye.

Following New's lead, other visionary farmers are raising quinoa throughout the Rocky Mountains, from the Mexican border up into Canada, as well as in western Washington State. East of the Rockies, the plant will grow as a decorative ornamental, but it will probably not set seed since it needs relatively cool summer nights for that.

Steamed Quinoa

At least once a week, I make a pot of quinoa to last for my next three meals. I sprinkle Gomasio (page 361) on it for breakfast, and then, for example, toss it with steamed vegetables for a lunch pilaf, and stir-fry the rest for supper. If the quinoa is to be used for a dessert, I cook it in water and season it only with salt and a little oil or ghee. Refrigerated grain loses its subtle flavor, so I just cover the cooked grain with a bamboo sushi mat or cotton cloth and leave it out on the counter.

Several factors affect the volume of the cooked quinoa. Letting the quinoa rest, covered, after cooking gives the grains a chance to swell. Fluffing the grain further increases volume. Also note that imported quinoa is slightly higher in volume than domestic.

Makes 3¹/₂ to 4 cups

2 cups Vegetable Stock (page 364) or water

¹/₄ teaspoon sea salt or 2 teaspoons tamari soy sauce

Freshly ground black pepper, to taste

1 clove garlic, minced

1 cup imported quinoa or 1¹/₃ cups domestic quinoa, well washed (see page 81)

Combine the stock, salt, pepper, and garlic in a 1-quart saucepan over high heat and bring to a rapid boil. Add the quinoa, cover, and lower the heat to a simmer. Cook for 12 minutes, or until all the water has been absorbed. The grain should be translucent and its thin germ curlicue white. Remove from the heat and let rest, covered for 5 minutes. Fluff with a fork. Serve with Miso-Walnut Topping (page 363) or Gomasio (page 361).

VARIATIONS: For a creamy breakfast cereal, substitute 3 cups milk for the 2 cups stock and increase the cooking time to 20 minutes.

Thoroughly drain the quinoa and toast it in an ungreased saucepan or a wok over medium-high heat, stirring constantly, for about 3 minutes, or until it turns a shade darker. Do not toast in the oven or in a cast-iron skillet, or you will dry the grain. What is more, oven toasting does not produce a uniform result.

Add minced shallot or onion to taste to the boiling stock.

Add 2 tablespoons toasted seeds or chopped nuts, such as sesame or sunflower seeds, pecans, walnuts, or hazelnuts at any point during the cooking time.

Season cooked quinoa with one tablespoon minced fresh herbs such as basil, dill, fennel, oregano, parsley, rosemary, tarragon, or thyme.

Spice blends such as curry or Garam Masala (page 358) are excellent in quinoa; use 1 tablespoon for 4 cups of cooked quinoa. Another good spice combination is $\frac{1}{2}$ teaspoon ground coriander, $\frac{1}{4}$ teaspoon ground cumin, and $\frac{1}{8}$ teaspoon turmeric to each cup uncooked quinoa.

Saffron flavors either domestic or imported quinoa, but its color is lost on domestic quinoa.

Quinoa Cooked Like Pasta

This method of cooking quinoa tempers the somewhat grassy taste of the grain and makes it denser and less fluffy.

Pour the water into a saucepan, place over high heat, and bring to a boil. Add the quinoa, lower the heat, and simmer, uncovered, for 10 to 12 minutes, or just until the grains turn translucent. Remove from the heat and pour into a strainer, draining well. Do not rinse. Use as you would steamed quinoa.

Makes 2 $^1/_2$ cups

4 cups water

1 cup imported quinoa or 1 $^1/_3$ cups domestic quinoa, well washed (see page 81)

Breakfast Quinoa

❦

This orange-flavored quinoa makes a good breakfast dish; it is also a great base for a fresh fruit salad.

Makes 3¾ cups

2 cups fresh orange juice

1 teaspoon ghee (page 359) or unrefined sesame oil

1 teaspoon honey

⅛ teaspoon sea salt

1 cup imported quinoa or 1⅓ cups domestic quinoa, well washed (see page 81)

2 tablespoons pecans, roasted and chopped very fine

Combine the orange juice, ghee, honey, and salt in a medium saucepan over high heat and bring to a boil. Watch closely to keep the orange juice from boiling over. Add the quinoa, cover, lower the heat, and simmer for 12 to 15 minutes, or until all of the juice has been absorbed. Remove from the heat and let rest for 5 minutes. Add the pecans and fluff with a fork.

Gingered Lamb
and Quinoa in Phyllo

❦

In these little rolls, the rich juices of the lamb are absorbed by the quinoa, creating a luxurious filling that is nicely offset by the crisp delicacy of phyllo. Phyllo dough can be found in the frozen food section of most supermarkets.

Heat the olive oil in a medium sauté pan over medium-high heat until hot. Add the onion and sauté for about 4 minutes, or until transparent. Add the mushrooms and sauté for about 5 minutes, or until the mushrooms give off their liquid. Add the lamb and sauté for 4 minutes, or until it begins to color. Season with thyme, salt, and pepper. Remove from the heat and let cool.

Combine the lamb mixture with the quinoa, red pepper, parsley, piñon, and ginger.

Preheat the oven to 375°F.

Unroll the phyllo sheets on a smooth dry surface. Cut the layered sheets in half to make 32 sheets 6 ½ inches wide. Cover tightly with plastic wrap and then cover with a damp towel to prevent phyllo from drying out.

Remove 4 half sheets of phyllo, one at a time. Brush each with melted butter and layer the buttered sheets one on top of another. Spread ½ cup of the filling along 1 end of the top sheet about 1 inch from the end, leaving ½ inch on each side free of any filling. From the end with the filling, roll 1 or 2 turns to totally enclose the filling. Then fold in the 2 long edges of the phyllo and roll to the end of the strip. Brush the outside with butter. Place on an ungreased baking sheet. Repeat with the remaining phyllo sheets and filling. Bake for 15 to 20 minutes, or until golden brown. Remove from the oven and serve hot.

Makes 16

2 tablespoons extra virgin olive oil

1 medium onion, finely chopped

3 ounces oyster mushrooms, chopped (see Note)

½ pound lean ground lamb

3 sprigs of thyme, leaves minced

Sea salt and freshly ground black pepper, to taste

3 cups cooked quinoa (see page 83)

⅓ cup minced roasted red bell pepper

¼ cup chopped fresh Italian flat-leaf parsley

¼ cup piñon (pine nuts)

1 tablespoon minced fresh ginger

16 sheets frozen phyllo dough, thawed

8 tablespoons (1 stick) unsalted butter, melted

Note: If oyster mushrooms are not available, substitute chopped shiitake or button mushrooms.

Quinoa Blinis
with Black Bean Caviar

❦

This is a lighthearted dish, an appetizer to serve to people with a sense of humor. The blini are thicker and lighter yet more substantial than those made with buckwheat. The pungent black bean mixture, which replaces Russian caviar, is creamy and flavorful.

Makes 12 blinis

2 cups cooked quinoa
  (see page 83)

2 large eggs, lightly beaten

½ cup minced onion

¼ cup minced fresh chives

1 tablespoon wine vinegar

2 tablespoons unbleached all-purpose
  flour

1 tablespoon water

Sea salt and freshly ground pepper,
  to taste

About 3 tablespoons unsalted butter

Black Bean Caviar (recipe follows)

½ cup Crème Fraîche (page 355)

Preheat the oven to 200°F.

Mix together the quinoa, eggs, onion, 2 tablespoons of the chives, vinegar, flour, water, salt, and pepper in a large bowl until well combined. Heat a large nonstick skillet over medium-high heat until hot. Add 1 tablespoon of the butter. When the foam subsides, pour four ¼-cup portions of quinoa batter into the pan. Cook each side for 3 to 4 minutes, or until well browned. Place cooked blinis in the oven to keep warm while you cook the rest, adding butter to the pan as needed.

Place 3 blinis on each of 4 plates. Top each with a spoonful of black beans, a dollop of cream, and a sprinkle of the remaining chives. Serve immediately.

Black Bean Caviar

Combine the beans with their liquid, the garlic, thyme, salt, and pepper in a small saucepan over medium heat and bring to a boil. Lower the heat and simmer for about 15 minutes, or until the flavors are well combined and the liquid has evaporated. Place about one third of the bean mixture in a blender and puree. Return the puree to the pot and stir to combine. Taste and adjust the seasoning if necessary. Cover and keep warm over hot water.

Makes about 1 ½ cups

2 cups cooked black beans, undrained

3 cloves garlic, minced

3 or 4 sprigs of thyme, leaves only

Sea salt and freshly ground black pepper, to taste

Quinoa and
Winter Squash Potage

❦

Serves 4

2 teaspoons unsalted butter

½ teaspoon yellow mustard seeds

1 cup minced onion

2 cups diced butternut, kabocha, or
buttercup squash

¼ cup uncooked quinoa, imported or
domestic, well washed (see page 81)

3 cups Vegetable Stock (page 364) or
Chicken Stock (page 366)

Sea salt and freshly ground black
pepper, to taste

2 tablespoons chopped fresh chives or
parsley

Potage, an old word for a hearty soup, somehow evokes the full-bodied goodness of this soup. It's one I make often during the cold months. It's satisfying and pleasing to the eye, with the quinoa, both the curlicues and the grains, standing out against the orange background.

Unless the skin is unusually thick, I don't bother peeling the butternut squash. When using a green-skinned squash such as kabocha or buttercup, I sometimes leave the skin on as well; the flecks of green add a welcome spark of color.

Melt the butter in a medium saucepan over medium heat. Add the mustard seeds and sauté for 1 minute. Add the onion and sauté for 5 minutes, or until translucent. Add the squash and sauté for 5 minutes more. Add the quinoa, stock, salt, and pepper and bring to a boil. Cover, reduce the heat, and simmer for 15 minutes, or until the squash is quite soft. Remove from the heat.

Use a potato masher to mash the squash until coarsely textured and creamy. The soup may also be pureed in a food processor, blender, or food mill. Be careful not to overprocess. (If using a green-skinned squash, do not puree.)

Taste and adjust the seasoning. Pour into a soup tureen or individual bowls. Serve garnished with chopped chives.

Quinoa Soup, Saigon Style

The tangy-hot but fresh flavor of this soup plays over the tongue with a round, pleasing aftertaste. It's quite light, so if you want to have it as a main course, serve it with Vietnamese Spring Rolls (page 182).

Heat 1 tablespoon of the sesame oil in a 2-quart saucepan over medium heat. Add the onion and sauté for about 10 minutes, or until well browned and very sweet tasting. Be careful not to let it burn. Add the stock and bring to a boil. Add the quinoa, red pepper, ginger juice, garlic, Tabasco, Sucanat, soy sauce, nuoc mam, salt, and pepper. Return to a boil, cover, lower the heat, and simmer for 15 minutes.

Heat the remaining sesame oil in a small sauté pan over medium-high heat until hot. Add the shrimp and sauté until just cooked. Remove from the pan and drain on paper towels.

Stir the lime juice, bean sprouts, and cilantro into the soup. Taste and adjust the seasoning. Ladle into soup bowls. Top each portion with a shrimp and serve immediately.

Serves 4

3 tablespoons unrefined sesame oil

1 cup chopped onion

6 cups Fish Stock (page 367) or Chicken Stock (page 366)

¹/₂ cup imported quinoa or ¹/₃ cup domestic quinoa, well washed (see page 81)

1 cup finely diced red bell pepper

1 teaspoon Ginger Juice (page 360)

2 cloves garlic, minced

¹/₄ teaspoon Tabasco Sauce

1 tablespoon Sucanat or light brown sugar

3 tablespoons tamari soy sauce

3 tablespoons nuoc nam fish sauce (see Note)

Sea salt and freshly ground black pepper, to taste

4 large shrimp, peeled and deveined

2 tablespoons fresh lime juice

1 cup bean sprouts

¹/₂ cup chopped fresh cilantro

Note: Nuoc nam fish sauce is available in Asian markets and some specialty food stores.

Cold Zucchini Soup
with Quinoa and Mushrooms

❦

This thick bright-green pureed soup is low in fat, low in salt, high in carbohydrates, high in fiber—and high in flavor. Make the soup at least three hours before serving and chill it quickly for best flavor and color. It is also good hot.

Serves 4

1 tablespoon extra virgin olive oil

¹/₂ cup diced onion

3 teaspoons minced garlic

3 small zucchini, thinly sliced

5 cups Vegetable Stock (page 364) or Chicken Stock (see page 366)

1 tablespoon minced fresh oregano

1 tablespoon minced fresh parsley

Sea salt and freshly ground black pepper, to taste

1 tablespoon Ghee (page 359) or unsalted butter

1 medium shiitake mushroom, finely diced

¹/₂ cup imported quinoa or ²/₃ cup domestic quinoa, well washed (see page 81)

Heat the olive oil in a 3-quart saucepan over medium heat until hot. Add the onion and 2 teaspoons of the garlic. Sauté for about 2 minutes, or until the onion wilts. Add the zucchini and sauté for 3 minutes. Add 4 cups of the stock, the oregano, parsley, salt, and pepper and bring to a boil. Cover, lower the heat, and simmer for 5 minutes, or until the zucchini is just tender. Remove from the heat and let cool for a few minutes. Put in a blender and process until smooth. Pour into a container, cover, and refrigerate for about 3 hours, or until well chilled.

Melt the ghee in a medium sauté pan. Add the mushroom and the remaining garlic. Sauté for about 3 minutes, or until the mushroom pieces have wilted. Add salt, pepper, and the remaining stock and bring to a boil. Add the quinoa and stir to combine. Cover, reduce the heat, and simmer over low heat for 12 minutes, or until all the liquid is absorbed. Remove from the heat and let rest, covered, for 5 minutes. Scrape into a container. Cover and refrigerate for about 3 hours, or until well chilled.

When ready to serve, divide the puree among 4 bowls. Top each serving with ¹/₄ cup of the quinoa mixture. Leave it in a mound or swirl it into the soup.

VARIATIONS: Substitute young beets, carrots, summer squash, or cucumbers for the zucchini.

Add 1 cup chopped ripe avocado or 1 cup light cream to the zucchini before pureeing.

Substitute fresh dill, basil, lemon grass, cilantro, summer savory, or sorrel for the oregano.

Quinoa Potato Salad

Created by Gisela Weischede, the German sub-abbess of the Crestone Mountain Zen Monastery in Colorado, this potato salad is much appreciated by the many people who have gone there on retreat, myself included. I leave the potato skins on for color, but you may peel the potatoes (after cooking them) if you prefer.

Put the potatoes in a large saucepan with water to cover. Place over high heat and bring to a boil. Cover and boil for 20 to 30 minutes, or until cooked through but still firm. Drain well. When cool enough to handle, cut into 1/2-inch cubes. Transfer to a mixing bowl, sprinkle with 2 tablespoons of the vinegar and salt and pepper, and toss. Let stand at room temperature for about 10 minutes, or until the potatoes are cool. Add the celery, quinoa, onion, pickles, and parsley to the potatoes. Gently toss to combine.

Combine the mayonnaise and mustard in a small bowl. Fold the dressing into the potato mixture. Garnish with olives, sprinkle with paprika, and serve.

VARIATION: Substitute 1 pound small pasta shells or gnocchi, cooked, for the potatoes.

Serves 6

1 1/2 pounds red new potatoes, scrubbed

1/4 cup balsamic vinegar

1/2 teaspoon sea salt

1/2 teaspoon freshly ground black pepper

2 stalks celery with some leaves, finely diced

2 cups cooked quinoa (see page 83)

1/2 cup minced red onion

3/4 cup chopped dill pickles

1/4 cup chopped fresh parsley

1/2 cup Tofu Mayonnaise (page 369)

1 tablespoon Dijon mustard

Sea salt and freshly ground black pepper, to taste

12 black olives, pitted

1 teaspoon paprika

Quinoa and Sweet Potato Salad with Mâche

❦

Serves 4

2 tablespoons white wine vinegar

1 tablespoon unrefined roasted sesame oil

1 teaspoon honey

1 teaspoon tamari soy sauce

$^{1}/_{2}$ teaspoon grated fresh ginger

Juice of $^{1}/_{2}$ orange

1 cup finely diced sweet potato

2 heads mâche

1 cup cooked and cooled quinoa (see page 83)

$^{1}/_{2}$ cup snipped chives

2 tablespoons slivered almonds, toasted

This piquant salad is a surprising combination of flavors. Serve it as a spring luncheon entree with a light soup or as a first course for an elegant dinner. If mâche is not available, substitute four ounces of mesclun (mixed baby lettuces). Chill the salad for at least one hour before serving.

Whisk together the vinegar, sesame oil, honey, soy sauce, ginger, and orange juice in a small bowl. Set aside.

Place the sweet potato in a steamer basket over boiling water and steam for $1^{1}/_{2}$ to 3 minutes, or until crisp-tender. Plunge into cold water to stop the cooking. Blot dry with paper towels. Set aside. Wash and carefully dry the mâche. Set aside.

Combine the sweet potato, quinoa, chives, and almonds in a mixing bowl. Toss in 3 tablespoons of the dressing. Cover and refrigerate for at least 1 hour, or until well chilled.

When ready to serve, toss the mâche with the remaining dressing and arrange equal portions on each of 4 salad plates. Place equal portions of salad on the mâche and serve immediately.

VARIATION: Substitute winter squash for yam.

Salad of Quinoa, Duck, and Greens

This easily made mélange blends robust flavors and great colors. It's perfect for either a casual Sunday supper or an elegant dinner party. Use whatever good greens are available. I prefer watercress, arugula, or mesclun, but even a fresh bunch of leaf lettuce from the supermarket will do.

Whisk together the vinegar, olive oil, zinfandel, garlic, soy sauce, thyme, and pepper in a small bowl. Add the duck breast to the dressing and toss to combine. Cover and let stand at room temperature for at least 1 hour.

Place the duck, quinoa, and greens in a large salad bowl and toss. Arrange on individual plates and serve immediately.

VARIATION: Substitute cooked game, poultry, or tempeh for the duck.

Serves 4

2 tablespoons balsamic vinegar

½ cup extra virgin olive oil

2 tablespoons zinfandel

1 clove garlic, minced

1 teaspoon tamari soy sauce

1 teaspoon minced fresh thyme

⅛ teaspoon freshly ground black pepper, or to taste

½ pound cooked duck breast, cut into small bite-size pieces

3 cups cooked quinoa (see page 83)

3 cups chopped mixed tender salad greens

Humitas with Zucchini, Black Olives, and Walnuts

❦

Makes about 20

1 package (6 ounces) dried corn husks

3 medium red potatoes, peeled and quartered

6 tablespoons (¾ stick) unsalted butter

1 large clove garlic, minced

2 tablespoons chili powder, or to taste

Sea salt and freshly ground black pepper, to taste

3 cups cooked quinoa (see page 83)

1 small onion, diced

2 small zucchini, chopped

¾ cup walnuts, toasted

½ cup chopped pitted black olives

I first feasted upon humitas in the Indian markets of Bolivia. They're lighter and moister than corn masa tamales. I like to spread the fixings on the table and soon everyone helps form the humitas. They are delicious with refried beans or Black Bean Caviar (page 89).

Remove any corn silk from the husks. Soak the husks overnight in cold water or for 1 hour in hot water. Drain and remove any remaining corn silk.

Put the potatoes in a medium saucepan with water to cover. Place over high heat and bring to a boil. Lower the heat, cover, and simmer for 20 minutes, or until tender. Drain well. Stir in 5 tablespoons of the butter, the garlic, 1 tablespoon of the chili powder, salt, and pepper. Mash together until creamy. Add the quinoa and stir to combine. Set aside.

Heat the remaining tablespoon butter in a medium sauté pan and sauté the remaining chili powder for 1 minute, or until aromatic. Add the onion and zucchini and sauté for 5 minutes, or until soft. Add the walnuts and black olives and set aside.

Take a large husk or overlap 2 small husks. Place 2 tablespoons of the quinoa mixture on the husk or husks and shape into a rectangle, leaving at least 1 inch on one side and 2 to 3 inches at the top and bottom ends of the husk. Bring the quinoa mixture close to the edge of the husk on the fourth side. Place the zucchini filling in the middle of the quinoa mixture. Fold 1 side of the husk over the quinoa and filling to the opposite side, overlapping the 1-inch border. Fold in the ends of the husk and turn the tamale over to hold the husks in place. Tie with long narrow strips of corn husk or with string. Steam for 30 to 45 minutes in a covered pot. Serve hot or at room temperature. To reheat, steam for 5 to 7 minutes over boiling water.

Annatto

In the altiplano highlands, humitas are colored and flavored with annatto. This South American flavoring (*Bixa orellana*), also called achiote, is available in Latin American and Asian markets and specialty food stores. The rust-colored seeds are quite small.

To use annatto, sauté $1/2$ teaspoon annatto seeds in 1 tablespoon oil or fat over low heat for 4 to 5 minutes, or until the oil turns a vivid scarlet-orange. Strain, and discard the seeds. Stir this seasoned fat into the quinoa mixture for the humitas. It may also be used in Quinoa and Winter Squash Potage (page 90), Red Sunset Soup (page 150), and Grilled Millet and Butternut Squash Cakes (page 158).

Shrimp, Fennel, and Quinoa Pilaf

❧

Serves 4

2 stalks fennel with several fronds

3 tablespoons extra virgin olive oil

1 onion, chopped

1 clove garlic, minced

½ teaspoon cayenne

1 cup imported quinoa or 1⅓ cups
   domestic quinoa, well washed
   (see page 81)

1 ripe tomato, peeled and seeded
   (see page 370), chopped and drained

2 cups water or stock

2 teaspoons Worcestershire sauce

½ teaspoon sea salt, or to taste

1 pound medium shrimp, peeled and
   deveined

Freshly grated nutmeg, to taste

I usually cook quinoa on stovetop, but here I bake it in an attractive casserole. The shrimp steam in it at the table. For a light supper, serve with a garden salad.

Preheat the oven to 350°F.

Chop the fennel stalks and fronds separately. Set aside. Heat the oil in a 2-quart ovenproof casserole over medium heat. Stir in the onions, garlic, and cayenne, lower the heat, and sauté for 10 minutes, or until the onions are tender. Add the fennel and quinoa and sauté for 1 or 2 minutes more. Add the tomato, stock, Worcestershire, and salt and bring to a simmer. Cover and bake for 25 minutes, or until the liquid has been absorbed.

Remove from the oven. Uncover, fluff with a fork, and stir in the shrimp. Cover and let stand for 10 minutes. The heat will cook the shrimp. Sprinkle with nutmeg and chopped fennel fronds. Serve hot or at room temperature.

Curried Quinoa
and Pistachio Pilaf

Quinoa adds new interest to this otherwise traditional Indian dish. For the roundest flavor, sauté the individual spices at the beginning and add the garam masala at the end. This curry makes a wonderful stuffing for eggplant or a large zucchini.

Melt the ghee in a large sauté pan over medium heat. Add the cumin and sauté for 2 minutes, or until light brown. Add the coriander and turmeric and sauté for 1 minute. Add the onion, and sauté for 3 minutes or until softened. Add the carrot and sauté for 3 minutes, or until it starts to soften. Add the quinoa and sauté for 3 minutes, or until each grain is heated through. Add the raisins, pistachios, stock, salt, and pepper, cover, and bring to a boil. Lower the heat and simmer, covered, for 12 to 15 minutes, or until the quinoa is cooked. Let stand, covered, for 5 to 10 minutes. Sprinkle on the garam masala and fluff with a fork before serving.

Serves 4

2 teaspoons Ghee (page 359) or unsalted butter

½ teaspoon cumin seeds

1 teaspoon ground coriander

¼ teaspoon turmeric

1 small onion, diced

1 small carrot, diced

1 cup imported quinoa or 1⅓ cups domestic quinoa, well washed (see page 81)

2 tablespoons raisins

¼ cup chopped unsalted pistachio nuts

2 cups Vegetable Stock (page 364) or water

Sea salt and freshly ground black pepper, to taste

1 teaspoon Garam Masala (page 358)

Scarlet Quinoa

✿

Serves 4

2 cups Vegetable Stock (page 364) or
Chicken Stock (page 366)

1 very small beet, peeled, trimmed,
and diced

1 cup imported quinoa or 1¹/₃ cups
domestic quinoa, well washed
(see page 81)

1 tablespoon extra virgin olive oil

1 tablespoon fresh lemon juice

¹/₂ teaspoon freshly grated lemon zest

Sea salt and freshly ground black
pepper, to taste

1 tablespoon minced fresh chives

Bold colors and flavors abound in this easy-to-make recipe. Scarlet quinoa is good hot as a side dish. It also makes a fine chilled salad scooped onto greens, and garnished with black olives, anchovy fillets, and a dollop of sour cream.

B ring the stock to a boil in a medium saucepan over high heat. Add the beet, quinoa, oil, lemon juice, lemon zest, salt, and pepper and return to a boil. Cover, lower the heat, and let simmer for 12 minutes, or until the stock has been absorbed. Let stand, covered, for 5 minutes. Fluff with fork. Scrape into a serving bowl, garnish with chives, and serve immediately.

Quinoa with Dried Cherries and Cashews

This simple side dish is about as good as a grain can get. For a more exotic flavor, substitute coconut milk for the water.

Whisk together the olive oil, orange juice, orange zest, 1 tablespoon of the mint, salt, and pepper. Set aside.

Bring the water to a boil in a medium saucepan over high heat. Add the quinoa and saffron and return to a boil. Cover, lower the heat, and simmer for 12 minutes, or until the water has been absorbed. Fluff and stir in the cherries and cashews. Let stand, covered, for 5 minutes. Stir in the orange mixture. Place in a serving bowl and garnish with the remaining mint. Serve hot or at room temperature.

Serves 4

3 tablespoons extra virgin olive oil

3 tablespoons fresh orange juice

2 teaspoons freshly grated orange zest

2 tablespoons minced fresh mint

Sea salt and freshly ground white pepper, to taste

2 cups water

1 cup imported quinoa or $1^1/_3$ cups domestic quinoa, well washed (see page 81)

$^1/_4$ teaspoon saffron threads, crumbled

$^1/_3$ cup chopped dried cherries

$^1/_4$ cup chopped toasted cashews

Chinese Greens
with Quinoa and Peanuts

❧

Serves 4

1 ½ cups chopped broccoli rabe or
   broccoli florets

3 tablespoons unrefined sesame oil

1 piece (2 inches) fresh ginger,
   peeled and grated

2 cloves garlic, minced

½ cup julienned daikon

4 leaves bok choy, cut crosswise into
   1-inch pieces

4 scallions, cut into 1-inch pieces

12 snow peas, stems removed

Tamari soy sauce, to taste

1 teaspoon five-spice powder (see Note)

2 cups cooked quinoa
   (see page 83)

¼ cup dry roasted peanuts

Note: Five-spice powder, a combination of star anise, cinnamon, Szechwan pepper-corns, fennel seeds, and cloves, is available in Asian markets and specialty food shops.

For this dish, have all the ingredients sliced and ready to go before heating the oil. Feel free to use other vegetables, such as mung bean sprouts, onion, carrot, celery, cabbage, or water chestnuts.

Steam the broccoli rabe over boiling water until tender but still bright green, about 5 minutes. Plunge into cold water and drain. Set aside.

Heat a large skillet or wok over medium-high heat until hot. Add the oil, ginger, and garlic and cook for 30 seconds. Add the daikon and stir-fry for 2 minutes, or until it softens. Add the bok choy and stir-fry for 2 minutes, or until crisp tender. Add the scallions and snow peas and stir-fry for 2 minutes, or until crisp tender. Season with soy sauce and five-spice powder. Stir in the quinoa and peanuts and stir-fry for 2 minutes more. Serve immediately.

Timbale of Quinoa, Currants, and Piñon

These timbales take but twelve minutes of cooking and a few minutes of preparation time. Unmolded at the table, they are impressive looking. Serve them warm with roast lamb in winter or at room temperature on a bed of lightly dressed greens in the summer. A large timbale can also be formed using a six-cup ring or fancy mold.

Combine the butter, stock, and a pinch of salt in a medium saucepan over high heat and bring to a boil. Add the quinoa and currants, cover, lower the heat, and simmer for 12 minutes, or until the liquid has been absorbed. Remove from the heat and let stand for 5 minutes, covered.

Whisk together the lemon juice, oil, mace, salt, and pepper in a medium bowl. Stir in the shallot, piñon, and parsley. Pour over the quinoa mixture and toss to combine. Pack into 6 oiled ²/₃-cup ramekins, timbales, or custard molds. The timbales may be served immediately by inverting them directly onto serving plates. Or they may be kept at room temperature, covered, for a few hours. To reheat, place the molds in a hot water bath in a preheated 350°F. oven for 15 minutes.

VARIATION: Chopped raisins or dried apricots or cranberries may be substituted for the currants.

Makes 6 timbales

1 teaspoon unsalted butter

2 cups Chicken Stock (page 366) or Vegetable Stock (page 364)

Sea salt, to taste

1 cup imported quinoa or 1¹/₃ cups domestic quinoa, well washed (see page 81)

¹/₂ cup dried currants

3 tablespoons fresh lemon juice

3 tablespoons extra virgin olive oil

¹/₄ teaspoon ground mace

Freshly ground black pepper, to taste

1 shallot, minced

¹/₂ cup piñon (pine nuts), roasted

1 tablespoon minced fresh parsley

Quinoa and Date Pudding

❦

This dessert is similar to rice pudding, but thanks to quinoa, which is smaller, lighter, and more nutrient dense, it is both more delicate and more substantial. I usually serve it as is, but you may want to top it with cream or whipped cream or, for breakfast, with sour cream or yogurt.

Serves 4 to 6

3 tablespoons unsalted butter, softened

¼ cup vanilla cookie crumbs or ground nuts

½ cup Sucanat or packed light brown sugar

2 large eggs, lightly beaten

1 cup milk or soy milk

1 tablespoon pure vanilla extract or liqueur, such as Grand Marnier

1 teaspoon ground cinnamon

Pinch of sea salt

2 cups cooked quinoa (see page 83)

½ cup chopped dates

½ cup chopped toasted hazelnuts

Freshly grated nutmeg

Preheat the oven to 325°F.

Using 1 tablespoon of the butter, grease a 1½-quart baking dish or soufflé dish or 6 individual ramekins. Coat the buttered surface with cookie crumbs. Set aside.

Cream the remaining butter and Sucanat. Stir in the eggs, milk, vanilla, cinnamon, and salt until blended. Add the quinoa, dates, and hazelnuts and mix thoroughly. Pour the custard mixture into the baking dish. Grate a little nutmeg over the top. Bake for 50 minutes, or until just barely set. Remove from the heat and let cool for 10 minutes. To serve, spoon from the dish or loosen the edges with a knife and invert onto a serving plate.

Quinoa Tarts with Kiwi Sauce

Don't expect traditional flaky tarts here. These are more like a pudding. Serve them after dinner or as a breakfast or brunch treat. For a full-blown char-treuse color, make the kiwi sauce just before serving.

Using both hands, moistened if necessary, compact the quinoa. Spread it out on the countertop ³/₄ inch thick. With a round 2 ¹/₂-inch cookie cutter, glass, or decorative shape, cut out 4 "tarts." Lift with a spatula, and slide each onto a dessert plate.

Trim both ends from the kiwis and peel. With a small spoon, remove the pith and most of the seeds. Cut into small pieces and puree in a food processor until smooth. Add the maple syrup and lime juice and puree for a few more seconds until the mixture is well combined. Divide the sauce among the tarts and serve immediately.

Makes 4 tarts

*2 cups Breakfast Quinoa
(page 86), cooled or still warm*

2 kiwis

2 tablespoons maple syrup

¹/₂ teaspoon fresh lime juice

Quinoa Carrot Cake

❦

Quinoa flour transforms this quick, citrusy carrot cake into an unforgettable orange breakfast cake. For a change of pace, substitute zucchini for the carrot.

Makes one 9-inch square cake

1 ¼ cups quinoa flour
  (see page 81)

¾ cup unbleached all-purpose flour

1 teaspoon baking soda

½ teaspoon sea salt

1 cup grated carrot

¾ cup honey

½ cup plain yogurt

½ cup frozen orange juice concentrate,
  thawed

4 tablespoons (½ stick) unsalted butter,
  melted

1 large egg, beaten

Neufchâtel Icing

¼ cup chopped toasted pecans

Preheat the oven to 350°F. Lightly butter a 9-inch square cake pan. Set aside.

Combine the quinoa flour, all-purpose flour, baking soda, and salt in a medium bowl. In a separate bowl, combine the grated carrot, honey, yogurt, orange juice concentrate, melted butter, and egg. Add to the dry ingredients and stir to combine. Pour into the cake pan and bake for about 40 minutes, or until a cake tester inserted in the center comes out clean. Remove from the oven and cool in the pan for 5 minutes. Cool thoroughly on a wire rack. Spread with icing and sprinkle with pecans. Cut into squares and serve.

Neufchâtel Icing

Makes ¾ cup

4 ounces Neufchâtel or cream cheese

½ cup honey

Put the Neufchâtel and honey in a small bowl. Using a fork, stir until they are well mixed and the icing is smooth. Spread with a spatula on the cake.

Gingered Lamb and Quinoa in Phyllo

Stuffed Artichokes, Sicilian Style

Warm Red Cabbage and Rye Berry Salad

Hawaiian-Style Grilled Halibut with Radish Rice

Barley Dolmadakia

Quinoa Butterscotch Brownies

This brownie, an adaptation of Nancy Baggett's brownie recipe in The International Cookie Cookbook, fills the house with enticing aromas as it bakes. Quinoa not only adds superb flavor to this dense brownie but deepens the color to a golden hue.

Preheat the oven to 350°F. Butter an 11 × 7 × 2-inch baking pan.

Melt the butter in a heavy saucepan over medium heat and bring to a boil. Lower the heat and simmer for 5 to 10 minutes, stirring occasionally. Adjust the heat if necessary so that the butter gently bubbles, turns slightly golden, and develops a butterscotch flavor. Be careful not to let it burn. Add the Sucanat, stirring to blend. Immediately remove from the heat and let stand until the mixture cools to lukewarm.

Sift together the flour, baking powder, and salt. Set aside. Combine the eggs and vanilla in a mixing bowl and stir to blend. Add the cooled butter mixture and stir to combine. Mix in the dry ingredients. Fold in the nuts. Pour the batter into the prepared pan, spreading it out evenly to the edges. Bake for 25 to 35 minutes, or until the top is golden brown and a cake tester inserted in the center comes out clean. Place the pan on a wire rack and let stand for at least 20 minutes. Invert the pan onto a wire rack to remove the brownie. Let the whole uncut brownie cool completely. When cool, place on a cutting board and cut crosswise into 6 strips and lengthwise into 4 strips.

Makes 24 brownies

½ pound (2 sticks) unsalted butter

1 ⅔ cups Sucanat or packed light brown sugar

2 cups quinoa flour (see page 81)

1 ½ teaspoons baking powder

½ teaspoon sea salt

3 large eggs, lightly beaten

2 ½ teaspoons pure vanilla extract

1 cup chopped toasted hazelnuts

Burnt Orange–Pistachio Swirls

Kiss-shaped, this fragrant butter cookie is a teatime favorite. It has a crisp edge and a moist interior.

Makes 24 cookies

6 medium organic oranges

8 tablespoons (1 stick) unsalted butter, softened

²/₃ cup pure maple syrup

1 cup quinoa flour (see page 81)

¹/₂ cup unbleached all-purpose flour

1 teaspoon baking powder

¹/₄ teaspoon sea salt

1 cup unsalted pistachios

Preheat the oven to 250°F.

Using a potato peeler, remove the zest from the oranges. Cut into very fine julienne strips. Reserve the oranges for another use. Spread the zest on an ungreased baking sheet and bake for 20 minutes, or until crisp and lightly browned. Remove from the oven. Grind the warm zest in a blender or food processor until very fine.

Cream together the butter and maple syrup in a mixing bowl. Combine the quinoa flour, all-purpose flour, baking powder, salt, and ground zest in a large bowl. Add the maple syrup mixture and stir until smooth.

Raise the oven temperature to 350°F. Lightly butter a cookie sheet.

Slice 24 pistachios lengthwise in half. Set aside. Finely chop the remaining nuts and stir them into the dough. Press the mixture through a pastry tube onto the cookie sheet. As each cookie is pressed, twist the tube about 90° to form a swirled round. Press two of the pistachio halves into the top of each cookie. Bake for about 12 minutes, or until very lightly browned at the edges and on the bottom. Remove to a rack to cool. (Cookies may be stored in an airtight container for up to 5 days.)

NATIVE ASIAN GRAINS

Buckwheat

Millet

Rice

Job's Tears

Buckwheat

MOST OF MY EXPERIMENTS with the native Russian grain, buckwheat, took place when I lived in Crestone, a rural Colorado village. One winter I was lucky enough to have as a neighbor Irina Sedokova, who was a visiting professor from the Institute of Slavic and Balkan Research at Moscow University. Irina and I share a love of good food and good talk and since we both had small children, we spent many winter afternoons cooking and talking as our children played at our feet. From Irina's knowledge of Slavic and Balkan languages and rituals flowed marvelous folk tales and simple peasant dishes filled with the bold flavors of her native land. When cooking buckwheat, I still imagine it as the staple food of Cossacks charging across the steppes.

People new to whole grain cuisine often find buckwheat overpowering at first taste. Even with my love of grains, I do not cook it every week. I am sure to use buckwheat, though, when I want a meal that is substantial and strengthening since, of all the grains, buckwheat is the heartiest. Because it is digested more slowly than other grains, it imparts a feeling of fullness and has medicinal benefits for people with blood sugar imbalances.

Although similar to wheat nutritionally, buckwheat (*Fagopyrum esculentum*) is not a grain but the seed of a weedlike plant related to rhubarb, which thrives in cold climates and poor soil. It originated in North Central Asia and reached overland into Central Europe sometime in the late Middle Ages. It is grouped with the grains because of its similar culinary profile and nutritional value. Buckwheat's name is derived from its similarity in shape and color to the three-sided, rust-colored beechnut. It is, so to speak, wheat that looks like a beechnut.

Buckwheat
Selection and Storage

Buckwheat, the substantial grain, is available in several forms.

Unroasted Buckwheat Groats

Pale tan and green hulled seeds. They have a mild flavor and may be cooked as is, but I recommend lightly toasting them first. This light toasting heightens the flavor and aroma. Buckwheat groats are available in natural foods stores and by mail order (see page 376).

Factory Roasted Groats

Usually referred to as kasha. The groats are a deep chestnut color with an assertive roasted flavor and aroma, which many people find overpowering. To my palate these groats taste stale, understandably so since there's no telling how many months prior to purchase they were toasted. Kasha is available in many supermarkets, natural foods stores, and by mail order.

Soba Gome

A tiny Japanese heirloom buckwheat with a distinctive flavor. It is available from Mountain Ark.

Kasha Grits

Available from coarse to fine in supermarkets. I find no advantage to grits since the primary reason for reducing a grain's size is to shorten its cooking time, which makes sense for some grains like corn and oats. Since buckwheat groats and kasha cook in ten minutes, the time saved in cooking grits is insignificant. Additionally the grits, like any broken grain, lack vitality and lose freshness.

Whole Buckwheat

The seed with its black hull intact, suitable only for sprouting. It is available in a well-stocked natural foods store which has a section of seeds and grains for sprouting and by mail order from the Sprout House and GoodEats. In quantity, seed buckwheat is available at a farmers' feed supply store. Be sure to purchase only that which is not treated with chemicals.

Buckwheat Flour

Buckwheat flour is made from unroasted groats. It is graded light, medium, or dark, depending on the amount of black hull the flour contains. Since the hull is rich in lysine, an important amino acid, I favor the darker flour.

To heighten the flavor of buckwheat flour, lightly toast the buckwheat in a dry skillet or wok until it releases its aroma. Buckwheat may be ground in a spice or coffee grinder or in a flour mill. One cup groats make 1 cup flour. Store buckwheat flour, tightly wrapped, in the refrigerator for 2 months or in the freezer for 6 months.

One of my treasured pastoral memories is of a field of buckwheat in bloom. Clusters of white blossoms delight the eye. Apparently they delight bees as well, for a dark and flavorful honey comes from the flower's nectar.

Astute farmers, however, keep light-colored horses and cows from grazing on buckwheat to prevent them from getting sunburned and suffering temporary hair loss. Buckwheat apparently inhibits the production of melanin, the tanning element in skin and hide, and intensifies the body's absorption of the sun's rays. Perhaps this is why buckwheat is a staple of the dark-complexioned Siberian peoples but not of the fair-skinned Scandinavians. According to the folk wisdom of the African-American South, buckwheat lightens the skin. When "black is beautiful" came into vogue, this rural lore was largely forgotten.

Buckwheat is particularly high in thiamin, riboflavin, and other B-complex vitamins, with exceptional amounts of calcium, phosphorus, and other minerals. Its most outstanding nutritional characteristic is its high lysine content (6.1 percent), greater than any of the cereal grains. Buckwheat is known as a blood-building food that neutralizes toxic acidic wastes; its rutin content benefits circulation. In Asian medicines, buckwheat is considered to be a strengthening agent for the kidneys. It is the one grain, however, that is not recommended for those with skin allergies or suffering from cancer.

The powers of buckwheat are no more evident than in Russia, where it is one of the oldest and most traditional of foods. In medieval Russia the word *kasha*, which now means only cooked buckwheat groats, signified "meal" or "feast." Today, it refers to any hot cereal, grain, pilaf, or stuffing. No Russian farmer would venture willingly into the snowy winter fields without a warming bowl of kasha. Rumor has it that Soviet athletes refused to participate in an Olympic event because there was no buckwheat for them.

There are several agricultural benefits to growing buckwheat: It naturally resists pests, thrives without the addition of fertilizers, and matures in fewer than sixty days so that a farmer can get two crops per growing season. Now grown primarily in New York State and Pennsylvania in the United States and in Canada, buckwheat is largely used as livestock feed or for soil enrichment in planned crop rotation. Because of Canada's cool climate, the buckwheat produced in the intense northern chill is of such exceptional character that over 80 percent of the crop is exported to Japan for use in making soba noodles.

The exotic yet wholesome goodness of buckwheat can broadly expand your grain repertoire. From the hearty kasha of the eastern Europe peasant to the airy golden blini and caviar of the Chekovian aristocrat to the fragrant soba noodles of the Japanese connoisseur to the buckwheat flapjacks of the American West, buckwheat will add substance and international flavor to your menu.

And on a hot summer night, buckwheat hulls provide cool comfort. Used as a stuffing for pillows in Asia, the hulls make a pleasant crinkling sound, and unlike down or feathers, do not retain body heat. Buckwheat hull pillows are available from futon shops.

Steamed Kasha

Traditional recipes for kasha call for an egg to be mixed with the buckwheat groats before cooking. I cook groats without the egg. I find the texture and deep flavor stand well on their own.

The fluffy texture of kasha belies its substantial, energy-imparting essence. I sprinkle breakfast buckwheat with Gomasio (page 361). I always make extra for the next meal or two. If only roasted buckwheat, also called kasha, is available, omit the toasting step.

Toast the groats in a saucepan or wok over medium-high heat, stirring constantly for 3 to 4 minutes, or until the color turns several shades darker and they give off a deep fragrance. For a stronger flavor, reduce the heat and toast for 2 to 3 minutes more, or until they turn a deep chestnut color.

Combine the water, oil, salt, and pepper in a medium saucepan over high heat and bring to a boil. Slowly pour in groats (dumping them in all at once will cause the pot to boil over). Cover, reduce the heat, and simmer for 10 minutes, or until all the liquid is absorbed. Remove from the heat. Let steam, covered, for 5 to 10 minutes. Fluff with a fork and serve. Place leftovers in a bowl, cover with a cotton cloth, and leave at room temperature for up to 24 hours. Within 4 hours, the kasha may be used in a salad; after that, use it in a filling, stuffing, croquettes, or loaf.

VARIATIONS: Stir ½ cup freshly toasted sunflower seeds into the boiling water.

Sauté ½ cup diced onion in the oil before adding the water or stock and groats.

Add 1 tablespoon chopped fresh herbs..

Replace the water or stock with whole milk or soy milk. Sweeten with honey to taste and add a pat of butter when ready to serve.

Makes about 2 ½ cups

1 cup unroasted buckwheat groats

2 cups water or Vegetable Stock (page 364) or Chicken Stock (page 366)

1 tablespoon unrefined vegetable oil, Ghee (page 359), or unsalted butter

Sea salt and freshly ground black pepper, to taste

Steamed Soba Gome

🌿

Makes about 2½ cups

1 cup soba gome (see Note)

1½ cups water or stock

1 teaspoon unrefined sesame oil (optional)

Sea salt, to taste

Note: A very small heirloom buckwheat imported from Japan, which is more flavorful and energizing. Soba gome's taste is smooth and satisfying, but its price is high.

To buckwheat connoisseurs, I recommend a tiny Japanese heirloom buckwheat called soba gome. Unlike common buckwheat, soba gome pops when it is toasted. Its initial chewiness quickly turns creamy, and while its flavor is more delicate than buckwheat, it has a rounder and more pleasing aftertaste. Soba gome may be substituted for buckwheat in any of the recipes that follow, but since it is such a treat unto itself, I usually have it unadorned, or with milk and honey for breakfast, or as a grain entree topped with a condiment such as Gomasio (page 361) or Miso-Walnut Topping (page 363).

Toast the soba gome in a saucepan or wok over medium-high heat, stirring constantly, for 3 to 4 minutes, or until most of the groats have popped.

Combine the water, oil, and salt in a medium saucepan over high heat and bring to a boil. Slowly pour in the soba gome (dumping it in all at once will cause the pot to boil over). Cover, reduce the heat, and simmer for 10 minutes, or until all the liquid is absorbed. Remove from the heat. Let steam, covered, for 5 to 10 minutes. Fluff with a fork and serve. Place leftovers in a bowl, cover with a cotton cloth, and leave at room temperature for up to 24 hours. Within 4 hours, the kasha may be used in a salad; after that, use it in a filling, stuffing, croquettes, or loaf.

Polenta Nera

When I found buckwheat polenta in an article by Jayne Cohen in Gourmet *magazine, I was thrilled to see this rather obscure use of buckwheat hitting the mainstream. Polenta Nera, or black polenta (gray is a more accurate description), made from buckwheat flour is a nourishing peasant food from the north of Italy. I consider it two dishes in one. I make it in the morning and serve some hot as a breakfast cereal with milk and maple syrup and use the rest for fried polenta at dinnertime.*

Whisk together the flour and water until smooth. Combine the stock, salt, and 1 tablespoon of the oil in a heavy saucepan over high heat and bring to a boil. Add the flour mixture in a steady stream, stirring constantly with a wooden spoon. Lower the heat and simmer, stirring as necessary, for about 7 minutes, or until quite thick and smooth. Pour into individual bowls as hot cereal or pour into an ungreased pan, smooth the top, and let cool at room temperature until firm.

Cut the polenta into squares. Heat the remaining oil in a large sauté pan over medium heat. When warm, add the polenta squares. Fry for about 3 minutes on each side, or until golden and crisp. Drain on paper towels. Serve hot.

VARIATIONS: Stir 1 tablespoon lemon juice and $^1/_2$ teaspoon lemon zest into the polenta as it cooks.

Fry the polenta in chili-flavored olive oil, Ghee (page 359), or butter.

Serves 4

1 cup buckwheat flour (see page 112)

1 $^1/_2$ cups water

2 cups Vegetable Stock (page 364) or Chicken Stock (page 366)

$^1/_4$ teaspoon sea salt, or to taste

2 tablespoons extra virgin olive oil

Easy Buckwheat Polenta

Serves 4

2 cups water

1 cup buckwheat groats, toasted

Sea salt and freshly ground black
  pepper, to taste

Polenta evokes images of laborious cooking and stirring, but not this one. It is a quick rustic dish, slightly grainy, with a marbled appearance. For a breakfast treat, I fry it in butter and serve it with maple syrup or honey. Or I'll season it with garlic for a unique grain entree served with tomato sauce or gravy.

Bring the water to a boil in a heavy saucepan over high heat. Stir in the buckwheat and season with salt and pepper. Lower the heat and cook, covered, for about 10 minutes, or until tender. Immediately remove from the heat and pour into a food processor. Process until of uniform consistency. Scrape onto a platter or baking sheet and form into a block about ³/₄ inch thick. When cool enough to handle, cut into uniform slices. Serve as is or fry for about 2 minutes on each side, or until crisp.

Homemade Buckwheat Noodles

✿

I go in spurts with pasta making. Months pass and I don't even consider making it, then I'll get a yen for great pasta and am amazed all over again at how easy pasta from scratch is. This soba, or buckwheat pasta, is hearty and aromatic. Buckwheat has much more flavor than wheat, and it requires different handling techniques. Once you get this buckwheat-to-wheat flour ratio down, you might want to start decreasing the wheat flour in subsequent batches for a more intensely flavored noodle.

Combine the flours. Whisk the water and egg together and stir into the flour, a bit at a time, working quickly so that all liquid is added within 1 minute. Do not allow lumps to form. Using both hands, work the flour until it feels evenly moistened. Squeeze fistfuls of dough together until a cohesive dough forms. Then knead for about 10 minutes, or until a large smooth ball has formed. Cover and let rest for 10 minutes.

Using a pasta machine, roll and cut the dough into the desired shape according to manufacturer's directions.

Cook the noodles in rapidly boiling salted water for about 1 minute, or until al dente. Drain and refresh in cold water. Drain again.

Makes about 1 1/2 pounds

*4 cups dark buckwheat flour
  (see page 112)*

*3 1/2 cups kamut, durum, or semolina
  flour*

2 cups water

1 large egg, beaten

Pirozhki

❧

Makes about 40

2 2/3 cups unbleached all-purpose flour

3/4 teaspoon sea salt

4 tablespoons (1/2 stick) cold unsalted
  butter

3/4 cup cold water

Kasha Filling, Orange-Squash
  Filling, and/or Fennel-Lamb
  Filling (recipes follow)

1 large egg

2 tablespoons milk or soy milk

3 tablespoons poppy seeds

These versatile rich pies are perhaps my favorite buckwheat dish. I didn't know until recently that in Russian pir *means "feast." Thus pirozhki, bite-size pies, are simply individual feasts.*

Frequently filled with kasha, pirozhki can be filled with poultry, meat, or vegetables. In fact, I often make an appetizer platter of pirozhki with the dough cut into both circles and squares and filled with a variety of stuffings.

Combine the flour and salt in a medium mixing bowl. Add the butter and using your fingertips, work it into the flour until coarse crumbs form. Stir in the water. Knead for about 5 minutes, or until a smooth, slightly stiff dough has formed. Shape into a ball. Wrap in plastic wrap and let rest at room temperature for 30 minutes.

Roll out the dough on a lightly floured surface until 1/8 inch thick. Using a glass or other round cutter, cut the dough into 2- to 3-inch circles.

Preheat the oven to 350°F. Lightly grease 2 baking sheets.

Place 1 rounded teaspoon filling on each circle, slightly off center. Fold the larger side over the filling to make a half-moon shape. Press edges together with the tines of a fork to seal firmly. Place on a baking sheet.

Whisk together the egg and milk. Using a pastry brush, generously brush the top of each pirozhki with egg wash. Sprinkle with poppy seeds. Bake for 20 minutes, or until golden. Serve hot.

VARIATION: Make 4- to 5-inch circles of dough for main course pies, to serve with sour cream and fried onions or applesauce. These will take 25 minutes to cook.

Kasha Filling

If using storebought sauerkraut, drain well before using. Combine the sauerkraut, kasha, and mustard in a small bowl and mix well.

Makes 1 1/2 cups, enough for 40 pirozhki

1/2 cup chopped sauerkraut, homemade (see page 362) or storebought

1 cup Steamed Kasha (see page 115)

2 tablespoons Dijon mustard

Orange-Squash Filling

Combine the squash puree, orange zest, and nutmeg in a small bowl and blend well. Add honey to taste.

Makes 1 1/2 cups, enough for 40 pirozhki

1 1/2 cups well-drained winter squash puree

1 teaspoon freshly grated orange zest

Freshly grated nutmeg

Honey, to taste

Fennel-Lamb Filling

Combine the lamb and fennel in a small bowl and mix well.

Makes 1 1/2 cups, enough for 40 pirozhki

1 cup finely chopped cooked lamb

1/2 cup minced fresh fennel

Kasha Knishes with Rosemary

🌿

Makes about 24

2 cups unbleached all-purpose flour

1 teaspoon baking powder

1/2 teaspoon sea salt

2 large eggs

4 tablespoons (1/2 stick) unsalted butter, melted

1/4 cup cold water

2 cups Steamed Kasha (page 115)

2 cups mashed potatoes

1/4 cup minced onion

2 tablespoons minced fresh rosemary

2 tablespoons minced fresh parsley

Sea salt and freshly ground black pepper, to taste

1/4 cup Dijon mustard (optional)

A dish that has come to us from the Ashkenazi, Yiddish-speaking Jews from eastern Europe, who emigrated to this country in the early part of this century, kasha knishes have become a favorite of mine as well. And I don't limit them to appetizers either—they make good travel food, an unusual breakfast, and a satisfying entree.

Combine the flour, baking powder, and salt in a mixing bowl. Make a well in the center and add the eggs, 1 tablespoon of the butter, and the water. Mix together to make a soft dough, adding additional water if necessary. Turn out the dough onto a lightly floured surface and knead for about 10 minutes, or until smooth and elastic. Place the dough in a clean bowl. Cover with plastic wrap or a damp towel and refrigerate for 1 hour.

Combine the kasha, mashed potatoes, onion, rosemary, parsley, and 2 tablespoons of the butter. Generously season with salt and pepper. Set aside.

Preheat the oven to 350°F. Lightly grease 2 baking sheets.

Remove the dough from the refrigerator and divide into thirds. Roll each piece of dough out on a lightly floured surface until 1/16 to 1/8 inch thick. Cut into eight 4-inch squares. Place about 2 tablespoons filling in the center of each square. Draw the edges up over the filling and pinch to enclose it. Place, sealed side down, on the baking sheets. Brush each knish with the remaining butter. Bake for 35 minutes, or until golden brown. Serve hot with mustard, if desired.

VARIATION: Spread each rolled piece of dough with one third of the filling. Roll up, jelly-roll fashion, and cut the rolls into 1 1/2-inch slices. Lay the slices on the baking sheets and slightly flatten them. Brush with butter and bake as in the main recipe. You may also brush the entire roll with butter and bake it whole for about 45 minutes. Cut into 1 1/2-inch slices after baking.

Jicama and Buckwheat Salad

✤

I think this salad's secret, flavor notwithstanding, is crunch, three distinct crunches in fact, from jicama, apple, and pumpkin seeds. Serve this in late summer or fall to take advantage of new crop apples.

Combine the kasha, sesame oil, and ginger juice in a small bowl. Cover and let stand for 1 hour.

Peel the jicama and cut into matchsticks. Place in a small nonreactive bowl with the lime juice and salt. Cover and marinate for 1 hour.

Toast the pumpkin seeds in a saucepan or wok over medium-high heat, stirring constantly, for about 3 minutes, or until the seeds begin to pop. Remove from the heat and set aside 1 tablespoon. When cool, coarsely chop the remaining seeds.

Combine the kasha, jicama, apple, chopped pumpkin seeds, cilantro, and Tabasco. Taste and adjust the seasoning with additional salt, Tabasco, and/or lime juice.

Line a serving platter or salad bowl with lettuce leaves. Mound the buckwheat salad in the center. Sprinkle with the whole pumpkin seeds and serve immediately.

Serves 6

1 recipe Steamed Kasha (page 115)

2 teaspoons roasted sesame oil

1 teaspoon Ginger Juice (page 360)

1 small (10 ounces) jicama

Juice of 1 lime, or to taste

$1/2$ teaspoon sea salt, or to taste

1 cup coarsely grated Granny Smith apple

$1/3$ cup pumpkin seeds

2 tablespoons chopped fresh cilantro

Tabasco Sauce, to taste

6 to 8 large red leaf lettuce leaves

Soba Salad

Serves 4 to 6

1 medium cucumber

5 cherry tomatoes

1 pound soba noodles

*6 ounces firm tofu, packed in water,
well drained*

2 tablespoons unrefined sesame oil

*1 ½ tablespoons white or yellow miso
(see Note)*

1 tablespoon brown rice vinegar

1 teaspoon grated fresh ginger

¼ teaspoon crushed red pepper

*Freshly ground black pepper,
to taste*

½ cup chopped scallions

1 cup fresh basil leaves, chopped

Romaine lettuce leaves

2 tablespoons chopped fresh parsley

Note: Miso is available in Asian and natural foods markets.

Cold soba always whets a flagging appetite, and the cucumber and tomatoes in this salad make it particularly refreshing. If company's coming, add a few more dishes to the menu and you'll have a feast.

Peel the cucumber, cut it in half lengthwise, and remove the seeds. Cut crosswise into thin slices. Set aside. Cut the tomatoes in half. Set aside.

Bring 2 to 3 quarts water to a boil over high heat. Add the soba noodles, stir gently, and reduce the heat slightly. Foam will form and swell to the top. Immediately add ½ cup cold water to prevent the pot from overflowing. Repeat with cold water 2 more times or until noodles are cooked al dente. Remove from the heat. Drain in a colander and rinse under cold running water. Plunge the noodles into cold water to chill. Drain well.

Combine the tofu, sesame oil, miso, vinegar, ginger, red pepper, and black pepper in a food processor. Process until well blended. Set aside. Combine the noodles, cucumber, tomatoes, scallions, and basil.

Line a serving platter, salad bowl, or individual salad plates with romaine. Mound the soba mixture on the romaine. Make a well in the center and fill with dressing. Sprinkle with parsley and serve immediately.

Beet and Kasha Salad

❦

In this salad I use yellow beets, which have a milder flavor than the red. As is typical of a Russian salad, this one is bound with mayonnaise and elaborately arranged. If like me you are a beet lover, do read Tom Robbins's shameless adoration of beets in his book Jitterbug Perfume.

Whisk together the mayonnaise, mustard, horseradish, and salt. Stir in the Kasha, pickle, onion, and mint. Mound the buckwheat mixture in the center of a serving platter or on individual salad plates. Place chopped lettuce around the edge. Arrange beets, carrots, peas, egg slices, and cherry tomatoes on the lettuce. Drizzle the olive oil and vinegar over the vegetables. Sprinkle with black pepper.

Serves 4

1 cup mayonnaise

¼ cup Dijon mustard

2 tablespoons bottled horseradish, well drained

Sea salt to taste

1 recipe, Steamed Kasha (page 115)

½ cup finely chopped dill pickle

½ cup minced red onion

¼ cup finely chopped fresh mint

4 cups chopped crisp lettuce

2 cups diced cooked yellow beets (see Note)

½ cup diced cooked carrots

½ cup sliced sugar snap peas or snow peas

2 hard-boiled eggs, sliced

6 to 8 cherry tomatoes

Extra virgin olive oil

Herbed vinegar

Freshly cracked black pepper

Note: If you use red beets, assemble the salad within an hour of serving to avoid having the beets' color bleed. Or substitute rutabaga.

Panfried
Buckwheat-Breaded Catfish

❧

My version of panfried catfish honors the Southern tradition of seasoning with an interesting variety of herbs and spices and adds the crunch of whole buckwheat groats to make a crisp crust that keeps the fish moist and flavorful.

Serves 4

4 catfish fillets

$^1/_2$ cup buckwheat groats, roasted

$^1/_2$ cup unbleached all-purpose flour

1 tablespoon Sucanat or light brown sugar

1 tablespoon dried chives

1 tablespoon dried marjoram

2 teaspoons paprika

1 $^1/_2$ teaspoons ground ginger

1 teaspoon crushed red pepper

$^1/_2$ teaspoon turmeric

$^1/_8$ teaspoon cayenne

$^1/_2$ teaspoon sea salt

1 large egg

$^1/_3$ cup water

Juice of 1 lime

$^1/_4$ cup peanut oil

Wash the catfish fillets and pat dry. Set aside. Combine the buckwheat groats, flour, Sucanat, chives, marjoram, paprika, ginger, red pepper, turmeric, cayenne, and salt in a shallow bowl. Set aside. Whisk together the egg, water, and lime juice until well blended.

Dip the fillets, one at a time, into the egg mixture. Roll in the buckwheat mixture to coat well.

Heat the oil in a large frying pan over medium-high heat until warm. Add the breaded fillets and fry for about 5 minutes, turning once, or until the fish is golden, crisp, and cooked through. Remove from the pan and drain on paper towels. Serve immediately.

Roast Duck with Kasha, Chestnut, and Parsnip Stuffing

❧

The rich flavor of duck is enhanced by the deep sweetness of chestnuts and parsnip. This technique of steaming and then baking brings up the flavor of parsnips. I learned it from Melanie Sachs, author of Ayurvedic Beauty Care.

Preheat the oven to 350°F.

Wash and trim the duckling of all excess fat. Pat dry and set aside.

Put the parsnip in a steamer basket over boiling water and steam for about 2 minutes, or until almost cooked. Plunge into cold water to cool. Place on a small baking dish, toss with 1 tablespoon of the butter, and spread out. Bake for 5 minutes, or until lightly browned. Remove from the oven. Raise the oven temperature to 400°F. Combine the parsnip, kasha, chestnuts, scallions, celery, parsley, thyme, and nutmeg. Stir in the remaining butter and season to taste with salt and pepper.

Lightly fill the duckling cavity with stuffing. Lace the opening closed. Place the duckling, breast side up, on a rack in a shallow baking pan. Roast for 15 minutes. Lower the oven temperature to 350°F. and roast for about 1 hour 45 minutes, or until a meat thermometer registers 180°F. for well done. Let rest for 5 minutes.

Place on a serving platter. Carve as desired and scoop stuffing from cavity. Serve immediately.

Serves 4 to 6

1 duckling, well cleaned (5 to 7 pounds)

1 large parsnip, peeled and cut into medium dice

4 tablespoons (¼ stick) unsalted butter, melted

1½ cups Steamed Kasha (page 115)

1½ cups chopped boiled chestnuts

3 scallions, trimmed and chopped

¼ cup chopped celery

2 tablespoons minced fresh parsley

2 tablespoons minced fresh thyme

½ teaspoon freshly grated nutmeg

Sea salt and freshly ground black pepper, to taste

Buckwheat Loaf

🌾

Makes 1½-quarter loaf

2 tablespoons unsalted butter

¼ teaspoon ground allspice

¼ teaspoon dried thyme

1 bay leaf, ground

½ cup minced onion

2 cloves garlic, minced

3 ounces shiitake mushrooms
  or other mushrooms, minced

1 large egg

1 pound turkey breakfast sausage meat,
  uncooked

2 cups Steamed Kasha (page 115)

¾ cup finely chopped walnuts

¼ cup chopped celery

¼ cup chopped fresh parsley

3 tablespoons brandy

1 tablespoon tamari soy sauce

Sea salt and freshly ground black
  pepper, to taste

½ cup prepared salsa

This has all the good flavor of a French country pâté, but thanks to hearty buckwheat, about half of the usual cholesterol. I always make a full recipe because it's good hot or as leftovers, especially with a smooth Dijon mustard. Slices of the chilled loaf will nicely anchor a cold plate of refrigerator finds and pantry staples like cheese, chilled steamed vegetables, lettuce leaves, tomato wedges, and marinated artichoke hearts.

If you have a favorite meat loaf recipe, adapt it by substituting cooked buckwheat for half the meat. It's an easy trick and one I wager you'll repeat.

Melt the butter in a medium sauté pan over medium heat. Add the allspice, thyme, and bay leaf and sauté for 2 minutes, or until aromatic. Add the onion and garlic and sauté for 3 minutes. Add the mushrooms and sauté for 6 minutes, or until they have given off most of their liquid. Set aside to cool.

Preheat the oven to 350°F.

Lightly beat the egg in a mixing bowl. Add the sausage, kasha, walnuts, celery, parsley, brandy, soy sauce, salt, and pepper and sautéed vegetables. Using your fingertips, mix the ingredients with a light touch until well combined.

Pack into a 1½-quart glass loaf pan and cover the pan with foil. Place the filled pan in a larger pan filled with water to come up at least 1 inch. Place both in the oven and bake for 30 minutes. Remove the foil, spread the salsa over the top, and return to the oven, uncovered, to bake for 30 to 45 minutes more, or until an instant-read thermometer inserted in the center registers 162°F. or until the juices run just barely pink. Cool on a wire rack for at least 20 minutes or up to 1 hour before serving. Or cool, remove from the pan, tightly wrap in aluminum foil or plastic wrap, and refrigerate until ready to serve.

Gisella Isidori's Pizzoccheri

Pizzoccheri are buckwheat noodles, a specialty of Valtellina on the Italian-Swiss border, home of Gisella Isidori. The dish that combines this pasta with a green vegetable and potatoes is also known as pizzoccheri. It has been in my repertoire ever since the day Gisella commandeered my kitchen to prepare it for a crowd of visitors. I often replace Gisella's savoy cabbage with kale. Like all the cabbage family, kale is a good source of the potent anticarcinogen indole and especially high in calcium. If you start with ready-made dried buckwheat pasta (there are several excellent brands available at natural foods stores), pizzoccheri is a surprisingly quick dish to make.

Cut the noodles into diamond shapes 1 inch wide and about 3 inches long. Set aside.

Melt the butter in a small sauté pan over medium-high heat. Add the onions, lower the heat, and sauté for about 15 minutes, or until onions are well browned and almost caramelized. Stir in the sage. Remove from the heat. Season with salt and pepper.

Preheat the oven to 400°F. Butter a 3-quart casserole.

Bring 4 quarts of water to a boil in a large saucepan. Add the potatoes and salt. Lower the heat and simmer, covered, for about 10 minutes, or until the potatoes are just tender. Add the kale and cook for 5 minutes. Add the homemade noodles and cook until al dente, 30 seconds. (Ready-made noodles will take longer.) Drain well. Pour into the casserole dish. Stir in the onions and Fontina cheese. Smooth the top and sprinkle Parmesan over all. Place on the top shelf of the oven and bake for 5 minutes, or until the cheese has melted. Serve hot.

Serves 4 to 6

$^1/_2$ pound Homemade Buckwheat Noodles (page 119), cut 1 inch wide, or dried buckwheat noodles

4 tablespoons ($^1/_2$ stick) unsalted butter

2 onions, diced

3 sage leaves, chopped

Sea salt and freshly ground black pepper, to taste

$^1/_2$ pound red potatoes, peeled and diced

2 cups chopped kale

$^3/_4$ cup finely diced Fontina

$^1/_4$ cup freshly grated Parmesan

Savory Kasha Croquettes

❧

Makes 10 croquettes

4 cups Steamed Kasha (page 115), just cooked and cool enough to handle

²/₃ cup minced fresh cilantro

²/₃ cup minced scallions

About 4 cups peanut oil

¹/₂ cup soy sauce

¹/₄ cup brown rice vinegar

1 tablespoon Sucanat or light brown sugar

Pinch of cayenne

Besides serving as a side dish, these croquettes also do duty as a main course accompanied by steamed greens and a carrot or sweet potato puree. The croquettes may also be panfried and topped with a slice of Swiss or Cheddar cheese.

Freshly cooked kasha needs no binder. If you use leftover kasha you will need to add half a cup of flour. Or you can pulse the kasha a few seconds in a food processor and then form it into shapes.

Combine the kasha, cilantro, and scallions. Form into triangles by gently shaping and packing ¹/₃ cup filling at a time into the angle formed by your right thumb and index finger when spread. Support the triangle with the fingers of your left hand and gently pack it with your left thumb.

Heat the oil to 360°F. in a deep-fat fryer over high heat. Fry the triangles, a couple at a time, for about 2 minutes on each side, until golden. Drain on paper towels. Keep warm while frying the remaining triangles.

Whisk together the soy sauce, vinegar, Sucanat, and cayenne. Pour into a small bowl.

When all the croquettes are fried, serve immediately with the soy mixture passed on the side.

Judith Choate's Kasha Paprikás

My mother, who serves meat as an entree, would serve this as a side dish to match an assertively flavored goose, roast meat, or salmon dish. I tend to serve it as an entree with a bowl of bean soup, baked squash, and a cooked salad. Cookbook author Judith Choate gave me this recipe.

Heat the ghee in a heavy saucepan over medium-high heat until hot. Add the onion, celery, and thyme, lower the heat, and sauté for 5 minutes. Stir in the paprika. When well blended, add the wine and stock. Raise the heat and bring to a boil. Add the groats, salt, and pepper. Lower the heat, cover, and simmer for about 15 minutes, or until the liquid is absorbed. Remove from the heat and let cool for 10 minutes. Stir in 3 to 4 tablespoons of the sour cream. When well blended, transfer to a serving bowl. Sprinkle with parsley and serve immediately. Pass the remaining sour cream at the table.

Serves 4

1 tablespoon Ghee (page 359) or unrefined sesame oil

1 onion, minced

$\frac{1}{2}$ cup minced celery

2 teaspoons minced fresh thyme

1 tablespoon Hungarian paprika

$\frac{3}{4}$ cup dry white wine

1 $\frac{1}{4}$ cups Chicken Stock (page 366)

1 cup buckwheat groats, toasted

Sea salt and freshly ground black pepper, to taste

$\frac{1}{2}$ cup sour cream

1 tablespoon minced fresh parsley

Sarrasin Crepes

Makes twelve 7-inch crepes

1 cup buckwheat flour
  (see page 112)

2 tablespoons unbleached
  all-purpose flour

1 teaspoon ground coriander

$^1/_8$ teaspoon sea salt

1 $^3/_4$ cups water

2 large eggs

4 tablespoons (1/2 stick) unsalted
  butter, melted and cooled

In their native Brittany, buckwheat crepes are used for savory and sweet dishes. They are often laced with an apple cider compote for a galette de sarrasin. In our house, the galette often shows up as a many-layered birthday cake. We heat up every available skillet and one person flips crepes while another slices fruit, someone chops nuts, and another whips cream. Many hands contribute to the layering of cake, cream, and fruit and the improvised decorating.

Combine the buckwheat flour, all-purpose flour, coriander, and salt in a medium mixing bowl. Whisk together the water, eggs, and 2 tablespoons of the butter in another bowl. Stir into the dry ingredients, mixing until no longer lumpy. Set aside for 15 minutes.

Pour the batter into a pitcher or a large measuring cup with a pouring lip. Heat a 7-inch crepe pan, brush it with some of the remaining butter, and grasp the pan in 1 hand. Fill a $^1/_4$-cup measure with batter, then pour it onto the pan while rotating it so that a thin layer of batter covers the surface. Return pan to the heat. Cook for 2 to 3 minutes, or until the top dries. Turn and cook 1 minute more, or until the bottom is just lightly browned. Repeat until all the batter is used, keeping cooked crepes warm. Serve warm with the filling of your choice.

VARIATIONS: For an egg-free crepe, decrease the buckwheat flour to $^3/_4$ cup and increase the all-purpose flour to $^1/_4$ cup. Allow the batter to rest for at least 1 hour or up to 8 hours.

Fill or top with any of the following or with your personal favorite crepe filling:

• Pickled herring in mustard sauce
• Caviar and sour cream
• Any smoked fish
• Asparagus or broccoli with an herbed béchamel sauce

Baked Blinis
with Strawberry Sauce

Blinis are golden pancakes traditionally served in Russia during Shrovetide. Melted butter, caviar, and sour cream were the toppings of choice—as much and as many as people could afford. I had once read that baked blinis are superior in texture. So I tried the oven method and found the blinis to be airier and more delicate than the griddle-cooked ones, probably because turning compacts the cake and makes it denser. This way, only one side is browned, so for a conventional-looking pancake, serve it browned side up. Serve the blinis hot with Strawberry Sauce, with melted butter, or with any of the toppings for Sarrasin Crepes (page 132). Or if you are feeling especially lavish, top each blini with a tablespoon of sour cream and a teaspoon of caviar.

If decent fresh strawberries are not available, substitute another seasonal fruit such as raspberries or blueberries. These cakes need a brightly colored fruit sauce.

Makes twenty-four 4-inch blinis

³/₄ cup buckwheat flour
 (see page 112)

³/₄ cup unbleached all-purpose flour

¹/₂ teaspoon sea salt

¹/₂ teaspoon freshly grated nutmeg

1 ¹/₄ cups milk or soy milk

1 teaspoon active dry yeast

²/₃ cup sour cream

3 large eggs, separated

About 2 tablespoons unsalted
 butter, melted

Strawberry Sauce (recipe follows)

Sift the buckwheat flour, all-purpose flour, salt, and nutmeg together in a mixing bowl. Heat the milk to 110°F. and stir in the yeast. When the yeast is softened, whisk in the sour cream and egg yolks. Stir into the flour mixture until the batter is just mixed but a bit lumpy. Cover and set aside in a warm spot for 1 hour or refrigerate, loosely covered, overnight.

Preheat the oven to 425°F. Place 2 baking sheets in the oven.

Beat the egg whites until stiff. Gently fold the egg whites into the batter. When the baking sheets are hot, remove from the oven and generously brush with butter. Pour the batter into 4-inch circles, keeping the edges from touching. Bake for 7 minutes, or until puffed and lightly browned on the bottom. Repeat with the remaining batter. Rotate the baking sheets, if necessary, for cakes to brown evenly. Serve hot with Strawberry Sauce.

Strawberry Sauce

Makes 1 1/2 cups

1 1/2 pints strawberries, washed

1/4 cup maple syrup or 1/3 cup Sucanat or packed light brown sugar

Hull the strawberries, cut in half lengthwise, and mix gently with syrup. Cover and set aside at room temperature for about 1 hour, stirring several times. If the strawberries are exceptionally ripe and fine, reduce the standing time to 30 or even 15 minutes.

Gost' na Poroge

Gost' na Poroge, or The Guest Is on the Threshold Cake, is so named because if you start mixing it as soon as you see guests coming up the walk, the cake can be in the oven by the time they reach the threshold. My former neighbor Irina Sedokova used no spices when making this cake. "I'm from new Russian generation," she explained, "so I have little familiarity with spices and other unavailable foodstuffs." I have added vanilla and ginger to Irina's recipe. Maybe it's because of the added ginger or because I have a very short path to my door, but I've never made this cake quite as quickly as Irina described. I use Jonathan apples for the cake. In Russia Irina would use Antonovka apples, which, she says, are inimitable.

Preheat the oven to 350°F. Butter and flour a 9½-inch springform pan.

Peel, quarter, core, and slice the apples into ¼-inch-thick wedges. Set aside.

Cream the butter and sugar until light and fluffy. Mix together the eggs, milk, and vanilla. Sift together the buckwheat flour, cake flour, baking powder, ginger, and salt. Alternately add the flour mixture and the egg mixture to the butter-sugar mixture, beginning and ending with the flour. Fold in all but 1 cup of the apples. Pour the batter into the prepared pan. Arrange the remaining apple slices decoratively on top and sprinkle with vanilla sugar. Bake for 30 minutes, or until a cake tester inserted in the center comes out clean. Cool on a wire rack for 10 minutes. Remove the sides of the pan and serve warm or cold, as is or topped with sweetened whipped cream if desired.

Serves 8

3 large tart apples

8 tablespoons (1 stick) unsalted butter

1 cup sugar (see Note)

3 large eggs

¼ cup milk or soy milk

2 teaspoons pure vanilla extract

1 cup buckwheat flour (see page 112)

1 cup cake flour (not self-rising)

2 teaspoons baking powder

2 teaspoons ground ginger

¼ teaspoon sea salt

2 tablespoons Vanilla Sugar (see page 269)

Sweetened whipped cream (optional)

Note: For a light colored cake, use refined (granulated) sugar. For a full-flavored cake, use Sucanat.

Buckwheat Rolls
with Thyme and Oregano

❦

Buckwheat has no gluten, so its dough won't rise high. It also needs a rather warm (80°F.) proofing temperature. I don't remember when I first made these rolls, but for years they've been one of our company's coming dishes. I line a basket with a white linen cloth, fill it with hot rolls, and watch them disappear. Allow several rolls per person.

Makes 24

1 teaspoon active dry yeast

1 ½ cups tepid milk or soy milk (110°F.)

3 tablespoons unsalted butter, melted

2 large eggs, beaten

1 ½ cups buckwheat flour, toasted (see page 112)

2 ¼ cups unbleached all-purpose flour (see Note)

1 teaspoon sea salt

1 ½ tablespoons chopped fresh oregano

1 ½ tablespoons chopped fresh thyme

Note: Whole wheat flour does not make a satisfactory substitute for all-purpose flour.

Soften the yeast in the milk. When softened, stir in 2 tablespoons butter and the eggs. Combine the buckwheat flour, all-purpose flour, and salt in a large mixing bowl. Stir in the yeast mixture until a soft dough is formed. Knead in the herbs. Cover and let rise in a warm (80°F.) place for about 1 hour, or until the dough has nearly doubled in bulk.

Preheat the oven to 425°F. Grease two 12-cup muffin tins. Divide the dough into 24 balls and place in the muffin tin. Cover and let rise for 15 minutes, or until the rolls have increased by a third in volume.

With a pair of sharp scissors, snip the top of each roll in 3 parallel lines. Bake for 15 to 18 minutes, or until the rolls pull away from the cups. Remove to a wire rack. Brush with 1 teaspoon melted butter. Serve hot or cold.

Buckwheat Waffles
with Peach Butter

❦

These buckwheat waffles are crunchy but soft, remarkable for buckwheat because its dense texture usually adds body and weight to a dish. Buckwheat flour takes more heat than wheat flour, so increase the cooking time. The waffles are ready when golden brown. Use a dead-ripe peach for the butter, and you'll be astounded at its sweet and creamy perfection. Another well-ripened fruit, such as apricot or mango, may be substituted.

Here's a less-work-for-mother idea: Leave the batter in a pitcher for late risers. Or bring it and the waffle iron to the table. Waffles are easier to make than pancakes, and everyone can make his or her own. Sometimes I make extra waffles at breakfast and serve them as bread for lunch. Unlike wheat waffles, these are still toothsome by noontime.

Soften the yeast in warm milk for 5 minutes. Combine the buckwheat flour, all-purpose flour, and salt in a large mixing bowl. Pour the yeast mixture into the flour and stir to mix well. Beat in the molasses and butter. Loosely cover and let rest for 1 hour at room temperature or refrigerate overnight.

Heat a nonstick waffle iron until hot. Pour the batter onto the iron. Bake until steam stops escaping from the iron, 5 to 6 minutes. Serve hot with peach butter and maple syrup.

Serves 2 to 3

1 teaspoon active dry yeast

3 cups warm milk or soy milk

2 1/2 cups buckwheat flour
  (see page 112)

1/2 cup unbleached all-purpose flour

1 teaspoon ground cinnamon

Dash of freshly grated nutmeg

1/2 teaspoon sea salt

2 tablespoons sorghum or other table
  molasses (not blackstrap)

2 tablespoons unsalted butter, melted

Peach Butter (recipe follows)

Maple syrup

Peach Butter

Makes about 1 cup

4 tablespoons (½ stick) unsalted butter, cold, cut into 1-inch pieces

2 tablespoons cream cheese, at room temperature

1 peach, peeled and chopped

2 tablespoons maple syrup

¾ teaspoon grated orange zest

Freshly grated nutmeg

Put the butter and cream cheese in a food processor and process until smooth. Add the peach, maple syrup, and zest and pulse until the fruit is finely chopped but not pureed. Scrape into a small serving bowl and sprinkle nutmeg on top. (The butter can be kept, well covered, in the refrigerator for 1 week.)

Buckwheat Pumpkin Muffins

❧

As I watch my pumpkins oranging on the vine, this is one of the recipes that I anticipate using as harvest nears. It has just enough buckwheat flour to enhance the sweet, earthy tones of the squash. These muffins are reminiscent of carrot cake only—in a word—better.

Preheat the oven to 400°F. Grease two 12-cup muffin tins. Combine the pumpkin, pecans, eggs, milk, butter, and orange zest in a medium mixing bowl. Put the buckwheat flour, all-purpose flour, Sucanat, baking powder, ginger, nutmeg, and salt in a bowl. Stir to combine and sift into the pumpkin mixture, a bit at a time, stirring to blend after each addition. When all the dry ingredients are incorporated, fill the muffin cups about two thirds full. Bake for about 25 minutes, or until lightly browned and a cake tester inserted in the centers comes out clean. Cool on a wire rack for 5 minutes. Remove muffins from tins and serve warm or cool thoroughly on the rack.

Makes 24

2 cups coarsely grated pie pumpkin, winter squash, or sweet potato

1 cup chopped pecans

2 large eggs

³⁄₄ cup milk or soy milk

3 tablespoons unsalted butter, melted

2 teaspoons freshly grated orange zest

¹⁄₂ cup buckwheat flour (see page 112)

1 ¹⁄₄ cups unbleached all-purpose flour

¹⁄₂ cup Sucanat or packed light brown sugar

1 ¹⁄₄ teaspoons baking powder

1 teaspoon ground ginger

¹⁄₂ teaspoon freshly grated nutmeg

¹⁄₂ teaspoon sea salt, or to taste

Millet

WHEN I COOK MILLET, I think of my friend Patricia Brewster, whom I met in 1972 when I was teaching macrobiotic cooking in Ireland. She was as interested in brown rice as I was in everything Irish. Patricia's interest in grains was not short term either—she eventually married Roger Wilkie, a millet and wheat farmer in Otis, Colorado, which lies just west of the Nebraska border. Montana may advertise that it is Big Sky Country, but eastern Colorado is a rival for that claim. Nothing but blue sky, an occasional farm house and silo on the horizon, and mile upon mile of ripening millet and wheat.

While the technical name of millet is proso, and the scientific name is *Panicum miliaceum*, hershey is what the farmers of northeastern Colorado call their crop. This was the name given to millet by the Russian Mennonites who introduced it to America's heartland over a century ago. Drought resistant and with a short growing season, millet has thrived in semi-arid conditions in Kansas, Colorado, and North Dakota. It can be planted as late as July 7 and still mature in time for an early fall harvest. Thus, if a farmer's wheat or corn is destroyed by a late frost, he can replant those fields with millet. In addition, millet does not drain the soil of its nutrients in the same manner that wheat does, so it can be planted three years in succession without the fallow period required after a season of wheat. In the United States, the millet we find in natural foods stores and supermarkets is proso. Elsewhere however, millet is a generic term for at least five different small and unrelated cereal grains.

Proso millet originated in Eastern Asia and remained the dietary staple of the northern Chinese until the Tang Dynasty, A.D. 618–907. Before then, China was divided north from south according to the principal grain of each region—millet in northern China and rice in southern China. As cold-withstanding rice varieties developed, rice moved northward and eventually became the preferred grain throughout most of Asia. Millet, however, remained an important food crop not only in pockets of Asia but elsewhere in the world. It is frequently cited in the New Testament. Millet flourished throughout the Roman Empire and was a dominant cereal crop into the Middle Ages.

Millet
Selection and Storage

Millet looks like a bright yellow mustard seed, but when cooked, it explodes into a pale yellow puff. When it is cooked with a little water (Steamed Millet), it is dry, light, and airy. When cooked with extra water (The Original Polenta) it fully dissolves into a moist, dense, uniform consistency.

Purchase millet from a natural foods store or a mail order supplier with a rapid turnover since millet easily turns rancid. I prefer purchasing grains from bulk bins because it's easier to see their quality and, in the case of millet, to put a few grains to the taste test. When fresh, this crunchy seed tastes mildly sweet with a very subtle alkaline aftertaste. When rancid, it tastes harsh and bitter.

I purchase a two-month supply of millet and store it in a glass jar in a cool and dark cupboard. If I were to purchase a larger supply, I would store it in a glass jar in the refrigerator for up to 4 months or tightly wrapped in the freezer for up to 6 months.

Like other grains, millet may be eaten alone as a cereal or a side dish or cooked in combination with other grains in breads, soups, stews, stuffings, and even in desserts. It's an excellent standby for those with wheat allergies.

Of the numerous varieties grown throughout the world, only proso millet is available for domestic consumption. The one exception is an heirloom glutinous millet available from Mountain Ark (see page 377).

Millet Flour

Millet flour gives a dry, soft crumb to baked goods and quick breads. Since it is gluten free, you need to combine it with a gluten-containing flour in a yeast product.

Millet flour is sold in natural foods stores, but since it turns rancid and bitter quite rapidly, I recommend grinding it as you need it in a spice or coffee grinder or even in a blender. Taste a few grains of millet first to be sure it is fresh. Grind $3/4$ cup millet to make 1 cup millet flour. Store the flour, tightly wrapped, in the refrigerator for up to 2 months. It is preferable, however, to grind as needed.

Extremely hardy, proso millet needs minimal care. The tiny seeds facilitate its spread and can be held in storage for years only to pop up like a weed when planted. Because of this, millet often offers salvation in times of famine. It remains the staple food for millions of people in India, Asia, and Africa. So valued are its life-giving properties that in Nigeria millet is called "hungry rice."

The smallest of the common grains, this tiny yellow seed has the most complete protein and significantly more iron than the other true cereal grains. It is gluten free and very rich in amino acids, phosphorus, and B vitamins. Due to its high alkaline ash content, millet is the easiest grain to digest. This unusual makeup also allows millet to be cooked without salt and yet be alkaline rather than acidic.

In North America, millet is now grown primarily for pasturage, silage, hay, or birdseed. I never plan to grow it in my garden at all, but every year it bursts forth nevertheless. Its presence has everything to do with the chicken feed that has found its way into the mulch and nothing to do with my garden plan.

I cook millet about once a week and enjoy it with a passion. I think my favorite way to eat millet is in a waffle—until I recall millet-stuffed onions. Cooked millet tastes sweet and has a light and dry nature.

I particularly like the nonhybrid millet grown in Saskatchewan, Canada, by Alvin Scheresky, who has been farming organically for more than thirty years. It is smaller than other millet, and its sweet flavor is without peer. It is available from the Gold Mine Natural Food Company (see page 377).

Millet is unusual among the grains in that if it is cooked with a little liquid it makes a light, dry, fluffy pilaf. Increase the liquid to 3 cups and the millet is no longer granular but cooks up like mashed potatoes or polenta.

Steamed Millet

✽

Millet is the only grain that responds best to toasting, rinsing, and then cooking. Since I started using this technique to cook millet, I cook it every week instead of just occasionally as before. These two preliminary steps may seem a bother, but they make the difference between a mediocre dish and a great-tasting one. Millet expands in cooking more than any other grain—one cup of raw millet turns into four cups of cooked grain. Serve millet as a side dish, alone or with any gravy, sauce, topping, or condiment.

Makes 4 cups

1 cup millet

2 cups Vegetable Stock (page 364), Chicken Stock (page 366), or water

1 tablespoon Ghee (page 359), unrefined sesame oil, or sunflower oil (optional)

Pinch of sea salt (optional)

1 tablespoon chopped fresh herb, such as cilantro, dill, or fennel fronds (optional)

½ teaspoon ground cumin or coriander (optional)

Put the millet in a saucepan or wok over high heat. Toast, stirring constantly, for about 4 minutes, or until the millet is aromatic. Remove from the heat when you hear the first grain pop. Immediately pour into a 1½-quart bowl. Fill with cold water and scrub the grains lightly between the palms of your hands for 5 seconds or so. Pour into a fine-mesh strainer and rinse under running water for 1 minute, or until the water runs clear.

Bring the stock or water to a boil in a medium saucepan. Add the millet, ghee, salt, and herb and/or spice, if using. Lower the heat, cover, and simmer for about 20 minutes, or until all the liquid is absorbed. Turn off the heat and let stand, covered, for 5 minutes.

Fluff millet with a fork and serve.

Put any leftover millet in a glass bowl, loosely cover with a cotton cloth, and leave out at room temperature for up to 24 hours. The millet may be used in salad, soup, croquettes, stir-fry, or bread.

VARIATION: Add ½ cup toasted chopped nuts or sunflower seeds when the millet is added to the boiling water for a soft texture. For a crunchy texture, add the nuts or seeds when fluffing the cooked millet.

Quick-Cooking Cracked Millet

If the millet you have has a bitter taste (a mild salty taste is normal), then prepare it this way. Besides a shorter cooking time, this method results in a light taste and texture, similar to couscous. If you have sweet-tasting millet, use the recipe for Steamed Millet (page 144) for a more nutritious and full-flavored grain dish.

Makes 3 cups

1 cup millet

1 ¼ cups Vegetable Stock (page 364) or water

Sea salt and freshly ground black pepper, to taste

Put the millet and ¾ cup water in a blender. Process for 10 to 15 seconds, or until each grain is broken into two or more pieces. Add cold water to fill the blender and stir once or twice. Using a fine strainer, drain off the opaque starchy water. Repeat this washing process 2 more times, or until the rinse water is clear. Drain well.

Bring the stock to a boil in a medium saucepan over high heat. Add the millet, cover, and bring back to a boil. Lower the heat and simmer for 7 minutes, or until all the stock has been absorbed. Remove from the heat and let stand, covered, for 5 minutes. Fluff with a fork and serve.

As for Steamed Millet, put any leftover millet in a glass bowl, loosely cover with a cotton cloth, and leave out at room temperature for up to 24 hours. The cracked millet may be used in salad, soup, croquettes, stir-fry, or bread.

The Original Polenta

❦

Serves 4

1 cup millet

3 cups Vegetable Stock (page 364), Chicken Stock (page 366), or water

¹/₂ teaspoon ground cumin or coriander (optional)

Sea salt and freshly ground black pepper, to taste

Centuries before corn was introduced to northern Italy, millet was the dietary staple and thus in all likelihood the original polenta. Polenta made from millet has the bright yellow color of that made from corn and is equally versatile but much easier to prepare. I often cook up an ample pot of millet in the morning, serve some as a hot breakfast cereal, and pour the leftovers into a pan. For dinner it takes only moments to cut the polenta into squares, panfry them, and top them with a sauce. Adding millet to cold (versus boiling) liquids and increasing the liquid measurement gives a soft, creamy texture.

Put the millet in a saucepan or wok over high heat. Toast, stirring constantly, for about 4 minutes, or until the millet is aromatic. Remove from the heat when you hear the first grain pop. Immediately pour into a 1¹/₂-quart bowl. Fill with cold water and rub the grains lightly between the palms of your hands for 5 seconds or so. Pour into a fine-mesh strainer and rinse under running water for 1 minute, or until the water runs clear.

Combine the millet, stock, spice, if using, and salt and pepper in a saucepan, cover, and bring to a boil. Reduce the heat and simmer for about 30 minutes, or until all the liquid is absorbed. Turn off the heat and let stand, covered, for 5 minutes. Scrape into an 8-inch square pan, smooth the top with a wet spatula, and let stand for 5 minutes. Cut into squares and serve hot. Or let stand, loosely covered, at room temperature for several hours, cut into squares, panfry, and serve.

VARIATION: Add 1 tablespoon chopped fresh herb, such as cilantro, dill, or fennel fronds.

Stuffed Artichokes, Sicilian Style

In 1972 I lived in Rome where I taught macrobiotic cookery at the Centro di Macrobiotica near Campo di Flores, the old market area. Previdènza, the head cook at the club, was Sicilian. She spoke no English, but I had acquired enough Italian to track her kitchen secrets. She was adept with fresh vegetables, especially artichokes, which she used in ever more interesting ways. Here's my favorite. The filling cooks on the heart of the artichoke and flavors each leaf. No dipping sauce is needed. When the last leaves are eaten then the filling tops the lush heart. Squisito!

Serves 4

¼ cup cooked and cooled millet (page 144)

2 chopped anchovy fillets

2 tablespoons fresh flat-leafed Italian parsley

2 cloves garlic, minced

4 medium-large artichokes

1 cup dry white wine

½ lemon, sliced

10 whole peppercorns

2 bay leaves

¼ cup extra virgin olive oil

Combine the millet, anchovies, parsley, and garlic. Set aside. Trim the artichokes, removing damaged lower leaves and removing enough stem so that the artichokes can stand straight. Using scissors, cut barbed points, if any, off the leaves. Press the tops of the artichokes down on a flat surface to slightly spread leaves, leaving an open flower shape. With a spoon, remove the choke. Divide the filling among the artichokes, placing it on the heart.

Place the artichokes in a heavy-bottomed pan just large enough to hold them comfortably. Place the pan on an unlit burner. Pour in the wine and add water to come up about 1½ inches on the artichokes, being careful not to let water get into the stuffing. Add the lemon, peppercorns, and bay leaves. Pour the oil over the tops of the artichokes so that each one gets a generous soak. Turn on the heat to high. Cover and bring to a boil. Lower the heat and simmer, covered, for 45 minutes, or until the artichoke center is tender but firm. Use a slotted spoon to remove artichokes from pot. Drain on a wire rack for 5 minutes. Serve hot or at room temperature.

VARIATION: Substitute bread crumbs or cooked bulgur, couscous, or quinoa for the millet.

Salmon Millet Rolls

❧

These bright tidbits are great as make-ahead cocktail snacks or as garnish on a big green salad. Millet's subtle taste won't assert itself over the more boldly flavored ingredients of the rolls, but you'll appreciate its texture and how it keeps the cream cheese from being cloying

Makes about 40

4 ounces cream cheese

3 tablespoons milk

1 1/2 cups Quick-Cooking Cracked Millet (page 145), cooled

1/4 cup minced black olives

1 tablespoon minced celery

1 tablespoon minced scallions

1 tablespoon minced fresh dill

1 teaspoon fresh lime juice

1/4 teaspoon Tabasco Sauce, or to taste

1/2 pound smoked salmon, thinly sliced and cut into 3 × 5-inch rectangles

Cream the cream cheese and milk together until smooth. Stir in the millet, olives, celery, scallions, dill, lime juice, and Tabasco. Taste and adjust the seasoning. Set aside.

Place a salmon slice on the work surface. Mound 3 tablespoons of the millet mixture down the center. Wrap the salmon lengthwise around the filling, overlapping the edges slightly. Using your fingertips, push the filling in from the ends to pack it firmly, adding additional filling if necessary. Place on a platter and continue making rolls until all the salmon and filling are used. Cover tightly and refrigerate for at least 4 hours or up to 8 hours.

When ready to serve, remove the rolls from the refrigerator. Unwrap and, using a serrated knife, slice rolls into 1/2-inch pieces.

VARIATION: Substitute cooked quinoa or steamed millet for the cracked millet.

Millet Madeleines with Crème Fraîche and Caviar

✹

Heavenly best describes these savory madeleines. I use tiny individual molds, about three tablespoons each for these. For more casual feasting, bypass the madeleines, bake the batter in a cake pan, cut the cake into fingers, and embellish. The sandy texture of millet makes a more interesting background for the caviar than does an all-wheat madeleine. You can use any caviar, from the finest beluga to those little jars on the supermarket shelf.

Melt 1 tablespoon of the butter in a small skillet over medium-low heat. Add the shallots and sauté for about 4 minutes, or until softened. Remove from the heat and let cool.

Combine the millet and all-purpose flour, the baking powder, and salt. Stir in the shallots. Add two tablespoons butter, cut into bits, and blend in until the mixture is mealy. Stir in the eggs, ¹/₂ cup of the crème fraîche, and Tabasco until well combined.

Preheat the oven to 400° F. Using the remaining tablespoon butter, generously grease 16 madeleine forms.

Place the pan on a baking sheet and heat in the oven for about 1 minute, or until very hot. Remove from the oven and put a rounded tablespoon of batter in each form. Return to the oven and bake for about 6 minutes, or until a cake tester inserted into the center comes out clean. Remove from the oven and turn out onto a wire rack to cool.

When ready to serve, garnish each madeleine with a dollop of crème fraîche, a dab of caviar, and a piece of chive.

Makes 12

4 tablespoons (¹/₂stick) unsalted butter, chilled

¹/₃ cup finely minced shallots

²/₃ cup millet flour (see page 142)

²/₃ cup unbleached all-purpose flour

¹/₂ teaspoon baking powder

Pinch of sea salt

2 large eggs

³/₄ cup Crème Fraîche (page 355)

Tabasco Sauce, to taste

About 3 tablespoons caviar

12 pieces (1 inch) fresh chive

Red Sunset Soup

❧

**Serves 4 as a main course,
8 as a first course**

1 large carrot

1 medium sweet potato

1 small butternut squash

2 tablespoons extra virgin olive oil or
unrefined sesame oil

1 large onion, chopped

3 cloves garlic, minced

1 very ripe large tomato, peeled, seeded,
and chopped

1/3 cup millet, toasted, washed, and
drained

5 cups Vegetable Stock (page 364) or
Chicken Stock (page 366)

1/2 teaspoon sea salt

1/4 teaspoon freshly ground black
pepper

1 small red bell pepper, roasted
(page 353), peeled, seeded, and
minced (optional)

4 to 8 fresh basil leaves (optional)

*The late Johna Albi, my friend from our days together in Boulder, Colorado,
created this harvest flavored and colored soup. A soup with grain makes an
ideal one-dish meal because the grain provides steady energy until the next
meal time. If the carrot, sweet potato, and squash are organic, use them
unpeeled; the skins will enhance the flavor, nutrients, and fiber.*

Peel the carrot, sweet potato, and squash if they are not
organic. If organic, scrub and dry them. Quarter the carrots
lengthwise and cut into a medium dice. Coarsely chop the
sweet potato. Cube enough squash to make 3 cups, reserving the rest
for another use.

Heat the oil in a large soup pot over medium heat. Add the
onion and garlic and sauté for about 4 minutes, or until softened.
Add and sauté the carrot, then the sweet potato, and then the squash
for about 7 minutes in all, or until lightly cooked. Add the tomato,
millet, stock, salt, and pepper. Bring to a boil, cover, and lower the
heat. Simmer for 30 minutes, or until the millet is cooked and the
vegetables are very tender. If the soup is thicker than you like it, add
water, 1/2 cup at a time. Taste and adjust the seasoning. Serve hot, garnished with red pepper and basil leaves, if desired. To serve cold, cover
and refrigerate for at least 2 hours. Taste for seasoning. Garnish with
red pepper and basil, if desired.

VARIATION: Puree the soup in a blender or food processor. Serve
hot or cold, garnished with pepper and basil, if desired.

Persian Yogurt Soup
with Garlic and Mint

I add millet, rather than rice, to this classic Persian soup because millet makes it smoother and richer tasting than rice.

Heat the ghee in a small sauté pan over medium heat. Add the garlic. Sauté for 3 minutes, or until softened. Stir in the mint. Remove from the heat and keep warm until ready to use.

Pour the water into a 2-quart saucepan. Vigorously whisk in the flour, then the egg until well combined. Add the chick peas, millet, dill, salt, and pepper. Bring to a boil over medium-high heat. Lower the heat, cover, and simmer for 10 minutes, or until the soup is thick and well flavored. Reduce the heat as low as possible and gradually whisk in the yogurt, scallions, and parsley. Continue to cook over very low heat for about 5 minutes, or until the soup is hot. Do not boil. Serve immediately with a spoonful of garlic-mint ghee floating on top of each portion.

VARIATION: Add tiny meatballs made with ½ pound ground lamb, ¼ cup bread crumbs, 1 beaten egg, ¼ cup minced onion, sea salt, and pepper when you add the chick peas, millet, and seasonings.

Serves 4

¼ cup Ghee (page 359) or unsalted butter

3 cloves garlic, minced

2 tablespoons chopped fresh mint

3 cups water

2 tablespoons millet flour (see page 142) or whole wheat flour

1 large egg

½ cup cooked chick peas

¼ cup cooked millet (see page 144)

2 tablespoons minced fresh dill

1 teaspoon sea salt, or to taste

½ teaspoon ground white pepper, or to taste

3 cups plain yogurt

½ cup chopped scallions

¼ cup chopped fresh parsley

Millet Watercress Salad
with Gingered Poppy Dressing

❧

Serves 4 to 6

⅓ cup extra virgin olive oil

3 tablespoons fresh lemon juice

¼ cup poppy seeds

2 cloves garlic, minced

1 tablespoon soy sauce

1 teaspoon Ginger Juice (page 360)

½ teaspoon sea salt

¼ teaspoon freshly ground pepper

4 cups cooked and cooled millet
  (page 144)

3 cups chopped watercress

¼ cup diced orange bell pepper

¼ cup diced red bell pepper

¼ cup chopped chives

8 leaves of red leaf lettuce

This salad is vibrant in color, pleasingly varied in texture, and bright in taste. Serve it as a first course or a light luncheon main course. Be sure to use freshly cooked millet for salads and serve them at room temperature. Millet does not stand up well to refrigeration.

Combine the oil, lemon juice, poppy seeds, garlic, soy sauce, ginger juice, salt, and pepper in a plastic or glass container with a lid. Tightly cover and shake to combine.

Toss the millet, watercress, orange and red bell peppers, chives, and dressing together. Let stand for 5 minutes at room temperature.

Place 2 lettuce leaves on each of 4 luncheon plates. Mound the salad onto the leaves and serve.

Millet Niçoise

The secret of this salad is the stalwart anchovy-based dressing. Although tomatoes are part of the classic formula, I omit them unless they are straight from the garden and dead ripe.

Preheat the grill.

Rub the tuna with 1 tablespoon of the olive oil and season with salt and pepper. Grill for about 7 to 10 minutes on each side, or until the center is just cooked. Remove from the grill. Break into bite-size pieces and set aside.

Trim the beans. Place on a rack in a steamer over boiling water. Cover and steam for about 3 minutes, or until bright green and crisp-tender. Remove from the heat and refresh under cold running water. Drain well. Cut into bite-size pieces. Set aside.

Soak the anchovies in water to cover for 5 minutes. Drain well.

If the cucumber is not organic, peel it. Cut the cucumber lengthwise in half and remove the seeds. Dice the flesh. Set aside.

Put the anchovies, remaining olive oil, lemon juice, garlic, and pepper in a blender. Process until smooth. Taste and adjust the seasoning.

Toss the millet, tuna, beans, cucumber, and dressing together. Mound in the center of a serving platter. Arrange the tomatoes and olives around the edge.

Let stand for 5 to 10 minutes at room temperature before serving.

Serves 4

1 piece (1 pound) tuna, about 2 inches thick

½ cup extra virgin olive oil

Sea salt and freshly ground black pepper, to taste

6 ounces green beans

1 can (2 ounces) anchovy fillets, drained

1 cucumber

⅓ cup fresh lemon juice

2 cloves garlic, minced

4 cups cooked and cooled millet (page 144)

2 ripe tomatoes, sliced

12 niçoise olives

Onions Stuffed with
Millet and Sun-dried Tomatoes

❧

The first time I tasted millet it was baked in an onion, and I still remember how it contrasted with the meltingly sweet onion. Here I've added sun-dried tomatoes and purple basil to enhance the flavor and add color and perfume. Serve the onions with a simple soup, like pureed carrot, and a black bean salad for a satisfying vegetarian supper.

Serves 4

4 large onions

2 tablespoons oil from sun-dried tomatoes

2 cloves garlic, minced

⅛ teaspoon crushed red pepper

½ cup julienned sun-dried tomatoes packed in oil

1 cup cooked millet (page 144)

¼ cup chopped pecans

¼ cup chopped fresh basil, preferably purple

Sea salt and freshly ground black pepper, to taste

Freshly grated nutmeg

4 basil leaves, preferably purple

Trim ½ inch off the top of each onion. Trim the root end slightly, to make the onion stand straight. Peel off the skins and any tough outer layers. Using the large end of a melon baller or a teaspoon, scoop out the onion centers leaving a ⅜-inch-thick shell. Chop enough of the scooped-out part to make 2 cups. Save the remaining onion pieces for another use.

Place the onion shells on the rack of a steamer over boiling water. Cover and steam for 10 minutes, or until just tender. Remove from steamer. Turn upside down on paper towels to drain.

Preheat the oven to 350°F.

Heat the oil in a large sauté pan. Add the chopped onion, garlic, and red pepper and sauté for 5 minutes, or until translucent. Add the tomatoes. Cover and cook 5 minutes more. Remove from the heat. Stir in the millet, pecans, and basil. Taste and adjust the seasoning with salt and pepper.

Pack the mixture into the onion shells, mounding slightly. Pour water into a dish large enough to hold the onions without crowding, to a depth of ⅜ inch. Place the stuffed onions in the dish, cover with aluminum foil, and bake for 30 to 40 minutes, or until very tender and heated through. Garnish with freshly grated nutmeg and basil leaves. Serve hot or at room temperature.

Red Radishes,
Water Chestnuts, and Tofu
on Millet Polenta

❧

Cooked radish is one of my favorite vegetables because the red softens to a rosy pink and it tastes so very sweet. Like a gaily colored pennant, the smallest leaf of each radish also helps transform this most common of vegetables.

Slice the tofu lengthwise into five 1-inch slices. Lay 5 or 6 layers of paper towels or a cotton towel on the work surface. Arrange the tofu slices on the towels, cover with additional towels, and place a heavy weight, such as a skillet, on top. Let stand for 30 minutes to press out the excess water.

Mash the miso and vinegar in a small bowl until pureed. Add the water, sugar, arrowroot, ginger juice and red pepper flakes. Blend well and set aside.

Remove all but the smallest leaf of each radish. Wash and set aside.

Warm the vegetable oil in a large sauté pan over medium heat. Add the tofu slices and fry until golden brown on both sides. Remove with a slotted spoon and drain on paper towels. When cool, cut into 1-inch cubes and set aside.

Heat the sesame oil in a wok or large sauté pan over medium heat. Add the garlic and mushrooms and sauté until tender. Add the radishes, water chestnuts, scallions, and tofu. Sauté until the radishes are pink and tender. Reduce the heat. Stir the miso sauce mixture again. Scrape the tofu mixture to the far side of the pan. Gently tilt the near side of the pan toward you. Pour the sauce into the empty side of the pan. Stir the sauce constantly until thickened, about 3 minutes, then blend with the tofu and vegetables. Remove from heat.

Cut the polenta into 4 squares or 12 fingers and divide among 4 dinner plates. Top with the tofu mixture. Garnish with black sesame seeds and serve immediately.

Serves 4

1 pound firm tofu, packed in water

2 tablespoons yellow miso

3 tablespoons raspberry vinegar

²/₃ cup water

3 tablespoons sugar

2 teaspoons arrowroot

1 teaspoon Ginger Juice (page 360)

³/₄ teaspoon crushed red pepper flakes

3 tablespoons vegetable oil

1 cup small radishes, with leaves

2 tablespoons dark sesame oil

2 cloves garlic, minced

4 ounces very small button
    mushrooms

1 cup whole fresh water chestnuts,
    peeled, or canned water chestnuts,
    drained

6 scallions cut into 2-inch lengths

1 recipe millet polenta (page 146)

2 tablespoons sesame seeds,
    preferably black

Millet and Sweet Potato Terrine with Garam Masala–Mushroom Sauce

❦

The elegant appearance of this dish makes it a very appealing dinner party entree or buffet dish. The Garam Masala–Mushroom Sauce is mildly pungent.

Serves 4

1 cup mushrooms, thinly sliced

1/2 cup water

2 tablespoons tamari soy sauce

1 tablespoon dry white wine

1 cup piñon (pine nuts), toasted

1 cup fresh parsley sprigs

About 2 3/4 cups Vegetable Stock (page 364)

1 1/2 cups millet, toasted, washed, and drained

2 cups peeled and diced sweet potatoes

1/2 cup minced onions

1/2 teaspoon ground coriander

1/4 teaspoon ground bay leaf (see Note)

Sea salt and freshly ground black pepper, to taste

Garam Masala–Mushroom Sauce (recipe follows)

Note: Grind bay leaves in a spice grinder, coffee mill, or blender. Ten whole leaves will make 1 teaspoon ground. Store in an airtight container in a cool, dry place.

Combine the mushrooms, water, 1 tablespoon of the soy sauce, and the white wine in a small saucepan over medium heat and bring to a simmer. Simmer, covered, for 15 minutes. Remove from the heat. Drain well, reserving the liquid.

Dilute the mushroom cooking liquid with enough stock to make 3 cups. Combine the liquid with the millet, the sweet potatoes, all but 1 tablespoon of the piñon, the onions, coriander, bay leaf, remaining 1 tablespoon soy sauce, salt, and pepper in a medium saucepan over high heat and bring to a boil. Lower the heat, cover, and simmer for 25 minutes, or until the millet and sweet potatoes are cooked and all the liquid has been absorbed. Remove from the heat.

Lay 3 mushroom slices, 1 tablespoon of the piñon, and 3 parsley sprigs in a decorative pattern in the bottom of a greased 9 × 5-inch loaf pan. Using a potato masher, mash the millet mixture. Pack half of the millet mixture into the loaf pan, gently pressing down to press out any air pockets. Make a layer of the mushroom slices, then pack the remaining millet mixture on top, tamping down and smoothing the top. Let stand, uncovered, at room temperature for 10 minutes or up to 1 hour. If the terrine must be made more than 1 hour in advance, cover and refrigerate, and then warm in a 325° F. oven for 20 minutes before serving.

Unmold onto a serving platter. Place the remaining parsley sprigs around the edge. Cut into 1-inch slices to serve. Pass the mushroom sauce at table.

Garam Masala–Mushroom Sauce

Heat the oil in a medium sauté pan over medium heat. Add the onion, garlic, and garam masala. Sauté for 5 minutes, or until onion is very soft. Add the mushrooms and sauté for 3 minutes. Sprinkle with flour and sauté for 2 minutes. Whisk in the stock. Cook, stirring as necessary, for about 5 minutes, or until thick. Season with salt, soy sauce, and wine. Reduce the heat to low and simmer, stirring as necessary, for 10 minutes. If the sauce gets too thick, thin with water, 1 tablespoon at a time. Keep warm until ready to serve.

Makes 1 1/2 cups

2 tablespoons extra virgin olive oil

1 small onion, minced

1 clove garlic, minced

1 tablespoon Garam Masala (page 358)

6 small mushrooms, thinly sliced

3 tablespoons unbleached all-purpose flour

1 3/4 cups Vegetable Stock (page 364)

1/2 teaspoon sea salt

2 teaspoons tamari soy sauce

1 tablespoon dry white wine

Grilled Millet and Butternut Squash Cakes

✦

Millet's light texture lends it to grilling. These sweet but pungent golden orange morsels may also be panfried. When I serve this dish to youngsters, I substitute a teaspoon of fresh Ginger Juice (page 360) for the minced ginger. Adults seem to prefer the direct ginger hit that minced ginger provides.

Serves 4

1 cup millet

1 teaspoon mustard seeds

1 teaspoon curry powder

2 ½ cups water

2 cups peeled and diced butternut squash

1 teaspoon minced fresh ginger

½ teaspoon sea salt

½ cup chopped fresh cilantro

Put the millet in a saucepan or wok over high heat. Toast, stirring constantly, for about 4 minutes, or until the first seed pops. Wash, drain, and set aside. Toast the mustard seeds and curry powder for 1 minute, or until aromatic.

Put the millet and spices, water, squash, ginger, and sea salt in a medium saucepan. Bring to a boil over high heat. Lower the heat and simmer, covered, for 25 minutes, or until the millet has absorbed all the water. Remove from the heat and let cool.

Preheat the grill.

Add the cilantro to the millet mixture. Wet your hands and blend the millet mixture to a fairly uniform consistency. Form into 12 cakes. Place on the grill and grill for about 3 minutes on each side, or until golden. Serve hot.

Millet, Quinoa, and Burdock Pilaf

When it comes to grain combinations, this is one of my favorites. Nutty quinoa rounds out the sweet millet, and burdock adds depth. The pilaf goes well with a meal of grilled winter vegetables or vegetable stew. It can also be used as a stuffing for baked vegetables.

Wash and trim but do not peel the burdock. Slice into thin rounds. Heat the ghee in a large saucepan over medium heat. Add the burdock and sauté for 5 minutes, or until it softens. Add the shallot and sauté for about 5 minutes, or until it is translucent. Add the salt, pepper, stock, and wine and bring to a boil. Add the millet. Lower the heat, and simmer, covered, for 10 minutes. Add the quinoa. Simmer, covered, for 15 minutes, or until the liquid is absorbed. Let stand, covered, 5 minutes. Add the sunflower seeds and tarragon and gently mix, fluffing rather than compressing the grains. Serve hot or at room temperature.

VARIATION: Black quinoa is especially beautiful in this dish. If using black or domestic quinoa, reduce the amount of stock by 2 tablespoons.

Serves 4

1 plump burdock root, about 10 inches long

2 tablespoons Ghee (page 359) or extra virgin olive oil

¼ cup chopped shallots or onions

1 teaspoon sea salt, or to taste

Cracked black pepper, to taste

2 cups Vegetable Stock (page 364) or Chicken Stock (page 366)

1 cup dry white wine

1 cup millet, toasted, washed, and drained

½ cup quinoa, rinsed and drained

¼ cup sunflower seeds, toasted

2 tablespoons minced fresh tarragon

Orange-Pecan Millet

$$\text{\textmd{❧}}$$

Serves 6 to 8

3 large organic oranges, scrubbed

*2 to 3 cups Vegetable Stock (page 364)
or water*

1/2 teaspoon sea salt

*2 1/2 cups millet, toasted, washed, and
drained*

2 tablespoons unsalted butter

1/2 cup chopped pecans

Freshly grated nutmeg, to taste

*This is adapted from a recipe by Annemarie Colbin. Her book, The
Natural Gourmet, is filled with imaginative ideas for healthy, grain-
centered meals. Orange brings out the sweetness of millet.*

Grate the zest of all 3 oranges and set aside.
Juice the oranges. Measure the juice and add enough
water to make 4 cups plus 2 tablespoons.

Pour the juice into a 3-quart saucepan. Add the salt and bring to
a boil over medium-high heat. Add the millet. Lower the heat, cover,
and cook for 30 minutes, or until the liquid is absorbed and the millet is done. Let rest, covered, 5 minutes.

Heat the butter in a small sauté pan over low heat. When warm,
add the pecans and lightly toast. Add the orange zest and nutmeg
and stir to blend. Remove from the heat. Fold into the millet and
serve immediately.

Millet Shortcake with Hot Caramelized Plums

Millet flour makes these shortcakes unique. They are light and dry with a subtle flavor.

Preheat the oven to 350°F. Grease a baking sheet and set aside. Cream together 8 tablespoons (1 stick) of the butter and ½ cup of the Sucanat until light and fluffy. Stir in the milk, eggs, almond extract, and lemon zest. Sift together the millet and all-purpose flours, baking powder, and ½ teaspoon salt. Stir into the batter. Stir in the ground almonds.

Drop dough in 6 tall mounds at least 2 inches apart on the baking sheet. Sprinkle ⅓ teaspoon Sucanat over each mound. Bake for about 30 minutes, or until golden. Remove and cool on a wire rack.

Wash, pit, and slice the plums. Set aside.

Melt the remaining butter in a large sauté pan over medium-high heat. Add the remaining ½ cup Sucanat and a pinch of salt. Cook, stirring constantly, for 3 minutes. Add the plums and the lemon juice and cook, stirring frequently, for about 10 minutes, or until the sauce is syrupy and bubbling. Remove from the heat.

Split each piece horizontally in half. Place a bottom half on each of 6 dessert plates. Spoon the plum filling over. Top each with the upper half of a biscuit. Garnish with a dollop of whipped cream. Sprinkle with toasted almonds. Serve warm.

Serves 6

12 tablespoons (1 ½ sticks) unsalted butter

1 cup plus 3 teaspoons Sucanat or packed light brown sugar

½ cup milk or soy milk

2 large eggs, lightly beaten

¼ teaspoon almond extract

1 tablespoon freshly grated lemon zest

1 cup millet flour (see page 142)

1 cup unbleached all-purpose flour

1 teaspoon baking powder

Sea salt

1 cup ground blanched almonds

3 pounds plums, such as Damson or Italian prune plums

1 tablespoon fresh lemon juice

½ cup heavy whipping cream, whipped

⅓ cup slivered almonds, toasted

Millet Horseshoe Cookies

Makes 2 dozen

8 tablespoons (1 stick) unsalted
  butter, softened

$^{1}/_{2}$ cup Sucanat or packed light brown
  sugar

3 large eggs

1 teaspoon pure vanilla extract

1 teaspoon freshly grated orange zest

1 $^{1}/_{2}$ cups millet flour (see page 142)

1 cup unbleached all-purpose flour

1 teaspoon baking powder

$^{1}/_{2}$ teaspoon ground coriander

$^{1}/_{4}$ teaspoon sea salt

$^{1}/_{4}$ cup hulled sesame seeds

These are very pleasing cookies, but a bit crumbly. When piped through a pastry bag, the cookies have a superior texture and appearance than when shaped by hand.

Preheat oven to 375° F. Grease 2 baking sheets and set aside. Cream the butter and Sucanat until very light and fluffy. Add 2 of the eggs, the vanilla, and orange zest and mix well. Sift the millet and all-purpose flour, baking powder, coriander, and salt together and stir into the batter until well combined.

Spoon the dough into a pastry bag fitted with a $^{3}/_{8}$-inch star-shape tip. Pipe into 4-inch long horseshoe shapes, 2 inches apart, on the baking sheets. Or shape the cookies by hand by rolling walnut-size pieces of dough into 4-inch-long logs and bending each into a horseshoe shape. Place 2 inches apart on the baking sheets.

Beat the remaining egg. Using a pastry brush, coat each cookie with egg. Sprinkle with sesame seeds. Bake for about 12 minutes, or until lightly golden. Cool on wire racks. (Cookies may be stored in an airtight container for 4 days.)

Crunchy Millet Bread

Millet gives the most surprising effect when kneaded into bread. Other grains add chewiness, but those little golden millet seeds add crunch. I've adapted this recipe from one from Greens restaurant in San Francisco.

Place the millet in a heatproof bowl and add the boiling water. Cover and let soak for 30 to 40 minutes.

Combine the yeast and warm water in a large mixing bowl. Stir to dissolve and allow to proof for 5 minutes. Beat in the honey, bread flour, and 1½ cups of the whole wheat flour until a smooth, thin batter is formed. Cover and set aside in a warm, draft-free spot for about 30 minutes, or until doubled in size.

Stir in the butter, salt, and millet, including any soaking water that remains. Blend well, then fold in 3 cups of the remaining whole wheat flour, ½ cup at a time. When the dough is too thick to add in more flour easily, scrape from the bowl onto a floured work surface. Begin kneading, adding enough flour to keep the dough from sticking. Knead for about 8 minutes, or until the dough is smooth and elastic. Place dough in a buttered bowl. Cover and let rise in a warm, draft-free spot for about 1 hour, or until doubled in bulk. Punch down the dough, round the dough, and return it to the bowl. Let rise again for about 30 minutes, or until doubled.

Butter two 9 × 5-inch loaf pans. Remove dough from bowl and shape into 2 loaves. Place the loaves in pans, cover, and let rise for about 25 minutes, or until doubled.

Preheat the oven to 350°F.

Beat the egg and milk together. Using a pastry brush, generously coat loaves with egg wash. Bake for about 50 minutes, or until browned and the edges pull away from the pan. Cool on wire racks.

Makes two 9-inch loaves

1 cup millet, toasted, washed, and drained

1 cup plus 2 tablespoons boiling water

2 tablespoons active dry yeast

2 cups warm water (100°F.)

2 tablespoons honey

1 cup bread flour

6 to 7 cups whole wheat flour

3 tablespoons melted unsalted butter

1 tablespoon sea salt

1 large egg

1 tablespoon milk or soy milk

Apricot Millet Breakfast Cake

❦

Makes one 9-inch loaf

1 ½ cups apple juice

½ cup chopped dried apricots

¼ cup currants

2 tablespoons dried cranberries

3 tablespoons melted unsalted
butter

3 tablespoons honey

1 large egg

1 cup cooked millet
(see page 144)

1 ½ cups whole wheat pastry flour or
unbleached all-purpose flour

½ teaspoon sea salt

½ teaspoon baking soda

½ teaspoon baking powder

¼ cup chopped pumpkin seeds

Here's a fine way to use leftover millet. The millet and apricots give a sweet-tangy flavor and a golden background for the red cranberries, green pumpkin seeds, and black currants. This is best served on a plate, as it tends to be crumbly.

Heat 1 cup of the apple juice in a small saucepan over medium heat. Put the apricots, currants, and cranberries in a heatproof bowl. Pour the hot apple juice over the fruit. Soak for about 15 minutes, or until the fruit is soft. Drain, reserving the juice. Measure it and, if necessary, add enough additional juice to make ¾ cup.

Preheat the oven to 375°F. Grease a 9 × 5-inch loaf pan.

Whisk together the butter and honey. When well blended, stir in the egg and juice. Add the millet and fruit. Sift the flour, salt, baking soda, and baking powder into the millet mixture. Stir just to blend. Fold in the pumpkin seeds.

Scrape into the loaf pan. Bake for about 30 minutes, or until a cake tester inserted in the center comes out clean. Cool on a wire rack.

Overnight Millet, Buckwheat, and Coconut Waffles

Here's a deceptive waffle. Deceptively easy, that is. The secret is soaked millet and buckwheat. Soaking encourages a grain's flavor to blossom. Early risers may want to soak the grains first thing in the morning for a later breakfast or brunch; for maximum flavor, though, be sure to soak the grains for at least three hours before making the waffles.

Put the millet and buckwheat in a blender. Add the milk, refrigerate, and let soak for at least 3 hours or up to 8 hours. (To reduce soaking time, soak at room temperature.)
Preheat the waffle iron.

Add the eggs, coconut, butter, baking powder, cinnamon, orange zest, coriander, and salt to the soaked grains in the blender. Process to combine. Pour into the waffle iron and bake according to manufacturer's directions. Serve hot.

VARIATIONS: Sprinkle the bottom of the waffle iron with sunflower, poppy, or sesame seeds before pouring in the batter.
Add ¼ cup chopped walnuts or pecans to batter.

Makes 4

1 cup millet, lightly toasted and washed

1 cup buckwheat groats, lightly toasted

2 ¼ cups milk, soy milk, or water

1 large egg

¼ cup unsweetened shredded coconut

2 tablespoons softened unsalted butter or unrefined corn oil

½ teaspoon baking powder

½ teaspoon ground cinnamon

½ teaspoon grated orange zest

¼ teaspoon ground coriander

¼ teaspoon sea salt

Rice

MOST OF WHAT I KNOW about whole foods I owe to rice. Not only has it fed me well, it has opened doors to knowledge and understanding that I otherwise could never have imagined. Beginning with my first scorched pot of brown rice in San Francisco, rice (*Oryza sativa*) has been the food through which I have learned to nourish the whole being.

In 1969, I moved to Boston so that I could live and study with Aveline and Michio Kushi in their, at that time, rather informal macrobiotic community. Short-grain brown rice was our daily fare; it was often served two or three times a day. More than any other cook I have met, Aveline could make a deeply satisfying dish with complex flavors using only two or three ingredients. What I learned most from watching and cooking with Aveline was how to show off rice to its maximum. For her, a simple pot of brown rice, cooked with reverence and cele-bration, needed no embellishment. Even if today brown rice is not on my table as frequently as it once was, I know that my respect for it is the source of my passion to experiment with and promote other grains and whole foods.

When you consider that rice is the heart of the meal for over half of the world's popula-tion, you don't need historical facts or statistics to recognize its significance. It is estimated that rice is eaten daily by six out of ten people worldwide and by most people throughout Asia. In China and Japan, in fact, the word for rice is synonymous with meal.

Rice is mainly grown in southern and eastern Asia where the annual rainfall pattern can supply the high level of water needed for its cultivation. It is also cultivated in more than one hundred countries on every continent except Antarctica. The United States is a leading exporter of all rice types.

The beginning of the cultivation of rice cannot be specifically dated. Archaeological evidence indicates that, in its wild form, rice was gathered by prehistoric people. It seems to have been cultivated more than four thousand years ago in southern Asia. Europe probably encountered rice as a result of diplomatic and trading contacts around the fifth century B.C. In the United States, rice came with colonization and was first grown in the South. Now it is also grown in Texas and California.

There are two basic species of cultivated rice: African red rice (*Oryza globerrina*), which was the foundation of west Africa's ancient civilizations, and Asian rice (*Oryza sativa*), which includes japonica (short- and medium-grain rice varieties) and indica (long-grain rice varieties). All rice is harvested with its hull intact; then it is removed. To refine the rice, machines strip off the bran layer, leaving a polished white kernel. Most of the vitamins, minerals, amino acids, and fiber go off with the bran. In America and some other places, several of these lost nutrients are subsequently replaced synthetically. For the cook's convenience, producers also have created converted (or parboiled) and precooked instant rice, which don't compare with the flavor and nutrition of less processed rice.

Rice is the principal sustenance for many millions of people, but it is not all that balanced in nutrients. Rich in fiber, extremely low in sodium and fat and cholesterol free, rice is composed almost 80 percent of complex carbohydrates with only a little protein, phosphorus, and potassium. And, since the time of Confucius, white or polished rice has been favored throughout Asia. This is unfortunate because the removal of the bran, a potent source of vitamins, contributes to beriberi, a vitamin deficiency disease. In fact, it was through the study of this disease that scientists discovered vitamins and the role they play in a balanced diet.

Although more than a hundred thousand varieties of rice are grown around the world, only a few types are available to the home cook. Until recently, long-grain white rice was the primary type used in the United States. Only 2 percent of the rice sold was brown rice. With the influx of immigrants from Asia in the 1970s, the proliferation of ethnic restaurants beginning in the 1980s, and a revitalized interest in good health since the 1960s, many other kinds of rice have made their way into the American kitchen.

My own rice pantry always includes either white jasmine or basmati rice and both brown and white sweet rice. My warm weather brown rice is basmati, though in cool weather I favor short-grain brown rice because it's more substantial. For special dishes I buy sushi rice, Arborio, Thai black sticky rice, or a specialty blend such as Christmas, Wehani, Wild Pecan, or Jubilee. The more common types are available in supermarkets, natural foods stores, specialty food shops, and Asian markets. Others are available through mail order.

Rice
Selection and Storage

All white rice was once brown or whole rice. Refining removes the germ and bran layers and makes a grain that requires less cooking time and is easier to digest.

Brown Rice

Quality brown rice contains a small percentage of green (chlorophyll-containing) grains because the kernels on any grain stalk mature at different rates. Grains at the bottom, the slowest to develop, are green and immature. If your brown rice has no green, the rice was gassed to yield a cosmetic monochromatic grain by eliminating the chlorophyll.

By buying quality brown rice and storing it in glass or tightly wrapped in a cool, dry, and dark cupboard, I've never lost any to bug infestation, but then I live in the arid mountainous West. Infestation (a sign that the rice is vital rather than sterile) becomes a problem when whole grain is old and/or when it is stored in a humid, especially a warm and humid, kitchen.

Unlike white rice, brown rice does have a finite shelf life, but if it is purchased as advised above, it will store without problems for ten months to a year in a cool and arid climate. If you do not have a cool, dry storage area, refrigerate or freeze your rice.

Rice, be it brown or white, is one of four types—long, medium, short, or sweet. (A different species, the West African red rice, *O. glaberrima*, is currently available only in Lundberg's Christmas Rice blend.)

Long-Grain Rice

The most popular rice type in the United States is long grain, which comprises 90 percent of all the rice used. Long-grain rice has slender kernels, four times longer than wide. It contains a high percentage of a starch, amylose, which keeps the grains separate after cooking. Most long-grain rice is grown in the southern United States and, historically, was favored in Iran, southern Asia, and India. Long-grain rice is preferred for pilafs, entrees, and salads. Some long-grain rice varieties are very perfumed; these include basmati, jasmine, popcorn, and wild pecan. Wehani, a recently developed variety, smells like popcorn.

Medium-Grain Rice

Medium-grain rice has kernels that are about twice as long as they are wide. Medium-grain rice has a more equal blend of amylose and amglopectin starches and so, in terms of size, cooking qualities, and starch composition, it has properties similar to both long- and short-grain varieties. In terms of stickiness, however, it is more similar to short grain.

Short-Grain Rice

Short-grain rice has almost round kernels that cling together once cooked because of its high percentage of the starch, amylopectin. This rice is slightly more nutrient dense than medium- or long-grain rice and is the preferred grain in the macrobiotic diet as it is considered more energizing. It is used as a side dish, in soups, risottos, puddings, and croquettes. Most U.S. short-grain rice is grown in California. In Asia, it is usually grown in colder climates such as Japan and northern China.

Sweet Rice

Also known as glutinous or sticky rice, sweet rice (*Oryza glutinos*) is a very sticky, sweet grain rice used in Asian cooking for sweets or snacks, and as the basis of rice wine, mirin, amasake, and mochi. The gluten in sweet rice is not the same gluten found in wheat; thus, sweet rice is an acceptable grain for people with gluten intolerance.

Specialty Rices

Thai black sticky rice is a long-grain glutinous rice imported from Thailand, where it is used primarily in sweets and snacks. It is a whole-grain rice.

Arborio rice is a medium-grain white rice from the Piedmont region of Italy. Because it absorbs a much greater proportion of liquid than other rices, it is the favored rice for risotto. Other Italian medium-grain rices include Vialone Nano and Carnaroli, which are not so commonly available as Arborio.

Parboiled or, to use Uncle Ben's trademarked term, "Converted" rice is usually long-grain white rice. Parboiled rice has been pressure-steamed before hulling. This hardens the starch and results in a grain that requires longer cooking and more liquid. Since the grains remain moist and separate, parboiled rice is favored in restaurants, where it holds up well on the steam table. This is the one rice that is not rinsed prior to cooking.

Instant rice has been thoroughly cooked and dried and so only requires rehydrating. I recommend this rice for traveling.

Be it white or brown, purchase rice directly from the bin in a natural foods store that has a rapid turnover. Select rice with few, if any, broken, chipped, or scratched grains. Good rice actually looks vibrant rather than dull.

Many supermarkets and natural foods stores carry specialty rice and rice blends in small cellophane packages. Asian markets and many natural foods stores sell jasmine, basmati, sweet, and Thai black sticky rice.

Other Rice Products

Rice vinegar comes in several qualities, colors, and strengths. My favorite, and one of the world's lightest, most mellow and delicious vinegars, is handcrafted in the traditional way on the Japanese island of Kyushu. Made from 100 percent brown rice sake, it is fermented in earthenware crocks which are buried outside in the ground. Kyushu Organic Brown Rice Vinegar is sold at large natural foods stores or by mail order. Harsh-tasting, inexpensive rice vinegars, from Japanese or Chinese commercial producers, are available in supermarkets and Asian markets. I do not recommend them.

Rice koji is the starter that catalyzes the fermentation of grains (or beans) into sake, amasake, miso, soy sauce, and tamari. Ready-made rice koji is available, refrigerated, in natural foods stores under the Cold Mountain label. It is packaged with simple instructions for its use. To make your own koji, purchase koji starter from Gem Cultures (see page 377).

Rice flour is used much like wheat flour in dumplings, cakes, and cookies, but not alone in bread since it is gluten free. The flour may be made from white rice or brown rice.

Rice pasta is made from rice flour and water. It comes in many shapes and forms, including rice noodles and rice paper.

Rice Flour

The difference in performance and color between white and brown rice flour is small. The white is a shade whiter, smoother textured, and less flavored. White or brown rice flour may be used interchangeably in any recipe.

There is a significant performance difference, however, between varieties. Flour made from any long-grain rice is suited to breading, sauces, and use as a thickener; it is not good for baking (brownies excepted) since it yields a wet, soggy product with a large crumb. Both medium- and short-grain rice flours are multipurpose and can be used as thickeners and in baked goods, where they give a sandy, dry crumb. Unfortunately, packages do not always specify the rice variety; you may assume it is multipurpose medium- or short-grain rice unless the package directions indicate that the flour is not to be used in baked goods.

Natural foods stores are more apt to stock brown rice flour and supermarkets white rice flour. Rice flour is also available by mail order. The advantage of white rice flour is its indefinite shelf life. Store brown rice flour, tightly covered, in the refrigerator for up to 5 months or in the freezer for up to 1 year.

I recommend using freshly milled rice flour if at all possible. Grind the rice in a home flour mill or a coffee or spice grinder. For 1 cup flour, grind a scant $^3/_4$ cup ($^3/_4$ cup minus 1 tablespoon) short-grain rice or $^3/_4$ cup long-grain rice.

Steamed Brown Rice

❦

Makes about 2 ¼ cups

*1 cup short-, medium-, or long-grain
brown rice*

2 to 2 ¼ cups cold water

Sea salt, to taste

My preference is always brown rice cooked in a pressure cooker. (I never boil rice, be it brown or white. Draining off extra cooking water drains off nutrients and flavor.) For my pleasure, the rice is short-grained. Expect pressure-cooked rice to be sweeter, stickier, and more flavorful, digestible, and energizing than rice cooked in a saucepan. Fluffy it is not. If you do not have a pressure cooker, use a heavy saucepan as directed. If you find that your rice always sticks to the bottom of the saucepan, place a Flame Tamer between the pan and the source of heat. You might also want to invest in a heavy enameled pot or pressure cooker.

It is difficult to provide an exact formula for the amount of water for cooking rice. Variables include the age and type of rice, the size and type of pot, and the humidity. Also, if rice is presoaked, it requires a little less water. Not to worry. Use the following finger-measuring technique (see Note), the same pot, and the same type of rice and soon your sixth sense will guide you better than a measuring cup. Once you've got a perfect pot of rice, rely on your finger and intuition for other rice varieties and for wheat, quinoa, and other grains.

Toast the rice in a saucepan or wok over medium-high heat, stirring constantly, until it gives off a pleasant aroma, about 5 minutes. Put the rice in a deep bowl. Add enough water to cover generously and gently scrub the rice for 5 seconds or so between your palms. Pour into a fine sieve. Repeat washing 1 or 2 more times, or until the water runs clear. Drain well.

To cook in a pressure cooker, put the washed rice in a 6- or 8-quart pressure cooker and add 2 cups water for short-grain rice or 2 cups minus 2 tablespoons for medium- or long-grain rice. Cover and soak for at least 1 hour or up to 8 hours. (In very hot weather, soak the rice in the refrigerator to prevent fermenting.)

Add the salt and lock the lid in place. Place over high heat and bring to high pressure. Lower the heat just enough to maintain medium pressure. Cook for 50 minutes. Remove from the heat and allow the pressure to come down naturally for 10 minutes. Remove the lid, tilting it away from you to allow any excess steam to escape. Using a damp rice paddle or large wooden spoon, mix the rice from the top down to the bottom. Lift into a serving bowl.

To cook in a saucepan, put the washed rice in a 1-quart heavy saucepan and add 2¼ cups water for short-grain rice or 2 cups minus 2 tablespoons for medium- or long-grain rice. Cover and soak for at least 1 hour or up to 8 hours. (If the weather is very hot, soak in the refrigerator to prevent fermenting.)

Add the salt and place over high heat. Cover and bring to a boil. Lower the heat and simmer, undisturbed, for 1 hour, or until the water is absorbed. Remove from the heat and let stand, covered, for 5 minutes. Using a damp rice paddle or large wooden spoon, mix the rice from the top down to the bottom. Lift into a serving bowl.

VARIATIONS: Add a 2-inch piece of kombu (see page 373) to the rice and water. When cooked, remove and compost the kombu.

For each ¼ teaspoon sea salt, substitute 1 teaspoon tamari soy sauce.

Add ½ teaspoon of any ground spice to the rice and water.

Add several tablespoons of minced watercress, parsley, or any other fresh herb when mixing the cooked rice.

Add up to ¼ cup chopped nuts or whole seeds, such as sesame, either with the rice and water or after rice has cooked.

Add a pinch of Sucanat or brown sugar and one ¼-inch slice of fresh ginger to the rice and water. When cooked, remove the ginger.

Replace the water with stock and reduce the soaking time and/or soak under refrigeration to prevent spoilage.

Note: When cooking more than 1 cup of rice, the amount of water slightly decreases and it's easier to measure by the inch. The first and second joints of the middle finger are a handy measuring tool and each measures, in fact, 1 inch. Stick your finger in the pot and let it rest on top of the rice, then add the water. For pressure-cooked short-grain brown rice, add water to a depth of 1½ inches, for pressure-cooked long-grain brown rice, add water to a depth of 1¼ inches. When short-grain brown rice covers the bottom of the saucepan by 1 inch or more, add enough water to cover the rice by 2 inches. For long-grain brown rice, add water to a depth of 1¾ inches.

Storing and Reheating Leftover Rice

To store leftover rice, put the cooked rice in a glass bowl, loosely cover with a cotton cloth, and leave out at room temperature for up to 24 hours. I compost rice not used within this time. To refrigerate or freeze rice, place it in a tightly covered container (it will keep for 3 days refrigerated or 1 month frozen) and use the rice in a highly flavored dish with other toothsome ingredients to mask its compromised flavor and texture.

Rice cooked within 4 hours may be used in any of the salad recipes in this book. After the rice is over 4 hours old, it invites reheating before serving it or using it in a soup, stir-fry, stuffing, bread, or pudding. Leftover rice may be used for Hash Brown Rice (page 195) or made into a breakfast porridge by simmering it with milk, raisins, and cinnamon.

The most flavorful way to reheat rice (about 2 cups) is to put it in a greased skillet over low heat for about 7 minutes, or until heated through; if you enjoy crisp rice, increase the cooking time to 12 to 15 minutes. Season to taste with tamari soy sauce.

When rice is reheated over steam or by adding water, it loses savor but is an acceptable accompaniment for a well-seasoned dish. To reheat rice in a steam basket, suspend it over boiling water for 5 minutes. A nonreactive steamer, such as bamboo or ceramic, yields the best-tasting rice. To steam rice in a saucepan, put $1/4$ inch of water in the pan and simmer until heated through, about 5 minutes.

To reheat rice in the oven, put leftover rice in a greased casserole, sprinkle with water, cover, and bake at 325°F. for 15 minutes or until heated through.

Cooking Brown Rice

There's one good reason why polished rice is eaten throughout Asia: It's more digestible. Undercooked brown rice challenges the digestive system. By using a pressure cooker, however, you can enjoy full-flavored brown rice that's easily digested. Pressure increases the boiling point from the standard 212° to 250°F., which adequately softens the bran. In addition, since a minimal amount of water is used, pressure-cooking concentrates the flavors.

For the most flavorful brown rice, pressure-cook it for a full 50 minutes. Yes, that sound like a long time, but it works. Be it short-, medium-, or long-grain, brown rice cooked by other methods tastes starchy and half-cooked. When it's brown rice, I pressure-cook.

Cooking Brown Rice in a Saucepan

If you want brown rice and do not have a pressure cooker, here are four steps to make it more digestible:

- Use your heaviest pot, one that has a tight-fitting lid, such as a Le Creuset pot.
- Lightly toast the rice.
- Allow generous (preferably overnight) soaking time
- Cook the rice with a 2-inch strip of kombu and a small knob of ginger.

I don't use an electric rice steamer for rice because such appliances are either made of aluminum or have a nonstick surface, neither of which enhances your health or the rice's flavor. I don't bake brown rice in the oven because I find whole rice tastes better with more direct contact with the heat source. If, however, using a rice steamer or baking rice is what works for you, then give its digestibility a boost by using toasted and well-soaked rice and by adding a strip of kombu and a small knob of ginger.

Pressure-Cooking Brown Rice in a Ceramic Insert Pot

When pressure-cooking small quantities of rice (2 cups or less), it often becomes dry on the top and scorched on the bottom. There's an easy solution. Cook it in a lidded ceramic pot, called an Ohsawa Ceramic Pot, inside the pressure cooker. The grain comes out fluffy, light, and cooked uniformly throughout. Besides, I use the ceramic insert for other pressure-cooked grains as well.

Put the washed and drained rice in a lidded ceramic pot. (You may also use a covered, heat-resistant glass bowl.) Add water to cover by $1^1/_4$ inches for short-grain brown rice, by 1 inch for long-grain. Cover and soak for at least 1 hour or overnight. (In very hot weather, soak the rice in the refrigerator to prevent fermenting.) Add the salt, cover with a ceramic lid, add 2 inches of water to the pressure cooker, and lock the lid in place. Continue as directed on page 177.

Pressure-Cooking Large Amounts of Brown Rice

To cook from $2^1/_2$ to 5 cups of rice in a pressure cooker, put the washed and drained rice in a 6- or 8-quart pressure cooker. Add water to cover by $1^1/_2$ inches for short-grain brown rice, $1^1/_4$ inches for long-grain brown rice, using the method of measuring with your finger described on page 173. Soak and cook as directed on page 177.

Ceramic pots, pressure cookers, and Flame Tamers are available from the Macrobiotic Company of America, Gold Mine Natural Food Company, GoodEats, and *Natural Lifestyle Magazine* and Mail-Order Market (see page 377).

Aveline Kushi's Pot of Rice

This is the rice Aveline Kushi cooked when she wanted to feed her students something special. It's an earthy brown color with rich, complex flavors, and it is oh, so filling.

Wash the rice as described on page 172 and drain.

To cook in a pressure cooker, put the rice in a 6- or 8-quart pressure cooker. Add the water and soak for at least 1 hour or up to 8 hours. (In very hot weather, soak the rice in the refrigerator to prevent fermenting.)

Add the walnuts and tamari and lock the lid in place. Place over high heat and bring to high pressure. Lower the heat just enough to maintain medium pressure. Cook for 50 minutes. Remove from the heat and allow the pressure to come down naturally for 10 minutes. Remove the lid, tilting it away from you to allow any excess steam to escape. Using a damp rice paddle or large wooden spoon, mix the rice from the top down to the bottom. When mixed, cover and allow to rest for another 3 minutes. Lift into serving bowl.

To cook in a saucepan, put the washed and drained rice in a 3-quart heavy saucepan and add the water. Soak for at least 1 hour or up to 8 hours. (In very hot weather, soak in the refrigerator to prevent fermenting.)

Add the walnuts and tamari and place over high heat. Cover and bring to a boil. Lower the heat and simmer, undisturbed, for 1 hour, or until the water is absorbed. Remove from the heat and let stand, covered, for 5 minutes. Using a damp rice paddle or large wooden spoon, mix the rice from the top down to the bottom. Cover and allow to rest for another 3 minutes. Lift into a serving bowl.

Makes about 2¹⁄₂ cups

1 cup short-grain brown rice, washed and drained

1 ³⁄₄ to 2 cups water

2 tablespoons chopped toasted walnuts

2 teaspoons tamari soy sauce

Note: When cooking more than 1 cup of rice, the water measurement slightly decreases and it becomes easier to measure by the inch. When the rice covers the pot's bottom by 1 inch or more, add enough water to cover the rice by 1¹⁄₄ inches for pressure-cooked rice, by 2 inches for rice cooked in a saucepan.

Steamed Long-Grain White Rice

❧

Makes about 3 cups

1 cup long-grain white rice

2 cups water (see Note)

Sea salt

*1 tablespoon Ghee (page 359) or
unrefined vegetable oil (optional)*

Note: When cooking more than 1 cup of rice, the water measurement slightly decreases and it becomes easier to measure by the inch. When the rice covers the pot's bottom by 1 inch or more, add enough water to cover the rice by 1 inch.

P lace the rice in a deep bowl. Add enough water to generously cover and scrub the rice for 5 seconds or so between your palms. Pour into a fine sieve. Repeat washing 1 or 2 more times. Drain well. Put the rice in a heavy 1-quart saucepan and add the water. Cover and let soak for at least 30 minutes or up to 1 hour.

Add the salt and ghee or oil, if using, and bring to a boil over high heat. Add the washed and drained rice and return to a boil. Reduce the heat, cover, and simmer for 15 to 20 minutes, or until the water is absorbed. Let stand 5 to 10 minutes. Fluff with a fork and serve.

Steamed Long-Grain
White Basmati or Jasmine Rice

P ut the rice in a heavy 1-quart saucepan and add the water. Cover and let soak for at least 30 minutes or up to 1 hour. Add the salt and ghee or oil, if using, and bring to a boil over high heat. Reduce the heat, cover, and simmer for 15 to 20 minutes, or until the water is absorbed. Let stand 5 to 10 minutes. Fluff with a fork and serve.

Makes about 3 cups

1 cup long-grain white basmati or jasmine rice

1 ³/₄ cups water (see Note)

Sea salt

1 tablespoon Ghee (page 359) or unrefined vegetable oil (optional)

Note: When cooking more than 1 cup of rice, the water measurement slightly decreases and it's easier to measure by the inch. When white basmati or jasmine rice cover the pot's bottom by 1 inch or more, add enough water to cover the rice by ⁷/₈ inch.

Thai Black Sticky
Rice Steamed in a Basket

❧

Makes 3 cups

1 cup Thai black rice

1 cup water

When cooked in water, sweet or glutinous rice, because it has no amylose, blends together into a very sticky mass. For this reason, glutinous rice is usually steamed so that the grains remain separate.

Thai steaming baskets are sold in many Asian markets in the United States. If you see one, buy it. It's the best way to cook sweet rice: Each grain remains separate yet still very tender.

Thai black sticky rice, which is a whole-grain rice, is available in Asian markets and natural foods stores, has a very fruity aroma, and, once cooked, is as black as blackberry jam. It is truly a unique taste experience. When you take the first bite or two, the rice is almost crisp and nutty. After three chews, it melts into your mouth. I serve the rice with Gomasio (page 361) as a dramatic entree, as a side dish, or as a dessert, like Coconut, Black Sticky Rice, and Banana Dumplings (page 200).

Spread the rice out on a plate or work surface and sort through it to remove any little stones or debris. Wash the rice as described on page 172. Soak the rice for no less than 8 hours or up to 12. Do not scrimp on soaking time, or the rice will not cook properly.

Line the rack of a steamer basket with dampened cheesecloth. Spread the soaked rice evenly on top. Or place the rice in a Thai steaming basket. Place the steamer over boiling water in a pot deep enough to enclose it. Cover and steam for 1 hour or until tender. Toward the end of the cooking period, begin tasting the grains for doneness. Serve the rice right from the steaming basket or place it in a serving bowl. It is most delicious when hot.

Store cooked rice in a glass bowl, loosely covered with a clean cotton cloth, at room temperature. To reheat rice, steam it for 5 minutes.

Note: Substitute brown sweet rice and steam for 1 hour. Substitute white sweet rice and steam for 30 minutes.

Risotto

The imported Italian short-grain rices, such as Arborio, Vialone Nano, and Carnaroli, are high in starch, which binds and absorbs the liquid in which the rice is cooked, resulting in a rich, creamy dish with a bit of a bite to the grain.

You can make risotto with water or any rich stock, with a taste of wine, and with the addition of any vegetable, meat, game, poultry, or fish you wish. When you make risotto, the rice may absorb more or less liquid than called for in any recipe. I always heat at least one extra cup of stock so that it will be at hand should I need it.

Combine the porcini and 2 cups very warm water in a small bowl. Let soak for 30 minutes. Strain through a double layer of cheesecloth, reserving the liquid. Chop the porcini and set aside.

Combine the mushroom soaking liquid, stock, and saffron in a medium saucepan over high heat and bring to a boil. Lower the heat to a bare simmer while you prepare rice.

Heat the butter and 1 tablespoon of the olive oil in a 2 ¹/₂-quart heavy saucepan over medium heat. When hot, add the shallot, garlic, and parsley. Sauté for 4 minutes, or until soft. Add the rice and stir until the grains are well coated. Add ¹/₂ cup of the simmering stock and cook, stirring constantly, until all the liquid has been absorbed. Continue adding stock, ¹/₂ cup at a time.

After 10 minutes of cooking, add the chopped porcini. After 20 minutes, taste for texture. Add the liquid in smaller increments until the rice is tender but firm to the bite and moist but not runny. Never stop stirring and never let the heat get too low. When the rice is done remove from the heat and stir in the remaining 1 tablespoon olive oil, ¹/₄ cup of the Parmesan, and the pepper. Taste and add salt, if necessary. Scrape onto a serving platter and serve immediately with additional grated Parmesan cheese at the table.

Serves 4 to 6

¹/₂ cup dried porcini mushrooms

4 cups Vegetable Stock (page 364)

¹/₂ teaspoon crumbled saffron threads

2 tablespoons unsalted butter

2 tablespoons extra virgin olive oil

1 large shallot, minced

1 clove garlic, minced

1 tablespoon minced fresh parsley

1 ¹/₂ cups Arborio rice (see Note)

¹/₂ cup freshly grated Parmesan cheese

¹/₂ teaspoon freshly ground black pepper

Sea salt, to taste

Note: Do not rinse Arborio rice before cooking. If you do, it will not accept the liquid properly.

Vietnamese Spring Rolls

❧

Makes 6

1 ½ ounces cellophane noodles
(bean threads)

6 round (8 ½ inches) rice paper
wrappers (see Note)

6 leaves butterhead or other tender
lettuce, washed and dried

6 large shrimp, cooked peeled, and
split lengthwise in half

½ cup mung bean sprouts

½ cup cilantro leaves

½ cup fresh basil leaves

6 sprigs of fresh mint

Spring Roll Dipping Sauce
(recipe follows)

Note: Rice paper wrappers are made of white rice flour and water. They look like brittle plastic but when moistened they become translucent and pleasantly chewy. They are available, dried, in Asian markets. A recipe for Fresh Rice Papers can be found in *Flatbreads and Flavors* by Jeffrey Alford and Naomi Duguid.

In Vietnam, spring rolls, called cha gio, *are made with transparent rice paper which makes them diaphanous, light, and fresh. Cha gio are always served on the Vietnamese New Year, which falls on the first day of spring, but they are also enjoyed at any time of the year.*

I often serve spring rolls at parties. For formal gatherings, I make the rolls ahead of time. For casual events, I arrange the ingredients on large platters and let my guests design their own. The dipping sauce may be made a day in advance and stored, covered, in the refrigerator. Bring it back to room temperature before serving.

Put the cellophane noodles in a large bowl and cover with hot water. Soak until pliable, about 3 minutes. Drain and cut with scissors into 2-inch lengths.

Moisten a clean kitchen towel and place a rice paper wrapper on it. Spray sheet on both sides using an atomizer bottle of water. Repeat with remaining wrappers. Wrap in a clean kitchen towel, and place in a plastic bag for several minutes, just until they become flexible.

Put a lettuce leaf on each softened wrapper. Top with a shrimp half, equal portions of each of the remaining ingredients, and the other shrimp half. Fold the sides of the rice paper over the filling and roll up to form a snug roll about 1 inch in diameter. Serve with dipping sauce.

Note: Rolls may be made up to 24 hours ahead. Cover with plastic wrap and refrigerate. For maximum flavor, bring to room temperature before serving.

Spring Roll Dipping Sauce

Whisk all ingredients together. Serve at room temperature.

Makes about ³/₄ cup

¼ cup nuoc nam fish sauce
  (see page 374)

2 cloves garlic, peeled and minced

2 teaspoons Sucanat or light brown
  sugar

¼ cup water

1 tablespoon grated daikon, red radish,
  or turnip

2 tablespoons grated carrot

Juice of 1 lime

Cayenne pepper, to taste

Nori-Maki

4 scallions, trimmed

1 medium carrot, trimmed, peeled, and cut into long thin strips

1 cup white sushi rice

1 ²/₃ cups water

1 strip (2 inches) kombu

1 tablespoon brown rice vinegar

1 tablespoon Sucanat or light brown sugar

³/₄ teaspoon sea salt

2 sheets of nori

2 tablespoons umeboshi paste (see page 374)

Note: Japanese ingredients—nori, umeboshi paste, and kombu—are available in Japanese markets and many natural foods markets. White sushi rice is also available in such markets.

❦

Nori-maki are attractive bite-size rice rolls studded with colorful bits of seasoned vegetables and enclosed in a black nori wrapper. I often bring nori-maki to potluck meals because they are easy to make and transport but look so elegant. For a festive brunch, I set out plates of nori-maki with different fillings.

I sometimes use short-grain brown rice which is very filling and flavorful, but when I want a really delicate dish, I use organic short-grain sushi white rice, available from Lundberg Family Farms (see page 376).

Freshly cooked rice that is a little chewier than usual is crucial to the success of nori-maki. Sushi rice needs to cool quickly so that each grain stays separate but still slightly moist. In Japan the sushi master has an assistant who fans the rice as the master gently tosses and stirs it. I spread the hot rice in a thin layer in my largest wooden salad bowl (the wood helps absorb the moisture) and enlist whoever is around to fan while I toss. When assistance is not at hand, I've used an electric fan.

Good-quality nori will guarantee that the rolls are easily shaped. If you buy sushi nori, it is already toasted, so you can skip the nori toasting step.

Make the nori-maki within two hours of serving and do not refrigerate. In hot weather, increase the rice vinegar by half a tablespoon.

Bring a saucepan of water to a boil over high heat. Add the scallions and carrot strips and boil for 1 minute, or until crisp-tender. Drain immediately and refresh under cold running water. Pat dry and set aside.

Place the rice in a deep bowl. Add enough water to generously cover and scrub the rice for 5 seconds or so between your palms. Pour into a fine sieve. Repeat washing 1 or 2 more times. Drain.

Bring the water and kombu to a boil in a 3-quart saucepan over high heat. Add the washed and drained rice and return to a boil. Remove and discard the kombu. Cover, reduce the heat to medium, and boil for 5 minutes. Then reduce the heat to very low and simmer for 15 minutes, or until the water is absorbed. Let stand for 10 minutes while preparing the vinegar mixture.

Combine the vinegar, Sucanat, and salt in a small saucepan over low heat. Warm slightly, just to dissolve the Sucanat and salt. When dissolved, remove from the heat and let cool.

Spread the rice out over a wooden surface. Sprinkle the vinegar solution over the rice. Cool the rice by cutting into it and tossing with a damp wooden rice paddle or large wooden spoon. Do not mash the rice. Toss until the rice has almost reached room temperature but still contains some warmth. Set aside.

Toast the shiny smooth side of the nori by passing it over a high flame or heated electric burner. The nori is ready when the color changes to a more brilliant green and it becomes crisp and fragrant. Place the sheet, toasted side down, on a sushi mat or dry work surface. Moisten your hands to keep the rice from sticking and spread half of the rice evenly over the nori, leaving 1 1/2 inches at the top edge, uncovered.

Starting about a third of the way up from the bottom, spread 1 tablespoon of the umeboshi across the rice. Position a line of carrot strips and 2 scallions on top of the umeboshi. Starting at the bottom edge, roll the nori and rice into a tight cylinder. If using a sushi mat, remove the mat as you roll. Let the roll rest on its seam. Repeat procedure for the second nori sheet. If not serving immediately, cover with plastic wrap.

Just before serving, use a wet, very sharp knife to cut each roll in half, wiping and wetting the knife between each cut. Cut each half into 4 pieces using the same cutting method. Place on a serving platter, cut sides up.

VARIATIONS: Replace the umeboshi with 1/2 teaspoon wasabi (see page 375).

Replace the scallions and carrots with thin strips of avocado, shiitake mushrooms, cucumber, cooked shrimp, fresh cooked tuna, or omelet.

Rice and Sorrel Soup

Serves 4

1 leek, trimmed, cleaned, and chopped

6 cups Shiitake Dashi Stock
  (page 368)

¹/₃ cup Arborio rice or short-grain
  white rice

6 cups finely chopped sorrel
  (about 8 ounces)

Sea salt and freshly ground black
  pepper, to taste

According to Oriental medical theory, sorrel, one of the first vegetables of spring, supports the liver's ability to "spring clean." This fat-free soup is a good first course for an otherwise rich meal. You can make this soup with watercress, purslane, or lamb's-quarter instead of sorrel.

Combine the leek and just enough stock to cover in a medium saucepan over high heat and bring to a boil. Reduce the heat, cover, and simmer for 5 minutes. Add the rice, the remaining stock, and salt. Raise the heat and bring to a boil. Reduce the heat and simmer for 20 minutes, or until the rice is tender. Remove from the heat. Stir in 5 cups of the sorrel. Sprinkle with black pepper. Adjust the seasoning. Ladle into individual soup bowls, garnish with the remaining sorrel, and serve.

Lemon Coconut Rice Salad

Southeast Asia meets the Middle East in this fragrant salad. I have served it with roast duck, with which it seems to be particularly appealing This salad is best when freshly prepared.

Put the fennel seeds in a small skillet or wok over medium-high heat. Toast, stirring constantly, for 2 minutes, or until aromatic. Remove from the heat and crush while still warm. Combine with the yogurt, coconut milk, orange juice, and lemon grass. Set aside.

Toss the rice with the coconut, melon, dates, cilantro, lemon zest and juice. Add the yogurt mixture and toss to combine. Serve at room temperature.

VARIATION: Substitute 4 cups cooked white or brown basmati rice or quinoa for the jasmine rice.

Serves 4

¼ teaspoon fennel seeds

½ cup plain yogurt

¼ cup fresh Coconut Milk (page 354) or canned coconut milk

2 tablespoons fresh orange juice

1 tablespoon minced fresh lemongrass (see Note)

4 cups freshly cooked jasmine rice (see page 179)

1 cup unsweetened coconut, toasted

½ cup diced cantaloupe or seedless grapes

½ cup chopped dates

2 tablespoons minced fresh cilantro

1 teaspoon freshly grated lemon zest

2 tablespoons fresh lemon juice

Note: Fresh lemongrass is available at Asian markets and some specialty food stores.

Grilled Turkey and
Short-Grain Brown Rice Salad

Serves 4

2 tablespoons extra virgin olive oil

1 teaspoon unsulfured molasses

Sea salt and freshly ground black
  pepper, to taste

1 pound thinly sliced turkey breast
  fillets

2 tablespoons unrefined walnut oil

2 tablespoons sherry wine vinegar

1 tablespoon fresh orange juice

1 teaspoon Dijon mustard

4 cups cooked short-grain brown rice
  (see page 172)

1 1/2 cups julienned snow peas or
  green beans

1/2 cup roasted piñon (pine nuts)

1/2 cup finely diced red onion

2 cups shredded radicchio

2 cups shredded Bibb lettuce

2 tablespoons julienned fresh basil
  leaves

*Turkey, an otherwise bland meat, becomes dark and sweet with a molasses
coating.*

Preheat the grill or broiler.
Whisk 1 tablespoon of the olive oil with the molasses,
salt, and pepper. Brush both sides of the turkey fillets with
the mixture. Place on the grill or under the broiler and grill for 3
minutes per side, or until done. Cut on the diagonal into thin strips.
Set aside.

Whisk together the remaining 1 tablespoon olive oil, the walnut
oil, sherry wine vinegar, orange juice, mustard, and salt and pepper to
taste. Combine the turkey, rice, snow peas, piñon, and onion. Add
the dressing and toss. Cover and let stand for 1 to 2 hours.

Spread radicchio and Bibb lettuce on a serving platter. Mound
the rice salad in the center. Sprinkle with julienned basil and serve.

Hawaiian-Style Grilled
Halibut with Radish Rice

Misoyaki, a Hawaiian marinade made of miso, mirin, and ginger, adds subtle sweetness and mild tanginess to fish. Served with rice made pink with radishes, this is a refreshing summer dish. It is my adaptation of one of Susan Herrmann Loomis's recipes from her Great American Seafood Cookbook.

Blend the miso, mirin, and ginger and pour the mixture into a glass or other nonreactive dish large enough to hold the fish in a single layer. Place the fish in the dish, turn to season both sides, cover, and marinate, refrigerated, for at least 1 hour or up to 24 hours.

Combine the grated radishes and vinegar and set aside while cooking the fish.

Preheat the grill or broiler to medium-high heat.

Scrape off excess marinade. Place the fish on the grill and grill for about 4 minutes on each side, or until it is just cooked in the center. Do not overcook.

Drain the liquid from the grated radishes. With a wooden rice paddle or spoon, gently mix the grated radishes into the rice. Place the rice mixture in the center of a serving platter and arrange the fish steaks around the edges. Garnish with the whole radishes. Serve immediately.

VARIATION: Substitute salmon, black cod, or tuna for the halibut.

Serves 4

$^1/_2$ cup light miso

3 tablespoons mirin

2 tablespoons minced fresh ginger

4 halibut steaks, (6 ounces each), cut 1 inch thick

1 cup grated red radishes (about 8)

1 tablespoon ume plum vinegar

2 cups freshly cooked basmati rice, hot (see page 179)

4 whole red radishes

Note: Japanese ingredients—miso, mirin, and ume plum vinegar—are available in Japanese markets and many natural foods markets.

Harvest Kabocha

❧

Although you could substitute a large buttercup squash for the kabocha, no vegetable is so dense and deeply sweet as the kabocha. I use it in this traditional Armenian pumpkin and rice side dish that is satisfying enough to stand as a meatless entree.

Serves 6

1 large kabocha (3 to 4 pounds)

2 tablespoons unsalted butter, softened

Sea salt and freshly ground black pepper, to taste

3 cups Vegetable Stock (page 364)

1 1/2 cups brown basmati rice, well rinsed

1 tart apple, diced

1/2 cup currants

1/4 cup dried cranberries

1 tablespoon pure maple syrup

1 teaspoon ground cinnamon, or to taste

1/4 teaspoon freshly grated nutmeg

1/4 cup fresh orange juice

Preheat the oven to 350°F.

Cut out the stem end of the kabocha, leaving a circle about 4 inches in diameter. Reserve the cut-out circle. Using a metal spoon, scoop out the seeds and membrane. Scrape out about 1 cup of the flesh, being careful not to break the shell. Chop and set aside. Rub the inside of the kabocha with butter, salt, and pepper. Place the squash and the stem "lid" on a baking sheet and bake for 40 minutes, or until the squash starts to soften.

Meanwhile, pour the stock into a large saucepan over high heat and bring to a boil. Stir in the rice and salt and pepper to taste. Lower the heat and simmer, covered, for about 40 minutes, or until the rice is still firm to the bite. Remove from heat and uncover. Add the reserved chopped squash, apple, currants, cranberries, maple syrup, cinnamon, and nutmeg. When well combined, taste and adjust seasoning.

Remove the squash from the oven. Spoon the rice mixture into the squash cavity. Do not pack too firmly. Sprinkle with orange juice and cover with the squash lid. Return to the oven and bake for 25 to 30 minutes, or until the squash is tender when pierced with the point of a knife. Remove from the oven and let stand for 15 minutes. Cut into wedges and serve.

Note: If all of the rice stuffing doesn't fit into the squash, put it in a buttered baking dish. Cover and bake with the squash.

Collard Rolls Stuffed
with Rice and Buffalo Meat

If you've never tasted buffalo, try this old recipe adapted to America's unique meat, which is low in fat and cholesterol. It is available in many natural foods stores and supermarkets.

Bring 4 quarts of water to a rapid boil. Put the collard leaves, 3 to 4 at a time, in the water for 1 minute to soften. Drain and pat dry. Cut off stems.

Combine the meat, rice, ½ cup of the onion, the parsley, egg white, tomato paste, salt, and pepper. Put a portion of meat mixture on each collard leaf. Fold over, fold in the sides, and roll up. Secure with toothpicks if necessary.

Preheat the oven to 350°F.

Combine the remaining onion, tomatoes, stock, Sucanat, salt, and pepper. Spread the sauerkraut in the bottom of a large heavy casserole. Lay the stuffed collard rolls on top. Carefully pour the tomato mixture over all. Cover and bake for about 1½ hours or until the collard rolls are cooked and the sauerkraut and tomato mixture is very thick. Remove from the oven and serve.

Serves 4 to 6

10 to 12 large collard leaves

1 pound ground buffalo meat (see Note)

1 cup cooked white rice (see page 178)

1 minced onion, large

2 tablespoons minced fresh parsley

1 large egg white

1 tablespoon tomato paste

Sea salt and pepper, to taste

3 cups chopped unsalted canned plum tomatoes with juice

1 cup Vegetable Stock (page 364)

2 tablespoons Sucanat or light brown sugar

2 cups sauerkraut, homemade (see page 362) or storebought, well drained

Note: If buffalo meat is unavailable, substitute any other ground meat or poultry.

Persian Rice
with Yellow Fava Beans

❦

Jewel-like in appearance and intriguing in taste, this exotic main dish is easy to make and perfect for company or a celebration. The bottom rice crust is valued throughout the Middle East as a crunchy and particularly flavorful treat. Fava is not an everyday bean in America, but its sweet flavor is one that my family appreciates Serve the dish with steamed greens or salad and an interesting wine, beer, cider, or iced tea. I adapted the recipe from Food of Life *by Najmieh Batmanglij.*

Serves 6

1 cup yellow dried fava beans
(see Note)

3 tablespoons extra virgin olive oil

1 tablespoon turmeric

1 teaspoon ground cinnamon

½ teaspoon freshly ground black
pepper

1 large onion, chopped

2 cups white basmati rice, well rinsed

6 cups water

¼ cup melted unsalted butter

1 teaspoon sea salt, or to taste

½ cup golden raisins

½ cup chopped dates

3 scallions, slivered

1 lemon, cut into 8 wedges

Note: Yellow (or peeled) dried fava beans are available at Middle Eastern markets. Or use brown dried fava beans, which must be soaked and then peeled. Dried La Sal or baby lima beans may be substituted for the fava beans.

Soak beans in water to cover for 8 hours or overnight. Drain well. Heat 2 tablespoons of the oil in a 3-quart heavy saucepan over medium heat. Add the turmeric, cinnamon, and pepper and sauté for 1 minute, or until aromatic. Add the onion and sauté for 15 minutes, or until well browned. Add the beans and 3 cups water and bring to a boil. Lower the heat and simmer, covered, for 45 minutes.

Meanwhile, combine the rice, the remaining 3 cups of water, and the salt in a bowl and let soak for at least 1 hour. Add to the beans, cover, and return to a boil. Reduce the heat and simmer for 20 minutes, or until the water is absorbed.

Pour the butter and the remaining 1 tablespoon oil on top of the rice and beans. Lay a paper towel across the top of the pot and fit the lid firmly on top to prevent steam from escaping. Using a Flame Tamer, place the pan over very low heat and cook for 40 minutes. Remove from the heat and let cool for 5 minutes.

Stir in the raisins and dates, being careful not to disturb the crust on the bottom. Remove the rice, a spoonful at a time, without breaking the crust. Mound the rice on a serving platter and garnish with scallions and lemon wedges. Remove the bottom crust. Slice and serve with the rice and beans.

Feta and Mint Rice

Some folks are not content to eat plain rice. For them, here's an anything-but-plain rice side dish for grilled meats or poultry. It also rounds out a main course of grilled eggplant, summer squash, and onions.

Heat the oil in a medium saucepan over medium heat. Add the onion and garlic and sauté for 5 minutes, or until translucent. Add the rice and stir to coat. Add the stock, salt, and pepper and bring to a boil. Lower the heat and simmer, covered, for 45 minutes, or until all the liquid is absorbed. Remove from the heat and let stand, covered, for 5 to 10 minutes.

Using a fork, fluff the rice and toss in the feta, mint, and orange zest just to combine. Serve hot or at room temperature.

Serves 4

2 tablespoons extra virgin olive oil

1 small onion, minced

1 clove garlic, minced

1 cup long-grain brown rice, well rinsed

1 ¾ cups Chicken Stock (page 366)

Sea salt and freshly ground black pepper, to taste

¾ cup crumbled feta cheese

3 tablespoons minced fresh mint

1 tablespoon freshly grated orange zest

Soubise

❧

Julia Child introduced this classic French side dish to the rest of the world. My version, unlike Julia's, contains zip cholesterol without sacrificing flavor. It is such an easy, no-fuss recipe that I often make a big batch for large gatherings when there is little time for last-minute cooking.

Serves 4

3 tablespoons extra virgin olive oil

1 onion, minced

½ teaspoon sea salt, or to taste

1 cup long-grain white rice, well rinsed

1 cup Chicken Stock (page 366)

1 cup water

¼ cup dry white wine

Freshly ground white pepper, to taste

Warm the oil in a medium saucepan over medium heat. Add the onion and sauté for 5 minutes. Stir in the salt. Cover and lower the heat. Cook the onion, stirring occasionally, for about 15 minutes, or until very soft but not brown. Uncover and cook for 5 minutes. Add the rice and stir to coat. Add the stock, water, and wine. Raise the heat and bring to a simmer. Stir, lower the heat, and simmer, covered, for 25 minutes, or until the rice is almost tender. Remove from heat and let stand, covered, for 15 minutes. Using a fork, fluff the rice. Taste and adjust seasoning with salt and pepper. Serve immediately.

Hash Brown Rice

✽

Leftover rice has been the inspiration for many innovative dishes in my home. This is one of the most successful. You could even serve it with eggs-over-easy and a rasher of bacon, just like hash brown potatoes.

Heat the oil in a 7-inch heavy skillet over medium heat. Add the onion and sauté for 5 minutes. Combine the rice, flour, milk, salt, and pepper and spread evenly over the onion, pressing down firmly to pack. Cover and cook for about 20 minutes, or until the bottom is golden and the rice is set. Carefully invert onto a serving plate. Cut into wedges and serve hot.

Serves 4

2 tablespoons unrefined sesame oil

1 small onion, chopped

3 cups cooked short-grain or other slightly sticky rice (see page 172)

2 tablespoons rice flour or other flour

$1/4$ cup milk or soy milk

Sea salt and freshly ground black pepper, to taste

Chinese Almond Cookies

❦

Makes 24

5 tablespoons unsalted butter

½ cup Sucanat or packed light brown sugar

1 large egg

½ teaspoon almond extract

1 ½ cups brown rice flour (see page 171)

¼ teaspoon sea salt

18 blanched almonds

1 large egg yolk

This cookie is the one cookie that I always make with brown rice flour rather than with wheat. Rice flour gives a perfect light and sandy texture. In addition, it is adequately leavened by the egg and doesn't require harsh-tasting baking powder. I like a buff-colored cookie, so I use Sucanat for both its color and its multidimensional flavor.

Preheat the oven to 350°F. Grease a cookie sheet and set aside. Cream the butter and Sucanat in a mixing bowl until light and fluffy. Mix in the egg and almond extract. Stir in the flour and salt until well mixed. (The dough may be baked immediately or refrigerated, tightly covered, for up to 5 days.)

Roll the dough into walnut-size balls. Place 2 inches apart on the cookie sheet. Flatten with your fingertips. Press an almond half into the center of each cookie. Bake for about 12 minutes, or until lightly golden. Cool on wire racks. (May be stored in an airtight container for up to 1 week.)

Purple Amasake

Amasake, which means sweet sake, is a creamy, rich beverage made from fermented rice. It is produced in the first fermentation period of sake making. Abundant in natural sugars as well as enzymes that aid digestion, it is a special treat for everyone, especially the very young or people with delicate digestion. Amasake is a favorite among fitness buffs and people in endurance training. During cold weather it is served warm; in hot weather it is served chilled, like a milk shake. If desired, you may season amasake with a pinch of freshly grated ginger, cardamom, or nutmeg, or vanilla extract.

Some regions have a local amasake producer; Grainassance, Inc., nationally distributes an amasake beverage in several different flavors. Look for it in the refrigerated section of your natural foods store. It is also found in Asian markets, where it usually contains added sugar.

I frequently make amasake to have on hand as a beverage and occasionally to use its base (before thinning) as a pudding, in custards, or in baked goods. I most often make white amasake, but for a special treat, I make it purple by using black Thai sticky rice.

For amasake recipes from cream puffs to brownies, see Jan and John Belleme's Cooking with Japanese Foods.

Yield: 15 cups

2 cups white sweet rice, well rinsed

5 cups water

¹/₂ cup Thai black sweet rice, well rinsed

1 cup rice koji (see page 171)

Pinch of sea salt

Put the white rice and 3 cups of water in a bowl and let soak for 1 hour. Put the Thai black sweet rice and the remaining 2 cups water in a 3-quart saucepan and let it soak for 1 hour. Bring the black rice to a boil. Cover, reduce the heat, and simmer for 20 minutes. Add the white rice and its soaking water and return to a boil. Cover, reduce the heat, and simmer for 20 to 25 minutes. Remove from the heat and scrape the rice into a glass bowl. Let cool for 5 minutes.

Beat the rice with a wooden rice paddle or a large wooden spoon for about 5 minutes, or until it is between 120° to 135°F., or when you can stick your finger into the rice and hold it there comfortably for 3 seconds even though the rice is still hot. The beating helps cool the rice quickly and breaks up the grains so the koji will be able to penetrate and work faster.

Add the koji and mix well. Cover and place in a warm spot, preferably an oven that is warm but below 140°F. Let stand for 6 to 10 hours. When it is done, the amasake will have a rich, sweet aroma and taste, so begin tasting after 6 hours so you will know how much fermentation you prefer. Add the salt. Transfer to a 3-quart saucepan and bring to a boil to stop the fermentation process. Let cool.

When ready, place a portion of the amasake in a blender and process until smooth. For each amasake drink, combine 1 part amasake with 1 to 1 1/2 parts water. Serve hot, at room temperature, or slightly chilled. (Undiluted amazake, which is puddinglike in consistency, may be stored in the refrigerator for up to 12 days. Once diluted, it may be stored for up to 1 week.)

Orchata

❦

This thirst-quenching drink is sold from street carts throughout Mexico. It is often made with melon seeds instead of almonds.

Combine the rice and almonds in a heatproof bowl. Cover with 2 ½ cups boiling water and let soak for 4 hours. Pour into a blender. Process for about 4 minutes, or until the rice and almonds are finely pulverized. Add the Sucanat and vanilla. Process to blend. Measure and add enough boiling water to make 4½ cups. Strain through a triple layer of cheesecloth. Pour into a glass container with lid and refrigerate for at least 2 hours or up to 3 days, or until chilled. Serve over ice cubes, garnished with an orange slice.

Serves 4

½ cup white basmati rice, well rinsed

⅓ cup whole blanched almonds

Boiling water

2 tablespoons Sucanat or light brown sugar or honey

¼ teaspoon pure vanilla extract

4 orange slices

Coconut, Black Sticky Rice, and Banana Dumplings

❦

Makes 6 dumplings

¾ cup fresh Coconut Milk
(page 354) or canned coconut milk

2 tablespoons Sucanat or light brown
sugar

2 slices (¼ inch thick) fresh ginger

1 cup freshly cooked black sticky rice
(see page 180), warm

1 teaspoon freshly grated orange zest

½ teaspoon freshly grated nutmeg

6 frozen banana leaves, thawed
(see Note)

1 banana

Notes: Frozen banana leaves are available in markets with a Central or South American clientele. For convenience, I always keep a packet of banana leaves in my freezer and thaw them just before use.

Parchment paper can be used instead of banana leaves, but the flavor will be less interesting. Cut six 8 × 6-inch pieces and six 8-inch lengths of butcher's twine. Proceed as with banana leaves.

I've adapted this recipe from traditional Laotian and Thai dessert techniques. In countries where ovens are scarce, dumplings like these replace the baked desserts Westerners are accustomed to.

Combine the coconut milk, Sucanat, and ginger in a small saucepan over medium heat and bring to a boil. Lower the heat and simmer for 5 minutes, or until the liquid is reduced to ½ cup. Remove from the heat and discard the ginger. Pour the hot liquid over the rice. Stir in the orange zest and nutmeg. Let stand for 15 minutes.

Cut the banana leaves into six 8 × 6-inch pieces. Pass each piece over a flame to soften it. Also cut six 8 × ¼-inch strips to use as ties. Peel and slice the banana crosswise in half. Slice each half lengthwise into quarters. Put 2 scant tablespoons of rice on each leaf. Top with a banana slice. Put another tablespoon of rice on top of the banana. Tightly wrap each packet by folding in the long ends and then folding over the short ends. (Eat the 2 extra pieces of banana or reserve them for another use.)

Place the packets on a steamer rack over boiling water and steam over medium-high heat for 20 minutes, replenishing the water if necessary. Remove from the steamer and serve warm, allowing guests to unwrap their own dessert packets.

VARIATIONS: For a quick dessert, skip the wrapping. Add the rice and seasonings to the hot milk and simmer for 5 minutes, stirring to prevent scorching. Remove from the heat. Cover and let stand for 15 minutes. Serve on fresh mango or papaya slices, or in a parfait dish with chopped fruit.

Milk can be substituted for coconut milk. It's not as good, but still tasty.

Job's Tears

J OB'S TEARS (*Coix lacryma-jobi*) is a tall grass that has been cultivated in Africa and Asia for centuries. Its name comes from the shape of the unhulled grain, which suggests a teardrop, an ebony-color teardrop. Throughout the world, rosary beads and other prayer beads are made from unhulled Job's tears. The grain is also used to make attractive, durable, and inexpensive necklaces.

Job's tears is one of the few nonhybridized grains available today. It has a distinctive and pleasing flavor. You won't find Job's tears at your corner market, but you may find it at a natural foods store, or you can order it by mail. It's worth the bother of seeking it out.

Here's why. Job's tears, more than any other grain, is reputed to strengthen the blood, the nervous system, and the stomach, to combat cancer, and to improve the skin. It is a premium medicinal in the Chinese pharmacopoeia and in macrobiotic regenerative cuisine. Job's tears has an excellent nutritional profile, being high in carbohydrates, iron, and calcium.

When hulled and polished, the grain looks rather like pearl barley, only it's more spherical, with a brown indentation down its middle. When not polished, Job's tears is a reddish brown color. I strongly recommend the unpolished grain for its superior nutritional value and flavor and also because the polishing process breaks and denatures many of the grains.

I find Job's tears more invigorating than other, more common grains. For several decades I've kept a small stash on hand. Sometimes I add a few tablespoons—the amount measured by its expense—to a pot of brown rice for an extra spark of energy. For more sustaining energy, I prepare Congee.

Job's Tears
Selection and Storage

The only Job's tears available is imported and probably will remain so for some time as attempts to grow the grain in North America have thus far failed. The polished Job's tears and the breakfast cereal preparations using Job's tears that are available in Asian markets are of poor quality. An excellent organic source of good quality Job's tears, both polished and unpolished, is the Macrobiotic Company of America (see page 377).

Store Job's tears in the refrigerator in an airtight glass jar for 3 months or tightly wrapped in the freezer for 6 months. Pick over the grain before cooking, discarding any discolored grains or any with signs of mold, as they will taste bitter. I find this easiest to do by pouring the grain out on a countertop or table.

Steamed Job's Tears

✾

Job's tears tastes best when freshly cooked; refrigeration toughens the grain. I use Job's tears in place of rice with Asian stir-fried vegetables or in place of barley in soups, salads, and pilafs. The grain invites bold flavors.

Put the Job's tears in a saucepan or wok over high heat. Toast, stirring constantly, for about 5 minutes, or until the grains are very dry and aromatic and begin to make crackling noises. Pour into a strainer and rinse well.

Bring the water and salt to a boil over high heat. Carefully add the Job's tears, watching that the water does not boil up. Add the garlic or ginger, if using. Lower the heat and simmer, covered, for 1 hour. Remove from the heat and let stand, covered, for 10 minutes. Serve hot.

Makes 3 cups

1 cup unpolished Job's tears, picked over

2 cups water

¼ teaspoon sea salt

1 clove garlic, minced, or 1 small knob of ginger (optional)

Congee

❦

Serves 2 to 3

1 cup Job's tears, picked over, rinsed, and drained

¼ cup chopped walnuts

1 stick (4 inches) cinnamon

3 slices (¼ inch thick) ginger

1 teaspoon Ghee (page 359) or butter (optional)

¼ teaspoon sea salt

3 to 4 cups water

1 teaspoon honey

Congee, also known as kichadi, is the Asian equivalent of mother's chicken soup, the Latin American equivalent of atole, and the British equivalent of barley water. I like this gruel made from any grain but use Job's tears for its extra energy boost. Congee is simmered in a covered pot for four to six hours. A Crock-Pot works well. People throughout Asia claim that this common medicinal dish becomes more "powerful" the longer it cooks.

Combine the Job's tears, walnuts, cinnamon, ginger, ghee or butter, if using, salt, and water in a 1½-quart heavy pot and bring to a boil. Reduce the heat to very low, using a Flame Tamer if necessary, and simmer, covered, for 4 to 6 hours, or until the grain is very soft. Add additional water if necessary. Stir in honey and serve warm.

VARIATIONS: Substitute ½ cup rice, ½ cup millet, ¼ cup barley, or 1 cup wheat for the Job's tears.

Substitute black beans or adzuki beans for the walnuts, omit the honey, add burdock or leek, and add the salt only after the beans are thoroughly cooked.

Native
Near
Eastern
Grains

Barley

Wheat

Barley

BARLEY (*Hordeum vulgare*) is possibly the oldest and certainly the most adaptable grain on the planet. It grows in the frigid Tibetan highlands and the blistering sea-level Sahara. Malted barley was—and still is—used for beer. In fact, beer making rather than use as a cereal was the impetus for its spread throughout the Western world. Even today innkeepers are often called John Barleycorn, after the personification of the spirit of barley liquor popularized by the Scots poet Robert Burns.

But for me, the mention of barley brings the warmth and enthusiasm of O.J. Locheed to mind. I finally met this king of barley lore in person after years of exchanging grain notes by telephone. His major interests—barley and minor crops for marginal areas—were fueled by his years as crops research director at the High Desert Research Farm at Ghost Ranch in Abiquiu, New Mexico. "The years of growing ancient crops taught me so much more about early cultures than I could have ever received from books," he says. "These plants are the living remnants of these primary civilizations. When you are out there in the fields you just *have* to think about what the early farmer/cultivators were thinking and how they were living as they nurtured their food crops. And, here you are, hundreds or perhaps thousands of years later doing the same thing."

Over a dinner of Southwestern Barley Salad and Barley Flatbread with Chilies, O.J. regaled me with tales of beans and barley. Probably the world's leading authority on beardless and hull-less barley, O. J. Locheed has spent most of the recent past teaching people around the world about sustainable agriculture. At the time we met, he was living in his old Volkswagen van in northern New Mexico. He was planning to fill the van with seeds and small agricultural equipment and ship it to the Ukraine. This would be his third trip back to a region deeply affected by radioactive contamination of the soil since the accident at Chernobyl. O.J. hoped to continue to pass on his knowledge about radioprotective foods such as barley and other whole grains and beans to the farmers of the area. He had found an old strain of beardless and hull-less barley, which makes it possible for the barley to be hand harvested, and to be eaten whole without pearling. Since harvesting bearded barley leaves your hands feeling as though they've disturbed a wasp's nest, this heirloom grain offers simple land-to-table nutrition.

Hull-less barley contains two or three times the protein of an equal portion of rice. Since it grows with no hull, its vital bran is not sacrificed by processing. When cooked, hull-less barley is similar to brown rice in appearance, but it is chewier and darker in color. It has a rich, whole-grain flavor with slightly nutty tones and a warmly inviting aroma.

Most of the barley grown in North America is destined for animal feed and for malting. The barley fields of the San Luis Valley of Colorado, where genetically engineered perfect barley is grown for the Coors Brewing Company, present a rather surreal view as every row is identical in height and every grain is identical in color, size, and shape. How different it is to trod the fields of Bud Clem in Bozeman, Montana, where hull-less barley is raised for the table. Diversity is its strength. Although he modestly calls himself "an old dirt farmer up here in barley country," Bud is producing some of the best hull-less barley in the world. His bronze, black, and gold varieties offer food rich in nutrients. Bud and his wife, Jean, offer whole-grain barley, barley grits, flour, and flakes as well as advice and good barley talk through their Western Trails, Inc. Their barley has 25 percent more protein and potassium, almost twice as much calcium and three times as much iron as pearl barley. Demand it from your local supplier—demand will eventually create a supply!

Barley
Selection and Storage

Although there are countless varieties of barley, because of barley's low demand the variety is not specified unless, that is, you purchase a specialty barley from a mail-order source. In natural foods stores, barley is differentiated by the degree it is processed rather than by variety. At a recent Cereal Chemists convention, a committee was formed to provide standard industry terms for barley and its degree of refining. At the time of this writing, however, the labeling of "pearled" or "whole" barley varies from manufacturer to manufacturer.

Barley for Seed or Sprouting

The grain is shaped like a plump grain of wheat, is usually tan in color, and has two inedible outer hulls. These outer hulls are removed to produce whole barley which is available primarily in natural foods stores.

Whole Barley

Also called Scotch or pot barley, whole barley has its bran intact and, like brown rice, is darker, chewier, and more nutritious than its refined counterpart. It also takes more time to cook.

Pearled Barley

This barley is further refined with its darker bran shaved off. Pearled barley in natural foods stores tends to be large, shaped like a grain of wheat, and buff in color due to the presence of some bran. Pearled barley from the supermarket has had all of its bran and fiber removed until only a small, round white pearl of starchy endosperm remains.

Hull-less Barley

This heirloom naked barley easily threshes free from the hull, and so is an ideal backyard grain for gardeners and subsistence farmers. This barley has a pleasantly chewy texture, like brown rice, and, unlike pearled barley, does not become sticky. Some specialty varieties, including hull-less barley, are available by mail order from Gold Mine Natural Food Company and Western Trails, Inc.

I store both pearled and whole barley up to 1 year in glass or tightly wrapped in a cool, dry, and dark cupboard. If I lived in a hot, humid area, I'd purchase a 2- to 3-month supply and refrigerate or freeze it during late summer when infestation is most apt to be a problem.

Barley Flakes

Like rolled oats, a thin grain flake. It's a tasty substitute for rolled oats in hot breakfast cereal and in granola and muesli.

Barley Grits

Tiny chunks of barley; because of their size, they are quick cooking. Barley grits may be used for a hot breakfast cereal. Although they are a little stickier than corn, they may be substituted for corn-meal in polenta. The size of the grit, and therefore the cooking time, varies from manufacturer to manufacturer.

Barley Malt

A sweetener, interchangeable with unsul-fured molasses. It is not so sweet as honey or sugar.

Barley Flour

Pearl barley flour is one of my favorite bak-ing aids. Starchy and soft with a sweet taste, it produces a moist texture, perfect for pancakes, cookies, and quick breads. I freely substitute it for wheat flour in cook-ies, quick breads, and sauces. Since it is low in gluten, though, generally no more than 15 to 20 percent barley flour should be added to a yeast bread.

Whole barley flour yields an even darker crumb than pearl barley flour and a moister quality. In flavor, aroma, texture, and ease of handling, the difference between pearl and whole barley flours compares to the difference between white and whole wheat flour.

Purchase at a natural foods store or grind your own as you need it in a spice or coffee grinder or in a home flour mill. To make 1 cup barley flour, grind $3/4$ cup lightly pearled barley (or $3/4$ cup minus 1 tablespoon highly pearled barley or $3/4$ cup plus 1 tablespoon whole barley). Freshly ground barley flour is curious among the flours in that it is airy and light. The flour made from $3/4$ cup barley will ini-tially measure $1 1/2$ cups flour, but after several days storage, it compresses to 1 cup. Before measuring freshly ground barley flour, I tap the container on the counter for a few seconds to settle the flour and get an accurate measure. Store barley flour, tightly wrapped, in the freezer for up to 4 months.

Steamed Whole Barley

Unlike most other grains, which always take about the same amount of time to cook, barley seems to have a mind of its own. Sometimes you have to add a few minutes more cooking time and sometimes it is ready before you are. Don't be intimidated! Here's the test: If the barley tastes rubbery, it is not done; increase the cooking time and, if necessary, the liquid. It takes well over an hour to overcook barley to the point of being soft versus al dente so a few minutes either way hardly make a difference.

Serve the steamed barley as a breakfast cereal with honey and milk, as a side dish, seasoned with Gomasio (page 361) or another savory topping, or add to soups and stews.

Makes 3¹/₂ cups

1 cup whole or hull-less barley

3 cups water

¹/₈ teaspoon sea salt

1 tablespoon unsalted butter or
unrefined sesame oil (optional)

Heat a saucepan or wok over high heat. Add the barley and toast, stirring constantly, for about 3 to 4 minutes, or until the grains become a shade darker and many of them have popped. Pour into a strainer and briefly rinse under running water, if you wish.

Combine the barley and water and let soak for 1 hour to overnight. Put in a medium saucepan over high heat, add salt, and butter, if using. Bring to a boil. Lower the heat and simmer, covered, for 50 to 60 minutes, or until the grains are tender but still chewy. If liquid remains, drain well. If the liquid is absorbed before the barley is tender, add hot water, about 1 tablespoon at a time. Let stand, covered, for 5 to 10 minutes. Fluff with a fork. Serve hot.

To store leftover barley, put it in a glass bowl, loosely cover with a cotton cloth, and leave out at room temperature for up to 24 hours. I compost barley not used within this time. If you must refrigerate or freeze barley, place it in a tightly covered container (it will keep for 3 days refrigerated or 1 month frozen) and use the barley in a highly flavored soup or casserole.

Barley cooked for breakfast or lunch is still fresh and delicious for the next meal when served at room temperature. Barley cooked within 4 hours may be used in a grain salad. After the barley is over 4 hours old, it needs to be reheated before serving it or use it as an ingredient in a soup, stuffing, bread, or pudding. Leftover barley may be made into a breakfast porridge by simmering it with milk, raisins, and cinnamon.

Steamed Pearl Barley

🌾

Though normally I favor whole grains, whole barley is decidedly brown when cooked. Sometimes white pearl barley is more aesthetically pleasing in a dish. To retain its whiteness, do not pre-toast.

Bring the water, salt, and butter or oil, if using, to a boil in a medium saucepan over high heat. When boiling, stir in the barley. Cover and lower the heat to a simmer. Simmer for 45 minutes, or until the grains are tender but still chewy. If liquid remains, drain well. If liquid is absorbed before barley is tender, add hot water, about 1 tablespoon at a time. Let stand, covered, for 5 to 10 minutes. Fluff with a fork.

Note: To store leftover barley, see page 213.

Makes 3 1/2 cups

1 cup pearl barley, well rinsed

2 1/2 cups water

1/8 teaspoon salt

1 tablespoon butter or oil (optional)

Tsampa

❦

Serves 2

½ cup hull-less barley

2 ½ cups water

Pinch of sea salt

Warm milk, to taste

Unsalted butter, to taste

Honey, to taste

In Tibet, high above the tree line where there is always a fuel shortage, Tsampa, the staple meal, is made by flash-toasting the barley in hot sand. The sand is sifted out and the grains are ground into meal. A tea made with yak butter is stirred into the meal to make porridge. My Americanized version is so tasty, warming, and invigorating, you'll feel like climbing Mount Everest!

Put the barley in a saucepan or wok over medium heat. Toast, stirring constantly, for 5 minutes, or until the barley has darkened, gives off a sweet aroma, and just begins to pop. Remove from the heat, and let cool.

Transfer to a grain or nut mill or coffee grinder and grind to the consistency of cornmeal.

Combine the ground barley, water, and salt in a medium saucepan over high heat and bring to a boil, stirring constantly. Lower the heat, cover, and cook, stirring occasionally, for about 10 minutes, or until thick.

Spoon into a serving dish and serve hot with warm milk, unsalted butter, and honey.

VARIATION: Substitute brown rice, rye berries, wheat berries, or wild rice for half the barley. Toast the grains separately. Proceed with the recipe.

Barley Dolmadakia

White rice is the grain commonly used to fill grape leaves in the popular Greek dish dolmadakia, but barley antedates rice in Greek culinary history. It makes a chewy, tasty filling. Dolmadakia are usually served as appetizers.

Heat 3 tablespoons of the oil in a medium sauté pan over medium-high heat. Add the onion and sauté for 5 minutes, or until translucent. Remove from the heat. Add the garlic and stir for 1 minute. Stir in the barley, mint, currants, piñon, and salt to taste until well combined. Set aside.

Preheat the oven to 320°F.

Arrange 32 grape leaves on a work surface, shiny side down.

Place 1 rounded tablespoon of the barley mixture in the center of each grape leaf. Fold the stem end up and the sides over and roll to the leaf tip to form a packet. Place in a baking dish or dishes in a single layer.

Combine the tomatoes, salt to taste, lemon juice, oil, and wine in a blender. Process until smooth.

Pour the tomato mixture over the packets. Tightly cover with aluminum foil. Bake for 1 hour. Remove from the oven and let cool. Serve warm or at room temperature. The dish may be refrigerated and served chilled, if desired.

Makes 30

4 tablespoons extra virgin olive oil

$^1/_2$ cup minced onion

3 to 4 cloves garlic, minced or pressed

2 cups cooked and cooled barley, any kind (see pages 213–215)

2 tablespoons fresh mint

$^1/_2$ cup currants

$^1/_2$ cup piñon (pure nuts)

Sea salt, to taste

32 bottled or fresh grape leaves, rinsed well and dried (8-ounce jar)

2 medium tomatoes, peeled and cored (page 370)

Juice of 1 lemon

$^1/_4$ cup red wine

Watercress
Garlic Soup with Barley

❦

I like this soup just as it is, but I often simplify it by using water instead of stock, omitting the lemon juice, and using leftover barley. I have also made it more filling and nutritious by adding poached eggs, the traditional Iberian accompaniment to garlic soup. That's the glory of a grain-based soup: It lends itself to simplicity and to embellishment. Like many soups, this one is better on the second day.

Pour the oil into a large pot over medium-low heat. Add the garlic and sauté for 5 to 7 minutes, or until lightly browned. Remove and set aside.

Add the bread to the oil and toast until golden brown on both sides. Remove and set aside.

Add the stock, barley, reserved garlic, and salt and pepper to the oil.

Raise the heat and bring to a boil. Immediately lower the heat, cover, and simmer for about 50 minutes, or until the barley is tender. Using a slotted spoon, remove and discard the garlic. Stir in the lemon juice and watercress. Simmer for 1 minute.

Divide among 4 warm soup bowls. Garnish each with a toasted bread slice. Serve immediately.

Serves 4

¼ cup extra virgin olive oil

10 cloves garlic

4 slices (1 inch thick) stale French or Italian bread

4 cups Vegetable Stock (page 364) or Chicken Stock (page 366)

½ cup pearl barley (see Note)

Sea salt and freshly ground black pepper, to taste

1 to 2 tablespoons fresh lemon juice

2 cups chopped watercress

Note: Substitute 1½ cups cooked pearl barley (see page 215) for the uncooked barley and simmer for 15 minutes.

Curried Barley and Cod Chowder

Miso turns this soup a warm golden color. Serve the chowder with crackers and a vegetable side dish—salad if the weather's hot, steamed greens if it's cold.

Heat the oil in a medium saucepan over medium-high heat. Add the mustard seeds and curry powder. Sauté for about 3 minutes, or until the seeds start to pop. Add the ginger and stir to combine. Add the onion and daikon and sauté for 4 minutes, or until softened. Add the stock and barley and cook for 15 minutes to allow the flavors to combine. Add the cod and cook for 5 minutes. Remove ½ cup of the soup and, using a fork, combine with the miso until smooth. Return the mixture to the pot and cook for 1 minute. Remove from the heat.

Serve hot, garnished with cilantro.

Serves 4

*1 tablespoon unrefined sesame oil,
unsalted butter, or Ghee (page 359)*

1 tablespoon mustard seeds

1 tablespoon minced fresh ginger

½ cup chopped onion

1½ cups diced daikon

6 cups Fish Stock (page 367)

*½ cup cooked pearl barley
(see page 215)*

*½ pound fresh cod, cut into
bite-size pieces*

*3 tablespoons light barley miso
(see page 220)*

1 tablespoon chopped fresh cilantro

Miso

Miso, which looks something like smooth peanut butter, is a fermented paste made of soybeans, a grain such as rice or barley, a catalyst, and salt. This traditional Japanese food is fast becoming an important staple in haute cuisine as well as for health-conscious people.

The preferred choice is domestic, unpasteurized, naturally fermented miso (rather than chemically processed), which is available in the refrigerated sections of natural foods stores. Many Americans favor a lighter-flavored miso, which is yellow or creamy beige in color. The strongly flavored red, dark amber, and brown miso varieties take more getting used to.

Store miso in an airtight container in the refrigerator for 1 year or more.

Barley, Fennel, and Beet Salad

Wonderful texture, gorgeous color, fabulous flavor, quick and easy to prepare. What more could anyone want from a salad?

Combine the barley and fennel. Whisk together the olive oil, lemon juice, salt, and pepper. Pour over the barley and toss to combine. Let stand at room temperature for at least 30 minutes or up to 4 hours. Stir in the piñon.

Separate the lettuce into leaves. Wash and dry well. Place the lettuce on a serving plate. Mound the barley mixture in the center and garnish with beets.

Serve immediately.

Serves 4

1 cup cooked and cooled pearl barley (see page 215)

1 cup diced fennel

2 tablespoons extra virgin olive oil

3 tablespoons fresh lemon juice

Sea salt and freshly ground black pepper, to taste

3 tablespoons piñon (pine nuts), toasted

1/2 cup julienned cooked beets

1 head Bibb lettuce

Southwestern Barley Salad

❦

A simple grain combined with zesty ingredients and attractively served is bound to please. This hearty main course salad can be converted into a side dish by omitting the shrimp or tempeh, a tasty soy food with a meaty texture.

Serves 4

2 cups cooked and cooled barley, preferably hull-less (see page 213)

1 cup cooked fresh corn kernels

1 red bell pepper, roasted (see page 353), peeled, seeded, and chopped

1 poblano chili, roasted (see page 353), peeled, seeded, and chopped

¼ cup diced jicama

2 tablespoons minced red onion

1 tablespoon minced fresh cilantro

1 teaspoon minced jalapeño, or to taste

¼ cup fresh lime juice

1 tablespoon cider vinegar

¾ teaspoon ground cumin

3 tablespoons extra virgin olive oil

¾ teaspoon sea salt and freshly ground black pepper, or to taste

1 head Bibb lettuce

1 pound grilled medium shrimp or tempeh strips

1 cup tortilla chips

Combine barley, corn, bell pepper, poblano, jicama, onion, cilantro, and jalapeño in a medium bowl.

Whisk together the lime juice, vinegar, cumin, oil, salt, and pepper. Pour over barley mixture and toss to coat.

Mound in the center of serving plate on top of lettuce leaves. Garnish with shrimp and tortilla chips. Serve right away.

Locro

Small rounds of corn—plucked from the soup and eaten with the fingers—make this substantial South America soup-stew an event. Locro, a meal in one, always contains a grain and sometimes meat or fish. Here, as a protein complement, I've used anasazi beans. They always remind me of the brightly colored and flavorful beans I marveled over at Indian markets in Bolivia. If you're new to kombu, here's a good introduction to it. A sea vegetable in a Latin dish? Yes. Not only were there unusual beans in the La Paz Indian markets but also several varieties of seaweed. The delicate tone of anise adds an authentic South American touch. As I prefer seasonal local corn—I find hybrids are overly sugary at the expense of flavor—I make this soup only in corn season.

Rinse the beans and put them in a 4-cup container with cold water to cover. Soak for 2 hours or overnight. Drain well.

Put the barley in a saucepan or wok over medium-high heat and cook for about 5 minutes, or until grains begin to pop and turn a shade darker. Combine the barley, beans, kombu, and stock in a soup pot over high heat and bring to a boil. Reduce the heat and simmer, covered, for 1 hour.

Warm the oil in a large sauté pan over medium heat. Add the anise seeds and cook for 1 minute, or until they become aromatic. Add the garlic, leek, mushrooms, celery root, and corn. Lightly sauté each one before adding the next. Sauté until vegetables just begin to soften, about 4 minutes. Scrape the vegetables into the soup, add the chili, and simmer for 30 minutes, or until the beans are soft. Remove and discard the kombu or chop it into bite-size pieces and return it to the pot. Add the collards and season with salt and pepper to taste. Cook 10 minutes more.

Ladle into bowls and serve hot, garnished with cilantro.

Serves 6

¹/₂ cup anasazi or Jacob's cattle beans

¹/₂ cup whole or pearl barley

1 stick (3 inches) kombu (optional) (see Note)

8 cups Vegetable Stock (page 364) or Chicken Stock (page 366)

1 tablespoon sesame oil or extra virgin olive oil

2 teaspoons anise seeds

2 cloves garlic, minced

1 small leek, sliced

2 shiitake mushrooms, chopped

¹/₂ cup diced celery root

1 ear fresh corn, husked and cut into 1-inch pieces

1 New Mexican chili, roasted (page 353), peeled, seeded, and chopped

2 cups chopped collard greens or kale

1 teaspoon sea salt

Freshly ground black pepper, to taste

¹/₄ cup chopped fresh cilantro

Note: Kombu is available in Asian and natural foods markets.

Christmas Hens with Spicy Barley

Serves 4

4 small Cornish game hens

1 tablespoon freshly grated lemon zest

2 teaspoons ground cumin

1 teaspoon Hungarian paprika

¼ teaspoon ground allspice

¼ teaspoon ground white pepper

1 tablespoon sea salt

1 medium onion, quartered

4 sprigs of sage

4 sprigs of rosemary

4 sprigs of parsley

4 tablespoons (½ stick) unsalted butter

1 teaspoon turmeric

2 cloves garlic, chopped

1 cup chopped leeks

1 cup chopped mushrooms

2 red New Mexican or poblano chilies, roasted (see page 353), peeled, seeded, and chopped

2 green jalapeños, roasted (see page 353), peeled, seeded, and chopped

1 cup pearl barley, well rinsed

2 ¼ cups Vegetable Stock (page 364) or Chicken Stock (page 366)

Sprigs of parsley, for garnish

I call these Christmas hens because of the red and green chilies. When there's leftover barley, I turn it into a salad the next day by adding some pickles, fresh herbs, and dressing. This dish was inspired by one produced by the late Peruvian chef Felipe Rojas-Lombardi, using quail.

Wash and dry the hens. Combine the lemon zest, cumin, paprika, allspice, pepper, and 2 ½ teaspoons of the salt. Sprinkle each hen, inside and out, with the mixture. Place an onion quarter and a sprig each of sage, rosemary, and parsley in each cavity. Tie the legs together with butcher's twine.

Preheat the oven to 375°F.

Heat 2 tablespoons of the butter in a large skillet over medium-high heat. Add the hens and fry, turning occasionally, for about 10 minutes, or until golden on all sides. Transfer the hens to a roasting pan. Roast for 15 minutes. Remove and set aside.

Meanwhile, heat the remaining butter in a Dutch oven large enough to hold the hens with room to spare over medium-high heat. Add the turmeric and garlic and stir for a few seconds. Add the leeks and sauté for 10 minutes, or until limp. Add the mushrooms, New Mexican jalapeños, and remaining ½ teaspoon sea salt. Sauté for about 10 minutes, or until the vegetables soften and the mushroom liquid cooks away. Stir in the barley and sauté for 3 minutes more, stirring as necessary. Add the stock. Raise the heat and bring to a boil. Lower the heat and simmer, covered, for 15 minutes.

Place the hens and their juices in the barley. Cover and continue to cook for 30 to 35 minutes, or until the hens and barley are cooked and all the juices have been absorbed.

Form a bed of barley on a large serving platter and arrange the hens on top. Garnish with parsley and serve.

Barley-stuffed Peppers

Mary Estella, author of the popular Natural Foods Cookbook, *inspired this recipe. If you think "Ho-hum, the same old stuffed peppers," think again. Adjourn to the kitchen and give this dish a try. Including both squash and sweet potatoes may seem a bother, but their color and flavor differences add depth.*

Put the barley in a saucepan or wok over high heat. Cook, stirring constantly, for about 5 minutes, or until the barley is toasted. Add the fennel and anise seeds and toast for 1 minute more. Put the barley and seeds in a heavy saucepan with a lid. Stir in 1 tablespoon of the oil, the currants, orange zest, and cloves. Add the water and ¼ teaspoon salt, place over high heat, and bring to a boil. Lower the heat and simmer, covered, for 45 minutes, or until the barley is cooked and all the liquid has been absorbed.

Meanwhile, cut off the tops of the peppers to make a wide opening. Core and seed the peppers. Trim the bottoms, if necessary, so that the peppers stand straight. Rinse inside and out. Turn upside down on a wire rack to drain.

Preheat the oven to 375°F.

Heat 1 tablespoon oil in a sauté pan over medium-high heat. Stir in the ginger and shallot and sauté for 2 minutes. Stir in the squash, sweet potato, and celery leaves and sauté for 3 to 5 minutes, or until crisp-tender. Scrape into the barley. Add the parsley, sunflower seeds, and cheese. Season with the tamari soy sauce. Toss to combine.

Pack the barley mixture into the peppers. Rub all surfaces with the remaining oil. Place in a deep casserole with a lid. Bake for 30 minutes, or until the peppers soften.

Serve immediately.

Serves 5 to 6

1 cup pearl barley

1 teaspoon fennel seeds

½ teaspoon anise seeds

3 tablespoons unrefined sesame oil or unsalted butter

¼ cup currants

1 teaspoon grated orange zest

¼ teaspoon ground cloves

2½ cups water

¼ teaspoon sea salt

5 to 6 large bell peppers, washed

1 teaspoon peeled and minced fresh ginger

1 shallot, minced

1 cup grated butternut squash

½ cup grated sweet potato

2 tablespoons minced celery leaves

2 tablespoons minced parsley

3 tablespoons sunflower seeds, toasted

½ cup grated white cheddar cheese

1 tablespoon tamari soy sauce

Barley Risotto with Mushrooms and Blue Cheese

🌿

Serves 4

1 tablespoon unsalted butter

1 tablespoon extra virgin olive oil

1 clove garlic, minced

1/2 cup minced onion

1/4 cup diced celery

1/4 pound mushrooms, chopped

1 1/2 cups pearl barley

*5 cups hot Vegetable Stock (page 364)
   or Chicken Stock (page 366)*

*Sea salt and freshly ground black
   pepper, to taste*

*1 cup crumbled blue cheese
   (6 ounces)*

2/3 cup pomegranate seeds (optional)

2 tablespoons minced fresh parsley

Earthier and more substantial than the traditional Italian rice risotto, barley risotto is also less fussy. While a rice risotto must be served immediately, barley risotto holds well with no loss of texture. For a dazzling garnish, stir in some pomegranate seeds just before serving.

Heat the butter and oil in a large heavy saucepan over medium-high heat. Add the garlic, onion, celery, and mushrooms and sauté for 5 minutes, or until soft. Stir in the barley and sauté for 3 minutes. Season with salt and pepper. Lower the heat and add the stock, 1 1/4 cups at a time, cooking and stirring frequently for about 15 minutes, or until stock is absorbed. If stock is absorbed too quickly, lower the heat. After 1 hour all the stock should be absorbed and the barley cooked. If not, raise heat to boil off the stock. Stir in the cheese and pomegranate seeds, if using. Taste and adjust seasoning, if necessary.

Serve hot garnished with parsley.

Barley Provençale

Barley, like most grains, is mild in flavor, but it's a fantastic base on which to glorify garden-fresh tomatoes, zucchini, and basil. That's why I serve this dish in Indian summer when all three are at their peak. It tastes best at room temperature.

Heat the oil in a large sauté pan over medium-high heat. Add the onion and saffron and sauté for 5 minutes. Add the zucchini and tomatoes and sauté for 10 minutes, or until just softened. Stir in the barley. Season with salt and pepper and cook for 5 minutes, or until barley is warmed through. Remove from the heat and stir in the basil, parsley, and nuts. Let stand at room temperature for at least 30 minutes.

Just before serving, drizzle with hazelnut oil.

Serves 4

2 tablespoons extra virgin olive oil

1 medium onion, diced

Pinch of saffron threads

2 cups julienned zucchini (2 medium zucchini)

10 cherry tomatoes, cut lengthwise in half

2 cups cooked pearl barley (see page 215)

Sea salt and freshly ground black pepper, to taste

$^{1}/_{4}$ cup julienned fresh basil leaves

$^{1}/_{4}$ cup minced fresh parsley

$^{1}/_{4}$ cup chopped toasted hazelnuts

1 tablespoon unrefined hazelnut oil

Barley Kuchen
with Hazelnut Streusel

🌾

Makes one 9-inch square cake

1 cup pearl barley

1 ⅓ cups water

5 tablespoons unsalted butter, softened

¼ teaspoon sea salt

1 teaspoon baking powder

2 large eggs

½ cup plus 2 tablespoons Sucanat or packed light brown sugar

½ teaspoon freshly grated lemon zest

1 teaspoon ground cinnamon

¼ teaspoon freshly grated nutmeg

2 tablespoons unbleached all-purpose flour or barley flour (see page 212)

½ cup chopped toasted hazelnuts

This Kuchen is a remarkable cake—spongy, moist, and delicately sweet, with excellent keeping qualities. At holiday time I like to splash the cake with brandy and let it sit, covered, for a day.

Soak the barley in the water for at least 8 hours or overnight. Preheat the oven to 375°F. Use 1 tablespoon of the butter to grease a 9-inch square baking pan. Set aside.

Put the soaked barley and soaking water in a blender and process until uniform in consistency. Add the salt, baking powder, 2 tablespoons of the butter, 2 tablespoons of the sugar, eggs, lemon zest, ½ teaspoon of the cinnamon, and the nutmeg. Process to mix. Pour into the pan.

Put the flour, remaining butter, remaining sugar, and remaining cinnamon in a bowl and use your fingers to combine. Sprinkle this mixture and nuts over the batter. With a butter knife, cut through the streusel and batter in a figure 8 to partially mix the streusel into the batter. Give the pan a quarter turn and repeat the figure 8. Bake for about 25 minutes, or until an instant-read thermometer inserted into the center comes out clean. Remove from the oven and cool on a wire rack.

Cut into squares and serve.

Barley Biscotti

Here's a barley version of the traditional crunchy Italian cookies. Barley gives biscotti a pleasing earthy flavor and a rustic texture that asks for dunking. In Italy, they're served alongside a glass of sweet wine, like vin santo or marsala. Americans are more likely to dunk them in coffee, espresso, tea, milk, hot chocolate, or dry wine or port.

Preheat the oven to 350°F. Grease a baking sheet and set aside. Lightly beat the eggs, lemon juice, and vanilla in a large mixing bowl. Stir in the barley and all-purpose flours, Sucanat, baking soda, salt, anise seeds, and lemon zest until well mixed. Turn the dough out onto a lightly floured work surface and knead into a smooth ball. Let stand for 5 minutes.

Divide the dough in half. Roll each half into an 8-inch log. Place the logs on a baking sheet, leaving 3 inches between them. Bake for 30 minutes.

Reduce the heat to 300°F. Remove the logs from the oven and cut on the diagonal into 3/4-inch slices. Place the slices on the baking sheet, cut side down. Return to the oven and bake for 15 minutes more. Cool on a wire rack. Store in an airtight container. The biscotti keep well for several weeks.

VARIATION: Substitute 1 cup barley flour for the all-purpose flour for a gluten-free cookie.

Makes about 24

2 large eggs

2 tablespoons fresh lemon juice

1 tablespoon pure vanilla extract

1 cup barley flour (see page 212)

1 cup unbleached all-purpose flour

1 cup Sucanat or packed light brown sugar

1 teaspoon baking soda

1/4 teaspoon sea salt

4 teaspoons anise seeds

1/2 teaspoon freshly grated lemon zest

Barley Flatbread with New Mexican Chilies

🌿

Jeffrey Alford and Naomi Duguid observe in Flatbreads and Flavors *that the key to full-flavored barley flatbreads is to toast the barley flour first. Following their lead, I've also toasted barley flour for bread and cookies with excellent results. A side benefit of toasting barley flour is that its smoky aroma pleasantly perfumes the kitchen for an hour or more afterward. These breads are most delicious when warm. Cooled, or reheated, they become even more chewy.*

Makes 6

1 cup barley flour (see page 212)

¼ teaspoon active dry yeast

1 teaspoon warm (100°F.) water

1 cup unbleached all-purpose or tortilla flour

½ teaspoon sea salt

¾ cup plain yogurt, at room temperature

1 fresh New Mexican green chili, roasted (page 353), peeled, seeded, and chopped

2 tablespoons minced fresh cilantro

Toast the barley flour in a saucepan or wok over high heat for about 4 minutes, or until the flour becomes several shades darker. If you stir very quickly, you may leave the heat at high; otherwise reduce the heat. Transfer to a medium glass bowl.

Combine the yeast and water in a small glass bowl and let stand for 1 minute to dissolve.

Add the all-purpose flour and salt to the barley flour. Stir in the yogurt and the yeast mixture. Knead together until soft but not sticky. Form into a ball and let stand, covered with plastic wrap, at room temperature for up to 3 hours. Or, wrap the dough in plastic wrap and refrigerate it for up to 3 days.

Knead the dough for several minutes. Divide the dough into 6 equal portions and form each into a smooth ball. Roll out each ball into a 4-inch circle on a lightly floured board. Spread an equal portion of chilies and cilantro on top of each round, rolling firmly into the dough. Cover with a cloth and let rest for 30 minutes.

Place, chili side down, in a hot skillet over medium heat. Bake for about 3 minutes, or until browned. Turn and, using a clean cotton cloth, press down on each bread for several seconds. The breads will puff up slightly and then deflate. Cook for 3 minutes more, or until browned. Wrap in a clean kitchen towel and keep warm and pliable. Serve warm.

Barley Poppy Bagels

Barley's soft and chewy nature makes it the ideal flour for bagels. I never bother making wheat or rye bagles, but I make these often. Have you ever noticed that a bagel is easier to digest than a hard roll? This is because boiled flour products—like pasta and dumplings—are easier to assimilate than baked. So boiling a bagel before baking lends more than texture.

Makes 12

4 teaspoons active dry yeast

2 cups warm water (110°F.)

2 teaspoons sea salt

3 cups barley flour (see page 212)

3 cups unbleached all-purpose or bread flour

3 quarts water

1 1/2 teaspoons sugar

1/2 cup cornmeal

1 large egg

2 tablespoons cold water

1/4 cup poppy seeds

Soften the yeast in warm water in a large mixing bowl. Stir in the salt and barley flour. When well combined, mix in the all-purpose flour, 1 cup at a time, until the dough is firm. Place the dough in an unoiled bowl. Cover with plastic wrap or a towel and let rise in a cool (not over 70°F.) spot until doubled in bulk, 2 1/2 to 3 hours.

Preheat the oven to 425°F. Grease a large baking sheet and dust it with cornmeal. Set aside.

Divide the dough into 12 portions and roll each into a ball. Let the balls rest for 5 minutes. Poke your thumb through the middle of each ball, twirling it on your thumb to enlarge the hole until the hole is about 1½ inches in diameter. Let the bagels rest for about 5 minutes.

Combine the water and sugar in a large saucepan and bring to a boil over high heat. Drop 3 or 4 bagels at a time into the boiling water. The bagels will sink and then, within a few seconds, rise. (If they do not sink, it means they rested too long. They will be fine but you have to turn them over so that both sides get immersed in hot water.) After 1 minute in the water, remove with a slotted spoon. Shake off excess water and place on the baking sheet.

Whisk the egg and cold water together. Using a pastry brush, generously coat bagels with egg wash. Sprinkle with poppy seeds. Bake for 35 minutes, or until browned. Remove from oven and cool on a wire rack.

Barley-Dandelion Coffee

❦

Makes 1 quart

$^1/_4$ cup whole barley

2 tablespoons roasted
dandelion root (see Note)

1 tablespoon roasted chicory root
(see Note)

6 cups water

2 dried figs, sliced

3 slices ($^1/_4$ inch each) fresh
ginger root

1 stick (3 inches) cinnamon

Cream or milk (optional)

Note: Roasted chicory and dandelion roots
are available in the bulk herb section of
natural foods stores.

My after-breakfast beverage is a cup of grain coffee, a habit from my Postum-drinking youth. Coffee it is not. A barley-based hot drink, though, has more body than tea, a coffeelike aroma, and a something-like-coffee flavor. Natural foods stores and some supermarkets have various flavors of instant barley coffees; my favorite is Yannoh, which also contains acorns. When I make barley coffee from scratch, I round out its flavor with medicinal roots such as chicory, dandelion, and ginger.

Roast the barley in a saucepan or wok over high heat, stirring constantly, for 5 to 7 minutes, or until the grains are chocolate brown. Lower the heat, if necessary, to prevent scorching. Put the barley and remaining ingredients in a large saucepan over high heat and bring to a boil. Reduce the heat and simmer, uncovered, for about 30 minutes. Remove from the heat and strain through a fine sieve.

Serve hot with or without a splash of cream or milk.

Iced Barley Tea
Mugicha

❧

I enjoy a good glass of chilled tea. In Japan mugicha, or roasted barley tea, is a popular summer beverage. It's especially mellow, rounded, and thirst quenching. In this recipe, I use roasted barley as the tea's base, but for a quick, lighter flavored tea, you can use unroasted barley.

Toast the barley in a dry saucepan or wok over high heat, stirring constantly, for up to 5 minutes, or until it turns several shades darker. Reduce the heat if necessary. Combine the barley and water in a small saucepan over medium-high heat and bring to a boil. Lower the heat and simmer, covered for 10 minutes. Remove from the heat. Add the honey, peppercorns, and lime zest. Stir to dissolve honey. Let cool. Strain through a fine sieve. Stir in lime and orange juices. Serve over ice with a sprig of mint, if desired.

Makes about 1 quart

2 tablespoons pearl barley

3 cups water

¼ cup honey

10 black peppercorns

Freshly grated zest of 1 lime

2 tablespoons fresh lime juice, chilled

1 cup fresh orange juice, chilled

Sprigs of mint (optional)

Wheat

IT'S A STELLAR JULY DAWN: soft blue and pink sky, cool morning air, hummingbirds zooming for nectar. The deep greens of summer predominate but for splashes of brilliantly colored flowers and my patch of golden wheat.

Over the past few weeks I've watched the green wheat spears gently bow back toward the earth with the increasing weight of the soft, juicy kernels. It's time to harvest when only a hint of green remains on the stalks and the kernels are no longer juicy but still soft. Mechanized harvesting demands dead ripe, hard, and crunchy wheat berries, and so, unfortunately, it's impossible to cure them on the stock the old way. The resulting flavor loss is significant.

I harvest my patch with a sharp kitchen knife and tie the sheaf around the middle with a piece of bindweed. Then I lean the sheaf against my patio wall, in a spot where it will get sun and protection from rain. There it takes its time to ripen and cure. Once the wheat is completely yellow and the berries hard and dry, my children and I thresh it by beating the wheat stalks against the inside of a dry clean barrel. To winnow the wheat, we pour it from one basket to another under a slight breeze (sometimes provided by an electric fan).

Granted, our token sheaf will not carry us through the year, but these few quarts of wheat do much more than merely feed us. While still on the stalk, some of our wheat is woven into a corn dolly. Despite the name, the dolly is made of stalks of wheat (called corn in Britain) braided into a variety of shapes—dolls, cornucopias, wreaths—with the grain heads, still attached to the stalks, woven into the design. The dolly will serve as a kitchen talisman through the fall and winter until the next spring's planting. Then its kernels will be stripped and laid back into the earth for another harvest. A bit of our threshed wheat will go into a Harvest Loaf and another bit into a Christmas Bambino Bread. Any extra will be placed in a jar and saved for a special occasion during the year.

I saw my first harvest loaf in Hartfordshire, England, in 1971 at a rural church festival celebrating the harvest. One side of the portal was bedecked like a cornucopia. The centerpiece was a bread shaped by hand into a four-foot-tall wheat sheaf. Flanking the bread were ribbons, banners, chrysanthemums, asters, apples, squashes, and real wheat sheaves.

Back in the United States, I fashioned a smaller version of that loaf and every Thanksgiving since then, this bread has adorned our table. I've even baked it and then packed it in a suitcase and taken it to Utah with my children to join my parents, brothers and sisters, nieces, nephews, cousins, aunts, and uncles on Thanksgiving day. One person at the table breaks off a piece of bread and passes it to the next person as we all sing a simple song that our friend Christine Palafox taught us many years ago:

From you, I receive
To you, I give
Together, we share
That we may live.

My children wouldn't have this bread without the song. Receiving this bread from the hands of another, breaking it, and offering it around the circle is in itself a nourishing act.

Wheat has fed humanity for centuries. Starting over ten thousand years ago when the inhabitants of Jericho laid out fields of two varieties of primitive wheat, einkorn (*Triticum monococcum*) and emmer (*Triticum dicoccum*), wheat has become the world's most widely distributed grain. Grown in every country in the world and in every part of the United States, power-packed wheat contains thirteen B vitamins, vitamin E, protein, essential fatty acids, and important trace minerals. It also contains phytic acid which binds with and prevents the absorption of phosphorus, zinc, calcium, and other minerals. Fermentation, soaking, and sprouting breaks down the phytates. It is important that children under the age of eighteen months eat soaked or fermented whole wheat and whole rye products if they are eating these foods on a regular basis.

The Romans perfected modern wheat and by establishing it as the predominant grain of the Mediterranean world, they displaced barley. This common wheat differed from earlier wheat in that it was a "naked" grain which easily separated from the husk of the glumes. Its most important trait was that it had a strong ear hinge, so that, unlike wild grasses, not even a high wind could lift the grains away.

Wheat came to the Americas with the colonists. The European varieties, however, were not suited to New World propagation; wheat remained expensive, and rye and corn were the typical staples. Roger Wilkie, who farms wheat and millet told me that his great-great-grand-father, a German immigrant who homesteaded the family farm in Otis, Colorado, planted wheat seed called Turkey Red, which he had obtained from the already established Russian Mennonites. This wheat from the Caucasus was well suited to the American soil and changed the face of farming. Roger also reported that, "In the next town, Yuma, there's a guy who has always grown Turkey Red. Did it since his Daddy got too old to do it. He plants a patch every year and sells it." It is through farmers such as these that heirloom seeds are preserved and our genetic biodiversity retained.

Although more than thirty thousand varieties of wheat are spread throughout the world, only three types are commonly used for human consumption. They are soft, hard, and durum.

Bronze-colored hard wheat has the highest protein content, therefore also the highest gluten content, and is used primarily for bread. Soft wheat, sometimes called white wheat because of its typical pale golden color, contains more carbohydrates and less gluten, making it ideal for cakes and pastries. The less chewy soft wheat berries are best for cooking whole in porridge, stuffing, or stew.

Both hard and soft wheat are further classified by growing season, as spring or winter wheat. Spring wheat grows fast; it is sown in the spring and harvested in the fall. It is usually the preferred grain for bread making because it is highest in flavorful protein and stretchy gluten content. Winter wheat requires a vernalization period. It is sown in the fall, when it germinates and leaves emerge. With cold weather, the plant lies dormant, and it then begins to grow again in the spring. Harvested in late spring or early summer, winter wheat has the highest mineral content because of its long growing season. It, too, makes good bread.

Durum wheat, a pale golden, high-protein, and high-gluten grain, is the hardest wheat grown. It is used almost exclusively for pasta. Grown in very cold climates, such as Montana and Manitoba, it has hard starch granules that hold pasta together in boiling water. Durum flour also makes wonderfully dense and flavorful breads that require special mixing and kneading techniques.

Two ancient wheats, kamut and spelt, are now making inroads into the natural foods market. Both are easily digestible and hypoallergenic. I have found both kamut and spelt workable and tasty in most recipes calling for common wheat.

Because of today's preference for bread and pasta, wheat is often thought of only as flour. Indeed, the word *flour* literally means the "flower," or best part, of a ground grain. If you grind wheat into a meal and then sift out the larger bran and germ particles, what remains is the starchy, nourishing, protein-rich endosperm, the flower of the staff of life.

In the 1845 edition of *The Young Housekeeper's Friend*, author Mary Cornelius writes,

"Good flour adheres slightly to the hand, and if pressed in the hand retains its shape, and shows the impress of the lines of the skin. . . ." To her, good flour was pale yellow, unadulterated, and did not require sugar to give it flavor. By 1880, though, Pillsbury had convinced the country that its chalk-white, starchy, lifeless flour was an improvement over the nutrient-packed flours of the past. The wheel of fortune has turned again in recent years with flavorful whole-grain and naturally aged flours gaining in popularity.

Wheat
Selection and Storage

Wheat offers a wide range of choices, each of which excels in specific foods. To some degree the different kinds are interchangeable. Once you learn the properties of each, you can use the different wheats creatively in your favorite recipes.

All natural wheat products are best purchased at a natural foods store or specialty market, where they are most likely to be organic and fresh because of high turnover.

Wheat Berries

At a casual glance, all wheat berries are similar in size and shape. Some are a light buff color, but most are various shades of brown, from tan to a deep red-brown. Whichever variety you select, look for grains that are a uniform color with few or no undersized or broken kernels and few or none with the husks still attached. There should also be little or no chaff visible as you let a few handfuls of wheat berries run through your hands.

Soft wheat berries, low in protein, which are used for flour for cakes, crackers, and pastries, are usually the lightest in color and thus sometimes called white wheat. However, soft wheat grown in the eastern United States is reddish brown in color. Unless you're shopping in an exceptionally well stocked natural foods store, whole soft wheat berries are not likely to be available, but their flour will be and it is usually labeled "whole wheat pastry flour." Soft wheat berries may be special-ordered from your natural foods store or by mail order from GoodEats, Gold Mine, Mountain Ark, and Shiloh Farms (see page 377).

Hard wheat berries, high in protein, are red or light tan in color. They are widely available in natural foods stores, Middle Eastern markets, and some food specialty stores.

Kamut is larger than other wheat varieties and some of the grains have a curved shape.

Spelt, distinctly red-brown in color, is unique among wheat varieties in that it immediately softens in the mouth.

Store wheat berries airtight In a cool, dark place for up to 1 year.

Wheat Germ

The embryo or heart of the wheat kernel, this is a widely available "health" product. I neither use it nor recommend it. Yes, it is a concentrated source of essential nutrients, vitamin E, and octacosanol (available as a food supplement), which enhances stamina and endurance. Unfortunately, most of what is available is rancid. Rancidity contributes to the formation of free radicals, which are carcinogenic.

Unrolled wheat germ, variously known as embryo, chunk, or unflaked wheat germ, is less apt to be rancid. When the package is opened, it will have a sweet, rather than an acrid, aroma. Store, tightly covered, in the refrigerator and use within 2 weeks.

Cracked Wheat

Cracked wheat is uncooked wheat berries that have been broken into pieces. It can be used as a hot cereal or in casseroles, soups, stews, and baked goods. It comes in coarse or medium grinds. Store airtight in a cool, dry place for up to 6 months.

Bulgur

Bulgur is whole wheat berries that have been steamed and hulled, then dried and cracked. Dark bulgur is made from hard red wheat, and white bulgur, with a more delicate taste, from soft white wheat. Whether dark or light, bulgur is graded according to texture, from fine to coarse. The finer the bulgur, the less cooking is required. As bulgur contains the wheat germ, it can turn rancid. Purchase bulgur that smells fresh and nutty. Store airtight in the refrigerator or freezer.

Couscous

A semolina product made with particles of durum wheat, couscous comes in both fine and medium grades. Yellow couscous is made from refined durum wheat; buff-colored couscous is made from whole durum wheat and has a richer, nuttier flavor. So-called instant and quick-cooking couscous are available, but I find they lack the flavor of traditional couscous, which is already quick cooking. Store refined couscous in a cool, dry place for up to 6 months. Store whole wheat couscous airtight in the refrigerator or freezer.

Steamed Wheat Berries

Makes about 3 cups

1 cup wheat berries, preferably soft

2 ½ cups water

Sea salt, to taste

Gomasio (page 361)

I used to read the Laura Ingalls Wilder books to my three children and I puzzled over the scene in The Long Winter *when the Ingalls family, as well as the rest of the town, was starving. Flour was unavailable, but Pa was able to purchase a fifty-pound bag of wheat berries.*

There was no gristmill in town so, using a small coffee grinder, Mary had to grind wheat all day long to get enough flour for bread. The author remarks, "The brown bread that Ma had made from the ground wheat was very good. It had a fresh, nutty flavor that seemed almost to take the place of butter."

Every day Mary, decidedly malnourished and lacking energy, would grind the wheat for the next day's bread. Having hand-ground wheat, I can appreciate the amount of energy the job took. Apparently, it never occurred to them to cook the wheat berries for porridge. They are chewier than brown rice, but still a pleasing dish. If you've found them too chewy, it was probably because they were not toasted first and then soaked. Try them again, my way.

Toast the wheat berries in a saucepan or wok over medium-high heat, stirring constantly, for about 5 minutes, or until they pop and give off a pleasant wheaty aroma. Rinse the berries in a strainer and drain. Put the berries in a medium saucepan, add the water, and let soak for at least 1 hour or overnight.

Bring to a boil over high heat, add salt, cover, lower the heat, and simmer for 1 hour, or until the berries are tender. Remove from the heat. Let rest, covered, for 10 minutes. Fluff with a fork. Serve hot with gomasio as a side dish.

Put any leftover wheat berries in a glass bowl, loosely cover with a cotton cloth, and leave out at room temperature for up to 24 hours. Within a few hours of cooking, the wheat may be used in salad; thereafter, use in a stir-fry, stuffing, or stew.

Steamed Spelt

✣

Makes 2 cups

1 cup spelt berries

1 ½ cups water

Sea salt, to taste

1 tablespoon unrefined sesame oil or unsalted butter (optional)

Gomasio (page 361)

*Spelt (*Triticum spelta)*, an ancient red wheat that thrived in Europe over nine thousand years ago, is mentioned by name in both Exodus and Ezekiel in the Bible. Although it is very popular in Switzerland, Austria, and Germany, where it is called* Dinkel*, and in central Italy, where it is called* farro*, spelt was not available in America until the late 1980s. Today spelt is grown in northeast Ohio, where poorly drained, low-fertility soils seem to offer the perfect culture for its growth.*

Saint Hildegard of Bingen, a twelfth-century mystic, cured every imaginable ailment with spelt. "When someone is so weakened by illness that he cannot eat," she wrote, "then simply take whole spelt kernels and boil them vigorously in water, add butter and egg … Give this to the patient and it will heal him from within like a good healing salve." Modern science has supported Saint Hildegard's theories by showing that spelt's water solubility is remarkably different from that of common wheat. It cooks in less liquid and in less time and is easily digested.

Toast the spelt in a saucepan or wok over medium-high heat, stirring constantly, for about 4 minutes, or until you hear many grains popping and it turns a shade darker. Put the spelt in a strainer and rinse it under running water for 5 seconds or so. Drain the spelt, put it in a medium saucepan, add the water, and let soak for at least 1 hour or overnight. Bring the spelt, soaking water, salt, and oil, if using, to a boil over high heat. Lower the heat and simmer, covered, for 45 minutes, or until tender. Serve hot with Gomasio as a side dish.

Put any leftover spelt in a glass bowl, loosely cover with a cotton cloth, and leave out at room temperature for up to 24 hours. Within 4 hours of cooking, the spelt may be used in salad; thereafter, use in a stir-fry or stuffing.

Kamut

Six thousand years ago, kamut (*Triticum durum*) was an important grain in the Nile region. For three millennia it thrived until the conquering Greeks displaced it with their favorite wheat, a red durum. In some isolated fields, however, farmers continued to grow kamut, until it was lost to the Green Revolution.

The Green Revolution, a Rockefeller Foundation project, promised to eradicate world hunger by replacing traditional grain crops with high-yielding hybrids. In the 1940s, the Foundation funded the cross-breeding of forty thousand different wheat varieties to create hybrids that would increase the per-acre crop yield by an impressive 250 percent. These "miracle wheats" were widely introduced throughout the world in the 1950s while the growing of traditional wheat varieties was discouraged. In a few decades, thousands of heirloom grain varieties were lost forever.

In Portugal in 1949, Earl Deadman, an airman from Montana, was given thirty-six wheat kernels, which, he was told, "were gathered from an excavated tomb near Dahshur, Egypt." Deadman mailed them to his father, a wheat farmer who promptly planted them. Thirty-two of the kernels germinated and grew. In six years, fifteen hundred bushels of this heirloom Egyptian wheat filled a Montana granary. At the county fair, it garnered some local attention as King Tut's Wheat, but the novelty soon wore off. The wheat went for cattle feed, and the grain was all but forgotten. Forgotten, that is, until 1977, when Bob Quinn, an organic wheat farmer with a doctorate in agricultural science, was drinking beer and eating corn nuts one night and remembered seeing King Tut's Wheat at the fair in his youth. He wondered if the corn nuts manufacturer would be interested in wheat nuts.

Quinn and his father, Mack, searched the Montana wheatland and found one single pint of the giant wheat. Over ten years—spring, summer, and fall—the Quinns carefully propagated and increased the grain. Kamut was once again saved from extinction. The Quinns took a sample of kamut to a natural foods trade show where its value was recognized.

Bob Quinn returned to his research. He learned that mummified wheat does not germinate, so the tomb story was discounted. However, taxonomists did determine that this giant wheat originated in Egypt and that it is an ancient durum with a wider genetic base than modern mono-cultured durum wheat. Quinn named and trademarked the grain as kamut, the ancient Egyptian word for wheat.

Steamed Kamut

Makes 2 cups

1 cup kamut berries

*1 ¹/₂ cups water or unsalted stock
(see pages 364–367)*

Sea salt, to taste

1 tablespoon unsalted butter (optional)

Gomasio (page 361)

Because it is less chewy than other varieties of whole grain wheat, kamut may be substituted for softer grains like brown rice in salads, pilafs, and stuffings. Since it is an heirloom food, many people with wheat allergies can tolerate it.

Toast the kamut in a saucepan or wok over medium-high heat, stirring constantly, for about 4 minutes, or until you hear many grains popping and the kamut is aromatic and turns a shade darker. Rinse and drain well. Put the kamut in a medium saucepan, add the water, and let soak for at least 1 hour or overnight. Bring the kamut, soaking water, salt, and butter, if using, to a boil. Reduce the heat and simmer, covered, for 50 to 60 minutes, or until the liquid is absorbed and the grains are tender but still a bit chewy. Remove from the heat and let steam, covered, for 10 minutes. Serve hot with gomasio as a side dish.

Put any leftover kamut in a glass bowl, loosely cover with a cotton cloth, and leave out at room temperature for up to 24 hours. Within 4 hours of cooking, the kamut may be used in salad; thereafter, use in a stir-fry or stuffing.

VARIATIONS: Cook with a bay leaf and/or 1 garlic clove, minced. Remove bay leaf before serving. After steaming, add ¹/₄ cup freshly grated Parmesan and 2 tablespoons minced fresh cilantro.

Pasta

Medieval Sicilians envisioned utopia as a land with mountains of pasta. By those standards, my kitchen is utopia. To determine the best ingredients and methods for pasta making, my children and I have for years been measuring flour, cracking eggs, and cranking machines to make pasta—and then, of course, feasting upon our creations.

At its best, fresh pasta is soft yet resilient. It invites comparison to a loaf of home-baked bread. But as with bread, just because it is fresh doesn't necessarily mean it is good. At its worst, fresh pasta is rubbery, dense, and heavy. I say this from experience.

I believe that I have found a foolproof way of making fine pasta at home. My rule is simple: Great pasta requires great ingredients and equipment that works. If I use eggs, they are local, organic, and fresh, from free-range birds. If I add vegetables, herbs, or spices, they are fresh and organic. If I add another flour such as tef, rye, or buckwheat to the basic wheat formula, I grind the organic grains myself. I always use spring water.

Durum wheat is universally acknowledged as the best for pasta. Durum's starch granules are such that they release negligible nutrients or flavor into the cooking water. Even though the best pasta is made from durum or semolina flour, it is simpler to make pasta from unbleached all-purpose flour, which is more readily available and easier to handle—if you are kneading and rolling the dough by hand. When you use mechanical aids, durum or semolina is better.

Pasta dough is dense, so dense, stiff, and tough, in fact, that it's easy to understand why before the Industrial Revolution commercial pasta was kneaded by foot. To produce consistently great pasta I now use my heavy-duty electric mixer with a dough hook and a hand-cranked pasta machine. The pasta may be run through cutters on the pasta machine or be cut by hand.

Fresh homemade pasta made with only wheat, eggs, and water will keep well for two days, covered, in the refrigerator. But since fresh pasta is best when cooked immediately, I recommend making a day's supply at a time, or if you must make it in advance, freezing it.

Kamut Pasta

❦

Makes about 1 pound

2 ³/₄ cups kamut flour (see Note)

1 ¹/₄ teaspoons sea salt

2 large eggs

1 to 2 tablespoons water

Note: Kamut flour is available at natural foods stores and by mail order (see page 378).

Kamut makes incomparable homemade pasta. The secret of fresh pasta is to add as little water as possible. A dry pasta dough will produce a light, rather than heavy and dense, pasta. If you are new to pasta making, wait for a dry day to begin.

TO MAKE THE PASTA BY MACHINE, combine 2 cups of the kamut flour and ¹/₄ teaspoon of the salt in the bowl of a heavy-duty mixer with the dough hook. Add the egg and 1 tablespoon of water and knead on low speed for 8 to 10 minutes. If necessary, add only enough of the second tablespoon of water to form a stiff dough. Form the dough into a ball, and put it in a plastic bag or wrap it in plastic wrap. Let rest at room temperature for 1 hour.

Divide the dough into 4 pieces. Sprinkle the work surface with the remaining flour. Using a rolling pin, flatten each piece into a rectangle the width of the rolling bars and thin enough to insert into the widest setting of a pasta machine. Roll the dough through the machine. Fold in thirds and roll it through 3 times. Proceed through all the settings, making the dough thinner and thinner each time. Cut the dough sheets into 8-inch lengths, then using the cutting attachments on the machine, cut into desired shape. Cook pasta within 1 hour of rolling it. Or dust the strands with flour and cover them with plastic wrap, refrigerate, and cook within 24 hours. Or hang the pasta until dry over a broomstick covered with plastic wrap and suspended between 2 chairs. (Store, tightly covered, in the refrigerator for 1 to 2 days.)

TO MAKE THE PASTA BY HAND, pour the flour onto a large work surface and shape it into a mound. Make a well in the center. Barely combine the egg, water, and ¹/₄ teaspoon of the salt and pour the mixture into the well. Work the mixture with your hands, folding the flour over the egg until a dry, stiff dough is formed. If more water is needed, add a few drops at a time. Knead the dough with your hands for 10 minutes, or until very smooth. Put the dough in a plastic bag or wrap it in plastic wrap. Let rest at room temperature for 1 hour.

Divide the dough into 4 balls and form each into a rectangular shape. Sprinkle the work surface with some of the remaining flour. Using a rolling pin, roll out the dough, stretching it with each roll. Continue to sprinkle it with flour to prevent sticking. Repeat rolling until the dough is paper thin. Repeat with the remaining dough. Allow the sheets to dry for about 3 minutes, or until dry but not brittle. Roll each sheet up, jelly-roll fashion, and cut crosswise into desired width.

To cook the pasta, place a large pot of water over high heat and bring to a boil. Add about 1 tablespoon sea salt. Unroll each nest of pasta into the pot and boil about 2 to 3 minutes, or until al dente. Drain and serve immediately with any sauce.

Fine- or Medium-Grind Bulgur

Makes 3 cups

1 ¾ cups boiling water or Vegetable Stock (page 364)

Pinch of sea salt

1 cup fine- or medium-grind bulgur

I once prepared bulgur from scratch. I found it to be a pleasant but time-consuming task. I boiled the wheat berries for about forty-five minutes, or until they were almost soft. Then, after a thorough drain, I spread them out on baking sheets and baked them at 200°F. for about two hours, or until they were very dry. I then cracked the berries in a hand mill. The flavor was terrific. If I used bulgur more frequently than I do, I would probably regularly make it myself. Use this recipe for tabbouleh and kibbeh.

Put the bulgur in large bowl. Pour boiling salted water over the bulgur, cover, and let sit until the grain has absorbed the liquid, 15 to 20 minutes for fine-grind bulgur, 20 to 25 minutes for medium-grind.

Steamed Coarse Bulgur

Unlike fine or medium bulgur, coarsely ground bulgur, also known as grade #3, needs to be cooked. It is usually served as a pilaf.

Makes 3 cups

1 ¾ cups water or Vegetable Stock (page 364)

Pinch of sea salt, or to taste

1 cup coarsely ground bulgur

Combine the water and salt in medium saucepan over high heat and bring to a boil. Stir in the bulgur, reduce the heat, and simmer, covered, for 15 to 20 minutes, or until the liquid is absorbed. Remove from the heat and let rest, covered, for 10 minutes. Serve hot or at room temperature.

VARIATIONS: Add 1 teaspoon minced garlic or ½ teaspoon minced fresh herbs to the cooking water.

Add any or all of the following to the cooking water:

1 teaspoon freshly grated citrus zest, ¼ cup chopped fruits, dried raisins or currants, or ¼ cup chopped nuts or seeds.

Add ¼ cup minced olives and 2 tablespoons minced sun-dried tomatoes after the bulgur is cooked.

Couscous

✦

The Berbers of North Africa created a wheat cereal more palatable and digestible than the coarse bulgur of the Middle East. They called it couscous—the name it still bears. Couscous is made from a mixture of coarse and fine granules of moistened semolina that are rolled together until clumps smaller than a pea are formed. This "pasta" is traditionally steamed over and served with a stew that is also called couscous.

Classic couscous is cooked in two steaming sessions. It is first washed, drained, and allowed to rest and absorb moisture for about fifteen minutes. It is then rubbed between the hands to break up any lumps. Then it is steamed, uncovered, in a couscousière, a two-part pot with a deep bottom pot and an upper basket, for about twenty-five minutes. The steamed grains are spread out in a shallow pan and worked between the fingers to separate them. This is followed by a ten-minute drying period. The grains are again placed in the couscousière to steam over a bubbling stew for twenty minutes. If you don't have a couscousière you can use a cheesecloth-lined steamer rack that fits tightly in a bottom pot or colander that fits tightly in a soup pot to cook couscous, either alone or over a stew. The top should never be covered and the grains should never touch the liquid of the stew.

If you lack the time to make couscous the traditional way, I recommend my simple method, which works for both whole wheat and refined couscous.

Makes about 3 1/2 cups

1 1/2 cups water or Vegetable Stock (page 364) or Chicken Stock (page 366)

1 tablespoon extra virgin olive oil

Pinch of sea salt, or to taste

1 cup couscous, refined or whole wheat

Bring the water, oil, and salt to a boil in a heavy saucepan with a tight-fitting lid over high heat. Add the couscous and cook for 1 minute. Remove from heat. Let stand, covered, for 10 minutes, or until all the liquid is absorbed. Just before serving, fluff with a fork. Serve as a cereal or side dish.

VARIATIONS: Add the following: 1/4 cup chopped nuts, 3 tablespoons chopped dried fruit, 1/2 teaspoon ground cinnamon, cardamom, allspice, or ginger, or 1 tablespoon freshly grated orange zest.

Grilled Bitter Melon
with Coconut Kamut

Cucumbers and melons originated in Asia, and in many Asian countries, the bitter melon is a popular vegetable. With a knobby, green skin just like a crocodile's back, it is a treat worth discovering.

For this recipe, I borrowed the stuffing technique from my Vietnamese friend TuAhn Holm. The flavorings are a mix of New Mexican and Bengalese, with the kamut holding it all together. An adult taste, with layer upon layer of surprising flavors.

Makes 20 appetizer servings

5 bitter melons (4 to 5 inches each)

2 teaspoons sea salt, or to taste

1 tablespoon Sucanat or light brown sugar

$1/2$ teaspoon turmeric

1 teaspoon fresh lemon juice

2 tablespoons unsalted butter or Ghee (page 359)

$1/4$ teaspoon ground coriander

$1/4$ teaspoon ground cumin

$1/8$ teaspoon ground cardamom

1 small onion, minced

1 jalapeño, minced

2 tablespoons unsweetened coconut flakes

2 tablespoons toasted piñon (pine nuts)

$1/2$ cup Steamed Kamut (page 244)

Freshly ground black pepper, to taste

2 tablespoons minced fresh cilantro

Cut both ends from the melons and, with your fingers, push the inner core of seeds to one end. Discard the melon tips, which tend to be particularly bitter, and the seeds. With a chopstick, finger, or the handle of a wooden spoon, push out all of the seeds to create a hollow channel.

Combine the salt, Sucanat, $1/4$ teaspoon of the turmeric, and the lemon juice in a small bowl. Rub this mixture into the core of each melon. Place the melons on a plate. Cover with plastic wrap and refrigerate for 8 hours or overnight.

Gently squeeze the melons to extract as much juice as possible, taking care not to crush them. Rinse thoroughly. Drain and set aside.

Heat the butter in a small skillet over medium heat. Add the coriander, cumin, cardamom, and the remaining turmeric. Sauté for about 2 minutes, or until the spices release their aroma and are a shade darker. Add the onion and sauté for 5 minutes, or until limp. Add the jalapeño, piñon, coconut, and kamut. Sauté for 2 minutes. Season to taste with salt and pepper. Remove from the heat. Stir in the cilantro and let stand until cool enough to handle.

Preheat the grill or broiler.

Divide the kamut mixture in five and tightly pack each melon center.

Place the melons over a medium-hot grill and grill, turning frequently, for about 8 minutes, or until evenly browned. Remove from the heat.

When cool enough to handle, slice each melon into 4 rounds. Arrange on a platter. Serve while still warm.

VARIATIONS: Substitute cooked barley, quinoa, wheat berries, or rice for the kamut. Panfry the stuffed melons in a skillet with 2 tablespoons ghee (page 359).

Minestrone with Spelt
Minestrone con Farro

I'm sure everyone has foraged, whether nibbling on a blade of grass or picking wild berries from a country lane. Foraging is mankind's oldest profession. And typically the medicinal and nutritional properties of a foraged food far exceed its commercial equivalents. But don't let any unusual vegetables in the following recipe put you off. Go foraging in your supermarket for substitutes to make this classic minestrone gone wild. The spelt, called farro in Italy, brings a perfect Italian note.

Heat the olive oil in a large soup pot over medium heat. Add the ramps and sauté until softened, about 5 minutes. Add the garlic and cattail root and sauté until softened, about 5 minutes. Add the mushrooms and sauté until softened, about 5 minutes. Add the beans, spelt, water, thyme, savory, soy sauce, vinegar, salt, and pepper. Raise the heat and bring to a boil. Reduce the heat and simmer, covered, for 20 minutes. Stir in the watercress. Taste and adjust the seasonings. Serve hot.

Serves 4

2 tablespoons extra virgin olive oil

3 chopped ramps or 1 leek

2 cloves wild garlic, minced

½ cup diced cattail roots, burdock, salsify, or celery root

1 cup sliced chanterelle mushrooms

1 cup cooked rice beans, great white northern or other white bean

1 cup cooked spelt or other wheat berry (see pages 241, 242, 244)

6 cups water or Vegetable Stock (page 364)

1 tablespoon minced fresh thyme

1 tablespoon minced fresh savory

1 tablespoon tamari soy sauce

1 tablespoon balsamic vinegar

Sea salt and freshly ground black pepper, to taste

1 cup coarsely chopped watercress

Mediterranean Kamut Salad

❧

I devised this recipe some years ago for Bob Quinn, the organic wheat farmer who saved kamut from extinction (see page 243), and it has remained in my repertoire ever since. Sometimes I make it with feta cheese and other times with miso-marinated tofu. Either adds the complex tang and depth of a fermented food.

Serves 8

4 cups Steamed Kamut (page 244)

1 fennel bulb and fronds, chopped

1 red bell pepper, diced

¹/₂ cup diced celery root

²/₃ cup crumbled feta cheese

¹/₂ cup chopped sun-dried tomatoes packed in oil

¹/₂ cup chopped fresh parsley

¹/₄ cup chopped fresh cilantro

¹/₄ cup olive oil

2 tablespoons balsamic or wine vinegar

Sea salt and freshly ground black pepper, to taste

Combine the kamut, fennel, bell pepper, celery root, feta, sun-dried tomatoes, parsley, and cilantro. Whisk together the oil and vinegar and pour over the mixture. Add salt and pepper and toss to combine. Let stand for 15 minutes before serving.

VARIATION: Substitute 4 ounces firm white tofu packed in water for the feta. (If using soft tofu, wrap in paper towels, place a weight on top, and press for 10 minutes). Cut the tofu into 1-inch slices. Mix 2 tablespoons miso with 2 tablespoons water and smear tofu slices with miso puree. Let rest at room temperature for 2 to 4 hours or refrigerate for 1 to 2 days. Discard any water that separates out. Crumble the tofu and add to the salad.

Yellow and Purple Bean Tabbouleh

In this salad, bulgur's nutty flavor is heightened by the hazelnuts, and their crunch nicely complements the juicy beans. It's perfect in Indian summer when colorful bean varieties are readily available. Serve as a salad side dish, or as a main course salad when accompanied with a bowl of soup.

P lace the beans in a colander and plunge into rapidly boiling water for 10 seconds. Immediately place in ice water to set the color. Drain and pat dry. Combine the beans, bulgur, hazelnuts, parsley, scallions, marjoram, and capers.

Whisk together the hazelnut oil, vinegar, garlic, salt, and pepper. Pour over the salad and toss to blend. Let stand for 10 minutes. Serve at room temperature.

VARIATION: Substitute green beans and half a red bell pepper, chopped, for the yellow and purple beans.

Serves 4

2 cups yellow string beans, frenched (see Note)

2 cups purple string beans, frenched (see Note)

2 cups Fine- or Medium-Grind Bulgur (page 248)

¹/₂ cup chopped toasted blanched hazelnuts

¹/₂ cup chopped fresh flat-leaf parsley

3 scallions, chopped

2 tablespoons chopped fresh marjoram

1 tablespoon capers, rinsed and drained

3 tablespoons unrefined hazelnut oil

2 tablespoons raspberry vinegar

1 clove garlic, minced

Sea salt and freshly ground black pepper, to taste

Note: To french beans, trim the beans and, using a vegetable peeler with a frenching end, cut the beans into thin strands. Or use a very sharp knife to slice the beans into very thin slivers.

Eggplant, Zucchini, Tofu, and Penne Salad

❦

Serves 4 to 6

1 medium (12 ounces) eggplant

2 teaspoons sea salt

$\frac{1}{2}$ cup extra virgin olive oil

1 small onion, diced

2 cloves garlic, minced

2 small zucchini, scrubbed and cut into small chunks

1 red bell pepper, roasted (see page 353), peeled, seeded, and diced

6 ounces firm tofu packed in water, drained and cut into 1-inch cubes

tamari soy sauce to taste

6 cups cooked penne (12 ounces uncooked penne)

$\frac{1}{4}$ cup plus 2 tablespoons minced fresh flat-leaf parsley

1 tablespoon fresh lemon juice

2 teaspoons balsamic vinegar

I serve this hearty and colorful salad whenever fresh eggplant and zucchini are both available. I advise salting eggplant before cooking it. The salt draws out the eggplant's bitter properties and makes it more tender and easier to digest.

Wash and trim the eggplant and cut it into small cubes. Put in a colander and toss with 2 teaspoons salt. Let drain for 2 hours. Rinse well, drain, and pat dry. Set aside.

Heat $\frac{1}{4}$ cup of the olive oil in a large sauté pan over medium heat. Add the onion and garlic and sauté for about 5 minutes, or until translucent. Add and sauté eggplant for about 7 minutes, or until the eggplant is just soft. Add the zucchini and sauté for about 5 minutes, or until soft. Add the pepper and the tofu and sauté for 3 minutes more, or until heated through. Add soy sauce to taste.

Put the penne in a bowl. Scrape in the eggplant mixture. Add the remaining $\frac{1}{4}$ cup of oil, $\frac{1}{4}$ cup of the parsley, lemon juice, and vinegar. Toss just to blend. Taste and adjust the seasoning. Place on an oval serving platter. Sprinkle with the remaining parsley and serve.

Angel Hair Pasta with Scorched Tomato Sauce

The inspiration for this dish comes from Rosemary Barron's Flavors of Greece. *The full-flavored kamut pasta is a good foil for the mellow tomato sauce.*

Preheat the broiler.

Lay the tomatoes on the broiler pan and place the pan as near to the flame as possible. Broil for about 5 minutes, or until tomatoes are black and very blistered. Remove from the heat and let cool. When cool enough to handle, core and remove the skin and seeds. Chop the pulp and put it in a fine sieve over a bowl. Let drain for 5 minutes, reserving the juice.

Transfer the pulp to a food processor, add the oil, honey, ¼ cup of the parsley, garlic, marjoram, and paprika, and process until smooth. Stir in the remaining parsley, salt, and pepper. Scrape into a small nonreactive saucepan and add the reserved juice to make a medium-thick sauce. Place the saucepan over very low heat just to warm the sauce.

Cook the pasta in lots of boiling salted water until al dente. Drain well. Gently toss with sauce and serve immediately.

Serves 4

6 large very ripe tomatoes

6 tablespoons extra virgin olive oil

2 teaspoons aromatic honey

¾ cup fresh flat-leaf parsley leaves

1 clove garlic, peeled

1 ½ tablespoons minced fresh marjoram

1 teaspoon sweet paprika

Sea salt and freshly ground black pepper, to taste

1 recipe Kamut Pasta (page 246), cut into capellini or thin strands

Shells and Scallops

❦

The success of this dish comes from the interplay of sweet scallops and wine, tart capers, and anise-flavored fennel. The pasta gives the dish body.

Serves 4

1 tablespoon sea salt

1 pound pasta shells

2 tablespoons extra virgin olive oil

1 onion, diced

3 cloves garlic, minced

2 stalks fennel with fronds or celery with leaves, chopped

1/4 cup minced fresh oregano

1/4 cup minced fresh flat-leaf parsley

1 pound bay scallops

3 tablespoons capers, rinsed and drained

1/2 cup sherry

Bring a large pot of water to a boil over high heat and add the salt. Stir in the pasta and cook for about 12 minutes, or until tender but still firm to the bite. Drain. Toss with 1 tablespoon of the olive oil and keep warm.

Heat the remaining oil in a large saucepan over medium heat. Add the onion and garlic and sauté for about 5 minutes, or until the onion is limp and translucent. Add the fennel and sauté for about 3 minutes, or until it softens. Add half of the oregano and parsley and sauté for 1 minute. Add the scallops along with any of their liquor, the capers, and sherry. Raise the heat and cook, uncovered, for 2 to 3 minutes, or until the liquid is reduced and scallops darken slightly in color and are cooked. Stir in the pasta and let heat through. Taste and adjust salt.

Serve immediately, sprinkled with remaining minced oregano and parsley.

Kamut Stuffing
with Vegetables and Fruit

One advantage of this stuffing is that you won't feel stuffed!

Bring the apple juice to a boil in a small saucepan over high heat. Add the dried apricots and remove from heat. Let soak for 10 minutes, or until softened. Drain well, reserving juice for another use, if desired. Set aside.

Melt the butter in a large sauté pan over medium heat. Add the giblets and sauté for 10 minutes, or until just cooked. Add the onion, celery, bell pepper, mushrooms, sage, and thyme. Season with salt and pepper and sauté for 5 minutes. Remove from the heat and stir in the kamut, apple, apricots, and pecans until well combined. Taste and adjust seasoning.

When cool, use the mixture to stuff a turkey, or place in a buttered 4-quart casserole. Dot with butter and tightly cover. Bake at 325°F. for 25 minutes. Uncover and bake for 10 minutes more, or until the top is crusty. Serve hot from the casserole or remove the stuffing from the bird, place it in a serving dish, and serve hot.

Makes enough for one 12-pound turkey

¹/₂ cup apple juice

¹/₂ cup chopped dried apricots

4 tablespoons (¹/₂ stick) unsalted butter

Turkey giblets, finely chopped

¹/₂ cup diced onion

¹/₂ cup finely diced celery

¹/₂ cup diced yellow or red bell pepper

¹/₂ cup coarsely chopped oyster mushrooms

1 tablespoon minced fresh sage

1 teaspoon minced fresh thyme

Sea salt and freshly ground black pepper, to taste

1 ¹/₂ recipes Steamed Kamut (page 244)

1 cup chopped Rome apple

¹/₂ cup coarsely chopped toasted pecans

Ableskivers

Serves 4

1 ½ cups unbleached all-purpose flour

½ cup whole wheat pastry flour

1 tablespoon Sucanat or light brown
sugar

2 teaspoons baking powder

1 teaspoon ground cardamom

¼ teaspoon sea salt

2 large eggs

1 ½ cups milk or soy milk

1 tablespoon unsalted butter, melted

½ teaspoon freshly grated
lemon zest

My mother and all my aunts have ableskiver irons because, the story goes, their great-grandmother, Ane Catrine Jensen, was in attendance on the Danish queen. Conversion by a Mormon missionary drew her to rural Utah, where she became the seventh wife of a polygamist named Abraham Hunsaker. What attending the queen had to do with making ableskivers I've never understood. Whatever the connection, Ane Catrine apparently arrived with ableskiver iron in hand since we were all raised on these Danish pancakes.

Each is the size and shape of a golf ball with a hollow inside, like a popover. The name means "sliver of apple" since a slice of apple is sometimes hidden in the center. Ableskiver pans, available in well-stocked kitchen supply stores, have seven wells for the batter. With a little practice and a seasoned pan, it is easy to form perfect balls. Open a steaming sphere, add a dab of butter, a dollop of jam, and enjoy.

Sift together the flour, sugar, baking powder, cardamom, and salt. Beat the eggs in a small mixing bowl. Add the milk, butter, and lemon zest and stir to combine. Stir into the flour mixture and beat just enough to make a smooth batter.

Heat an ableskiver iron over medium heat. Thoroughly grease each well. Fill each well three quarters full of batter and cook for 3 minutes, or just until the surface contacting the pan has browned. With a skewer or nut pick, pierce and lift the cooked side up to a right angle. The batter will pour out into the well to form a second surface. When the second surface browns, turn again. A total of 4 turns produces a hollow ball. Serve hot.

VARIATION: Add a small sliver of apple before making the first turn.

Couscous Marmalade Torte

❧

I've been making this cake for more than twenty years and am always surprised at how good it is. It has no eggs and no fat and is made within fifteen minutes. I serve it as a dessert as well as a breakfast cake. My daughter Roanna has more than once requested it as her birthday cake.

Organic apple juice made from whole apples gives the best flavor. Either whole wheat or regular couscous can be used. The whole wheat couscous has more flavor, the refined a lighter, more yellow color.

Combine the apple juice, couscous, orange juice, orange zest, and salt in a medium saucepan over medium heat and bring to a boil. Reduce the heat and simmer, stirring occasionally, for 10 minutes, or until thickened.

Press the couscous mixture into a 9-inch springform pan. Smooth the top. Allow to cool for 2 hours.

Cover the top of the cake with marmalade and sprinkle with nuts. Remove from the pan. Slice into wedges and serve with a dollop of whipped cream, if desired.

VARIATION: Stir 1 cup fresh blueberries into cooked couscous. Served topped with slices of poached peaches or pears.

Serves 8

2 cups apple juice, preferably organic

1 cup couscous, whole wheat or refined

Juice and grated zest of 1 orange, preferably organic

Pinch of sea salt

1 cup orange marmalade

½ cup chopped roasted pecans

Whipped cream (optional)

Dutch Apple Pie

❦

Serves 6 to 8

6 cups peeled and thinly sliced Granny Smith apples

3 tablespoons unsalted butter, melted

1/2 cup plus 1 teaspoon Sucanat or packed light brown sugar

1 tablespoon arrowroot

3/4 teaspoon plus 1 pinch ground cinnamon

1/2 teaspoon freshly grated nutmeg

1/8 teaspoon ground cloves (optional)

1 teaspoon freshly grated lemon zest

1 recipe Wheat Pastry for Pies and Tarts (recipe follows)

1/4 cup heavy cream

In this classic pie, cream is poured into the filling for the last few minutes of baking. This pie is a standout when served warm.

Combine the apples and butter in a large bowl. Add 1/4 cup of the Sucanat, the arrowroot, 3/4 teaspoon cinnamon, the nutmeg, cloves, if using, and lemon zest. Toss until the apples are evenly coated.

Preheat the oven to 400°F.

Divide the pastry dough into 2 balls, one slightly larger than the other. Flatten into 2 disks. Wrap each in plastic wrap and refrigerate for 30 minutes. Roll out larger disk into a 12-inch circle to line a 9-inch pie plate. Roll out the other disk into a 10-inch circle. Scrape the filling into the pastry-lined pie plate. Place the pastry circle over the apples. Press the edges together. Fold under and crimp together with thumb and forefinger.

Cut leaves out of the pastry scraps and score a vein pattern on each leaf with the back of a knife. Brush the bottom with a bit of water and press the leaves onto the pie surface. Cut a vent 1 inch in diameter in the center of the pie. Lightly brush the crust with 1 tablespoon of the cream. Combine the remaining Sucanat and pinch of cinnamon and sprinkle over the crust.

Bake for 15 minutes. Lower the heat to 350°F. and continue to bake for 30 to 35 minutes, or until the crust is golden. Pour the remaining cream into the vent. Bake for 5 minutes more. Let cool slightly before cutting into wedges to serve.

Wheat Pastry for Pies and Tarts

**Makes enough dough for one
9-inch double-crust pie**

*2 cups whole wheat pastry flour, or
1 cup unbleached all-purpose flour
and 1 cup whole wheat pastry flour*

¼ teaspoon sea salt

*12 tablespoons (1½ sticks) cold
unsalted butter, cut into small cubes*

About ¼ cup ice water

When I was fifteen years old, I won a state cherry pie baking contest and a trip to Chicago to compete in the national bake-off. In those more innocent days, the national winner was to travel to the White House and bake a pie for the president, then President Eisenhower. In the hope of baking for Ike, I practiced with pie after pie after pie. Though I didn't win the contest, I did learn a few things about pie crusts.

In the 1960s I adapted my techniques for the more flavorful whole wheat pastry crust. This is now my all-purpose pastry dough, which can be used for either sweet or savory pies or tarts. When the fare is robust, I cut the whole wheat with white flour for a lighter crust; otherwise, I prefer the full flavor of whole wheat, which, if handled delicately, yields a tender crust.

To make the dough in a food processor, put the flour, salt, and butter in a food processor with the metal blade and pulse 5 or 6 times to mix. Add the ice water and pulse 2 or 3 times. If a handful of dough just holds together when lightly pressed, turn the dough out onto a floured work surface. If the dough is too crumbly, pulse in additional water, a few drops at a time. Using the heel of your hand, push the dough into a mass. Gently form the dough into 2 balls.

To make the dough by hand, measure the flour and salt into a mixing bowl and toss with your fingers to blend thoroughly. Cut the butter into ¼-inch cubes and add to the flour mixture. Using a pastry knife or two butter knives, cut the butter into the flour until it is pea size. Pour in the water a little at a time, mixing lightly with a fork, until the dough comes together into a ball. Gently form into two balls, one slightly larger than the other.

Wrap the dough in plastic wrap and refrigerate for at least 2 hours but preferably for 24 hours.

Flatten the larger piece of dough into a disk on a lightly floured work surface. Sprinkle some flour on top and roll the dough away from you once. Rotate the dough and repeat 5 more times (over-rolling will toughen the dough) or until the circle is 11 inches in diameter. Fold the circle in half, pick it up, and unfold it in the pie plate. Roll out the remaining dough to cover pie filling, if required. (The dough may be stored, tightly wrapped in plastic wrap, for up to 5 days in the refrigerator or up to 1 month in the freezer.)

Note: To bake an unfilled pie shell, weight the crust with a pie plate of slightly smaller size or with parchment paper and fill with a layer of dried beans or peas, rice, or metal pie weights made specifically for this purpose. Bake in a preheated 450°F. oven for about 15 minutes, or until the edges are brown and the bottom is cooked.

Peggy Markel's Renaissance Plum Pie

My friend Peggy Markel, who directs the cooking school La Cucina al Foco-lare in Florence, Italy, introduced me to this pie. It's simultaneously elegant and rustic in appearance. A large crust is filled with orange- and mace-flavored plums and the excess dough is folded up over the fruit. Plums, because of their royal color and because they're less juicy than other fruits, are perfect for this dessert. But if fresh cherries or peaches are on hand, then don't wait for plums. And don't wait for a special occasion—this pie is easier to assemble than a double-crusted pie. You'll need a large, shallow earthenware baking dish, twelve to fourteen inches in diameter.

Serves 6 to 8

2 cups unbleached all-purpose flour

¼ teaspoon sea salt

12 tablespoons (1 ½ sticks) unsalted butter, quartered lengthwise and diced

5 to 6 tablespoons ice water

Plum Filling (recipe follows)

TO MAKE THE DOUGH IN A FOOD PROCESSOR, combine the flour, salt, and butter in a food processor with the metal blade and pulse 5 or 6 times to mix. Add the ice water and pulse 2 or 3 times. If a handful of the dough just holds together when lightly pressed, turn the dough out onto a floured work surface. If the dough is too crumbly, pulse in additional water, a few drops at a time. Using the heel of your hand, push the dough into a mass. Gently form the dough into a ball.

TO MAKE THE DOUGH BY HAND, measure the flour and salt into a mixing bowl and toss with your fingers to blend thoroughly. Cut the butter into ¼-inch cubes and add to the flour mixture. Using a pastry knife or two butter knives, cut the butter into the flour until it is pea sized. Pour in the water a little at a time, mixing lightly with a fork, until the dough comes together into a ball. Gently form into a ball and, using the palm of your hand, flatten into a disk.

Wrap the dough in plastic wrap and refrigerate for at least 2 hours but preferably for 24 hours.

Preheat the oven to 400°F.

Place the disk on a lightly floured work surface. Sprinkle some flour on top and roll the dough away from you once. Rotate the dough and repeat 5 more times (over-rolling will toughen the dough) or until the circle is 18 inches larger than your dish. Fold the dough in half, pick it up and unfold it in the dish, leaving the excess hanging over the edge. Add the plum mixture. Fold the crust up and over the plums. The crust will meet in some places but not in others. With a toothpick or a fork, poke out a lacy design.

Bake for 10 minutes. Lower the heat to 350°F. and continue to bake for 50 minutes, or until the crust is golden. Serve warm or cold.

Plum Filling

Makes about 6 cups

2 ½ pounds dead ripe Damson or prune plums, pitted and quartered (about 6 cups)

½ cup Sucanat or packed light brown sugar

2 tablespoons fresh orange juice

1 tablespoon unsalted butter, cut into small pieces

1 teaspoon freshly grated orange zest

½ teaspoon ground mace

About 2 tablespoons unbleached all-purpose flour

Toss the fruit with the Sucanat, orange juice, butter, orange zest, and mace. Add flour if the mixture is very juicy. Set aside while you roll out the dough.

Pueblo Bread Pudding
Capirotada

Adobe bread, for sale in every pueblo I've ever visited, is a heavenly white flour and lard bread, generously salted, that is baked in the horno, *a large, beehive-shaped outdoor adobe oven. Often the vendors are wizened grandmothers patiently sitting at a card table by the roadside. I like to buy bread from the hands that have baked it, so I always buy two loaves: one for eating on the car ride home and a second to savor once we get there. When I don't have adobe bread for this traditional Rio Grande Valley dish, I use a loaf of whatever home-baked bread I have on hand.*

Break up the bread into little pieces. Layer half of the bread pieces in the bottom of a buttered 2-quart casserole. Top the layer of bread with half of the cheese and raisins. Repeat with a second layer. Set aside.

Preheat the oven to 350°F.

Put the Sucanat in a medium-size heavy sauté pan over medium-high heat. Cook, stirring constantly, for about 5 minutes, or until the sugar starts to melt and caramelize. Slowly whisk in the hot water, taking care not to allow the sugar to sputter up. Stir in the cumin and cloves and bring to a boil. Boil for 10 minutes. Pour the syrup over the bread, sprinkle evenly with pine nuts, and dot with butter. Cover with the casserole lid or with aluminum foil.

Bake for 30 minutes, or until all the liquid is absorbed and the cheese is bubbling. Serve warm or cold.

Note: This pudding is at its best made a day ahead and reheated just before serving.

Serve 6

6 slices homemade bread, toasted

1 cup crumbled queso blanco or mild domestic goat cheese or grated Monterey Jack

1 cup raisins

½ cup Sucanat or packed light brown sugar

2 cups hot water

2 teaspoons ground cumin

⅛ teaspoon ground cloves

½ cup piñon (pine nuts)

2 tablespoons unsalted butter

Charlie Papazian's Arme Ritter

Serves 4

3 large eggs, separated

¾ cup Bavarian-style wheat beer, such as Paulaner Hefe-Weizen or Hacker-Pschorr Weisse

4 slices, ¾ inch thick, day-old French bread

½ cup water

½ cup fine bread crumbs

½ teaspoon ground cinnamon

3 tablespoons unsalted butter

¼ cup Vanilla Sugar (recipe follows)

1 ½ cups applesauce

Bavarian-style wheat beer with its banana and clove essence transforms an otherwise mundane French toast into a first-class dish. If a Bavarian specialty beer is not available, any good stout will work. Arme Ritter, which means "poor knights" in German, presumably was devised by knights too impoverished to afford fresh bread. Charlie Papazian, who gave this recipe to me, is the founder of the American Homebrew Association and a key figure in the revival of home brewing and the microbrewing industry.

Whisk together the egg yolks and beer. Pour into a shallow dish. Add the bread. Soak the slices until most of the egg mixture has been absorbed. Beat the egg whites with water until frothy. Add the bread crumbs and cinnamon. Stir until just mixed.

Remove the bread slices from the beer mixture with a slotted spoon, and dredge both sides in the egg white mixture.

Heat the butter on a griddle over medium-high heat. Add the bread slices, reduce the heat to medium, and fry until golden brown on both sides. Remove from pan. Serve immediately, sprinkled with vanilla sugar and with applesauce on the side.

Vanilla Sugar

Makes 2 cups

1 vanilla bean

2 cups Sucanat or packed light brown sugar

Split the vanilla bean in half and place it in a pint-size jar. Add the Sucanat. Cover tightly. The flavored sugar will be ready to use in 5 days. As the sugar is used, replace it with new sugar until the bean loses its flavoring power.

Instant Vanilla Sugar

Makes ¼ cup

¼ teaspoon pure vanilla extract

¼ cup Sucanat or packed light brown sugar

Rub the vanilla into the Sucanat with your fingertips until it is uniformly mixed.

Wheat Flour
Selection and Storage

Many kinds of wheat flour are available to the interested cook, from the five-pound paper bag of white flour stacked on a supermarket shelf to an increasing number of specialty flours. If it is stoneground, it will say so on the label. Always favor stoneground, which is the superior flour.

White flour has had the bran and germ removed. It comes in several forms. As with other foods, I always recommend organic.

Bleached All-purpose Flour

A blend of hard and soft wheat, intended, as its name suggests, to be used for all baking needs. Self-rising bleached all-purpose flour includes $1^1/_2$ teaspoons baking powder and $^1/_2$ teaspoon salt per cup of flour. It is mainly available in southern markets.

Unbleached All-purpose Flour

A blend of hard and soft wheat. Unlike bleached flour, it has not been treated with chemicals to age, bleach, whiten, and preserve it. Organic unbleached all-purpose flour is available in natural foods stores and by mail order. This is what I use, even for pastries. As soon as there is an organic unbleached cake flour on the market, I'll switch to that.

Bread Flour

A specially formulated high-gluten blend of 99.9 percent hard-wheat flour with malted barley added to improve yeast activity and often potassium bromate to increase the gluten's elasticity and the dough's gas retention. There is no industry standard for bread flour; King Arthur (see page 377), for example, includes only the malted barley.

Gluten Flour

A high-protein hard-wheat flour treated to remove most of the starch. It is used mainly as an additive to dough made with low-gluten flour (such as rye flour) and to make low-calorie breads. I don't recommend this product both because it is super-refined and because it toughens bread.

Tortilla Flour

A low-gluten hard-wheat flour that is excellent for quick breads, including chapatis, tortillas, fritters, muffins, dumplings, and biscuits. It is available in Latino and some specialty food markets or by mail order from Valencia Flour Mill (see page 378).

Cake Flour

A bleached and refined fine-textured soft-wheat flour with a high starch content, which makes particularly light and airy cakes and pastries. Self-rising cake flour contains $1^1/_2$ teaspoons baking powder and $^1/_2$ teaspoon salt per cup of flour.

Semolina Flour

Made from refined durum wheat with a hard, dense, starchy kernel. It is excellent for pasta and some desserts. A bright yellow color, semolina flour is usually available in a coarse grind. For a fine semolina, process the flour for 5 minutes in the food processor.

Whole Wheat Flour

Made from the whole hard wheat berry, whole wheat flour is best for bread. Unless otherwise specified, it is made of red wheat.

White Whole Wheat Flour

Made from hard white winter wheat. It is lighter in color and texture and has a milder flavor than whole wheat flour made of red wheat.

Bolted Flour

Whole wheat flour which has had 80 percent of its bran sifted off. Each mill gives it a proprietary name such as Giusto's Old Mill Reduced Bran Flour and Walnut Acres Unbleached Bread Flour. To make your own bolted flour, combine 3 cups all-purpose flour with 1 cup whole wheat flour.

Whole Wheat Pastry Flour

Made from whole soft wheat berries. It gives good flavor but a less airy cake, cracker, or pastry crumb than white flour.

Kamut Flour

Made from whole grain, kamut is a pale yellow-colored granular, hard flour which may be used for pasta or bread. In a yeasted bread, kamut performs best when there are no chunky ingredients like cracked wheat, raisins, nuts, or seeds which would tear its gluten and interfere with leavening. Substitute $^7/_8$ cup kamut flour for 1 cup whole wheat flour.

Spelt Flour

Made from the whole spelt berry. In function and appearance, it is most similar to whole wheat flour.

Sifting

Most flour on the market today is pre-sifted, requiring only that it be stirred, then spooned into a measuring cup and leveled off.

Measuring Homemade Freshly Ground Flour

Because just-made flour contains a higher percentage of air than what you buy, lightly tamp it down in the measuring cup to slightly compress the flour and give a uniform measurement.

Leavened Breads

An unleavened bread made of flour, water, and salt would be dense as a brick and taste like flour and salt. Leaven those same ingredients with baking soda or powder, and you'll have a lighter bread. Add yeast or sourdough to flour, water, and salt, and permit a leisurely fermentation period, and you'll create a crusty loaf of bread with good texture and complex flavors.

The breads in this book use two different agents to start the fermentation—yeast and sourdough. A sponge method, which further enhances fermentation, may be used with either method.

Yeast Bread

Using yeast is the easiest and most convenient technique for leavening bread. Yeast is a living community of one-celled microorganisms, which when added to warm water and flour awaken and consume the flour's available sugar to produce fermentation.

I recommend using the dry baker's yeast found in natural foods stores because it contains no preservatives or additives, is long-lived (when refrigerated in an airtight container, it will last for 6 months), and is economical. Do not use quick-rising yeast: It does not permit adequate fermentation and it produces exceedingly light bread with an undeveloped flavor and poor keeping quality.

Sourdough Leavening

Sourdough is an intensely alive mass of fermenting yeast, flour, and water that is used as the seed or starter to leaven a larger amount of dough. Rye makes a superior sourdough starter for both rye and wheat sourdough breads. It is available by mail order or you can easily make it yourself. Allow several days for the process. For a wheat sourdough, you may substitute all-purpose whole wheat, kamut, or spelt flour.

Day 1: Combine 1 cup spring water with 1 cup organic rye flour and 3 grains dry yeast. Keep at room temperature in a nonmetal container with a tight-fitting lid for about 24 hours.

Day 2: The starter will have a slightly tangy taste. Vigorously stir in $^1/_4$ cup rye flour and 3 tablespoons spring water. Cover and keep at room temperature for about 24 hours.

Day 3: The starter will have a definite sour taste and aroma and large and small bubbles. Vigorously stir in $^1/_4$ cup rye flour and 3 tablespoons spring water. Cover and keep at room temperature for another 24 hours.

Day 4: The starter will be honeycombed with holes and have a tangy but not bitter sour taste. Again add $^1/_4$ cup rye flour and 3 tablespoons spring water and stir vigorously. Let stand for 8 hours, or until the mixture is almost doubled in volume.

Stir the starter to expel any gas bubbles, measure out 2 cups for use in bread and feed and nourish the small amount of leftover starter for the following batch of bread.

Refrigerating Dough

I often lengthen the fermentation period of a dough by putting it in the refrigerator during one of its rises. To make a bread in one day takes some doing. But to mix it in the evening, let it rest overnight (or even two nights) in the refrigerator, and then continue the next day makes bread making seem effortless. Knead up a normal recipe and place the dough, tightly covered, in the refrigerator. If it rises before you're ready to work it, punch it down. When you're ready to bake, remove the dough from the refrigerator and allow it to warm through. If it has risen once or more in the cold, it will be ready to shape. It may require another rising period, which you can determine by the feel of the dough. Shape, proof, and bake as usual.

Stone Hearth

To best approximate in a home oven the brick oven of an Old World bakery, place clay quarry tiles on the floor of the oven. These tiles absorb and hold the heat, making the oven temperature even. When the bread is baked directly on them, it gets a robust look, rich color, and chewy texture. My quarry tiles remain on the floor of the oven. Because the tiles take a while to heat, allow at least twenty minutes to preheat the oven. Clay quarry tiles $^3/_8$ inch thick are available from a tile or building supply store. They come in different widths and you can easily "tile" your oven for a few dollars. Be sure to allow at least two inches between the sides of the oven and the tiles so that the rising heat can circulate.

100% Whole Wheat Bread

Makes two 8¹/₂-inch loaves

2 teaspoons active dry yeast

2 ¹/₂ cups warm water (110°F.)

2 tablespoons unsalted butter, melted

2 tablespoons honey

2 tablespoons unsulfured molasses

2 ¹/₂ teaspoons sea salt

6 to 6 ¹/₂ cups whole wheat flour

This is my mother's recipe and one of the few I've ever found that doesn't require at least a small portion of high-gluten white flour. It doesn't rise quite as high as one with white flour, but the sweet wheat taste keeps you from noticing.

Combine the yeast and ¹/₂ cup of the warm water in a large warm bowl. Let stand for about 10 minutes, or until the yeast is softened. Stir in the butter, honey, molasses, and salt. When well combined, stir in the remaining warm water. Add the flour, 1 cup at a time, beating vigorously with a wooden spoon, until the dough becomes too stiff to stir. Turn out the dough onto a lightly floured work surface. Knead for about 10 minutes, adding any remaining flour as necessary, until the dough is smooth and elastic. Place the dough in an ungreased bowl. Cover with plastic wrap or a clean damp towel and let rise in a warm draft-free spot for about 2 hours, or until doubled in bulk.

Grease two 8¹/₂ × 4¹/₂ × 2¹/₂-inch loaf pans. Punch down the dough and divide in half. Form each half into a smooth loaf and place in a pan. Cover and let rise in a warm draft-free spot for about 1 hour, or until the dough has risen to the top of the pan.

Preheat the oven to 350°F.

Using a sharp knife, slash the loaves with 3 parallel ¹/₂-inch deep cuts along the surface. Bake for 45 minutes, or until light brown and crusty. Tap the bread out of the pans. Turn off the oven and place breads on the oven rack to crisp for 5 minutes. Remove from oven and cool on a wire rack.

VARIATION: Add 1³/₄ cups roasted sunflower, pumpkin, or sesame seeds, or 1¹/₂ cups raisins just as you begin to mix in the flour.

Note: The dough may also be kneaded in a heavy-duty mixer with a dough hook.

My Thin-Crust Pizza

On any bread-making day, pizza is the obvious and most effortless meal to prepare. It's as simple as reserving some dough for the crust. Besides, pizza is my best ploy for having fresh, aromatic bread without breaking into a cooling loaf. While Italian-type doughs are more common, I've made pizza from every bread dough in this book. If the bread is without oil, I slather it more generously onto the dough before adding the topping. For a more traditional pizza crust, however, I use the Italian variation of the Whole Wheat Baguette.

Pizza toppings can range from just sea salt and an excellent olive oil to a traditional tomato-based sauce. The topping in this recipe is from last night's pizza, which looked and tasted great. I like to serve pizza without the expected cheese and tomato sauce. The flavors of the crust and other ingredients can then shine through.

Makes one 14- to 15-inch pizza

2 tablespoons extra virgin olive oil

3 tablespoons cornmeal

½ recipe bread dough, such as Whole Wheat Baguette (page 276)

½ red bell pepper, thinly sliced

6 anchovy fillets

1 clove garlic, minced

¼ cup chopped fresh basil or cilantro

Preheat the oven to 500°F. Lightly grease a 14- to 15-inch pizza pan and dust it with cornmeal.

On a lightly greased surface, roll out the dough into a 13-inch circle. Brush the dough lightly with oil, then transfer it to the prepared pan. Crimp the edge to form a slight lip. Arrange the pepper and anchovies in a decorative pattern on the pizza. Sprinkle with garlic and basil. Bake for about 15 minutes, or until the crust is set and edges are browned.

Serve hot, cut into wedges.

Whole Wheat Baguette

✦

Makes 2 small loaves

1 ²/₃ cups warm water (110°F)

2 teaspoons active dry yeast

4 cups whole wheat flour

1 ¹/₂ teaspoon sea salt

¹/₄ cup cornmeal

Here's a whole wheat baguette with the crisp crust of French bread and even more flavor than a white bread. The flavor develops during the long rising time. The bread is traditionally baked in a steam-filled brick oven, but I have had good success using baking tiles in my home oven. Because of the high temperature at which the bread is baked, it does dry quickly and so is best eaten the day it is baked.

Combine the yeast and water in a medium bowl and stir to dissolve the yeast. Add 3 cups of the flour or enough to make a stiff sponge. Cover with a damp cloth or plastic wrap and place the sponge in a warm draft-free spot for 1 hour, or until it has risen 1 inch.

Stir the salt into the sponge. Gradually stir in enough of the remaining flour to form a dough. Turn the dough out onto a lightly floured work surface, knead until smooth and elastic, about 10 minutes, adding flour as necessary to keep the dough from sticking. When the dough is ready it will be quite alive and will almost pull away from your kneading. Form it into a ball and place in a lightly floured bowl. Cover with plastic wrap or a damp cotton cloth and place in a cool (70°F.) draft-free spot for 2 to 3 hours, or until it is almost doubled in bulk and does not spring back when pressed. Punch down, form into a smooth ball, cover, and set in a cool place to rise again, about 1 ¹/₂ to 2 hours.

Dust 2 baguette pans or a baking sheet with cornmeal.

Remove the dough from the bowl. If you are making pizza, set aside half the dough and form the rest into a loaf. If not, place on a lightly floured surface and divide in half. Press the air out of each piece and shape into a tight ball. Cover with plastic wrap or a damp cotton cloth and let rise for 10 minutes. Flatten each ball to make a thick oblong. Fold the top down to the middle lengthwise, then fold the bottom up to the middle. Press the dough until it is 1 inch thick. Fold in half lengthwise and seal the edges. Turn the loaf, seam side down, into the pan. Or if baking directly on a stone, place it, seam side up, on a clean surface. Cover with a damp cloth or plastic wrap and let proof for 30 minutes, or until nearly doubled in bulk.

About 20 minutes before baking, preheat the oven to 450°F. and place the oven rack and baking stone in the center of the oven. Place a pan on a lower rack and fill it with boiling water.

Make 5 diagonal $\frac{1}{4}$-inch-deep slashes in the tops of the loaves with a razor or sharp knife. Spray with cold water from a spritzer bottle and place in the oven. Spray the inner walls and the oven floor with cold water. (Be careful not to spray the oven's electric light bulb). Spray for several seconds or until steam fills the oven. Quickly close the oven door. After 5 minutes, repeat the spraying process. After a total of 15 minutes baking time, remove the pan of water. Bake for 20 to 25 minutes, or until the bread is a rich caramel color, the crusts are firm, and the bread sounds hollow when you thump the bottom with your fingertips. Remove from oven and cool on wire racks. (Once cooled, tightly wrap and freeze any bread that will not be consumed the same day.)

VARIATION: For Italian bread, add 2 tablespoons extra virgin olive oil when mixing in the salt.

Note: The dough may also be kneaded in a heavy-duty mixer with a dough hook.

Aunt Anna's Chewin' Bread

❦

Makes 3 loaves

3 cups warm water (110°F.)

2 tablespoons active dry yeast

*¼ cup Sucanat or packed light brown
sugar*

*3 cups bread flour, plus extra for
kneading (see Note)*

5 cups whole wheat flour

3 teaspoons sea salt

*1 tablespoon unsalted butter, softened,
or unrefined vegetable oil*

½ cup poppy seeds

½ cup sunflower seeds

½ cup pumpkin seeds

½ cup hulled sesame seeds

Note: Unbleached all-purpose flour may
be substituted for the bread flour. Do not
use kamut flour; it is not suitable for bread
containing seeds and nuts, which would
stress its delicate gluten structure.

*My Aunt Anna, who is an unusually creative baker, devised this dense,
almost dessertlike bread, which she serves with her own Oregon grape jelly or
with cream cheese.*

Pour the water in a warm large bowl. Sprinkle the yeast over
the top, then sprinkle in the Sucanat. Add the bread flour
and 3 cups of the whole wheat flour and stir to blend. Cover
with plastic wrap or a damp cloth and let rest for 1 ½ to 2 hours or
until nearly doubled in bulk.

Add salt, butter, poppy seeds, sunflower seeds, pumpkin seeds,
and sesame seeds and stir until well combined. Work in the remaining flour. Turn out onto a lightly floured work surface and knead for
10 to 15 minutes. Place in a bowl. Cover with a damp towel or plastic wrap and let rise in a warm draft-free spot for about 1 ½ hours, or
until dough has visibly increased in bulk.

Punch down the dough and put on a floured surface. Knead
briefly. Divide into thirds and shape each into a tight ball. Cover
with plastic wrap or a damp towel and put in a warm draft-free place
for 45 minutes, or until visibly increased in bulk.

Grease 3 baguette pans or a large baking sheet. If using baker's
stones, position them in the middle of the oven.

Flatten each ball to make a thick oblong. Fold the top down to
the middle lengthwise, then fold the bottom up to the middle. Press
the dough until it is 1 inch thick. Fold in half lengthwise and seal the
edges. Turn the loaf, seam side down, into the pan. Or if baking
directly on a stone, place it, seam side up, on a clean surface. Cover
with a damp cloth or plastic wrap and let proof for 30 minutes, or
until visibly increased in bulk.

Preheat the oven to 375°F.

Cut 5 or 6 shallow diagonal slashes evenly spaced along the length of the bread. Bake for 20 minutes, or until light brown and crusty and the bread sounds hollow when thumped on the bottom. Remove from the oven and cool on a rack.

VARIATION: Either flax, chia, canola, or black sesame seeds may be substituted for the poppy, sunflower, pumpkin, or hulled sesame seeds. All of these seeds are available at well-stocked natural foods stores.

Kamut Pita Bread

Makes six 8-inch breads

1 teaspoon active dry yeast

1 cup warm water (110°F.)

2 1/2 cups kamut flour (see Note)

1 teaspoon sea salt

Note: Kamut flour is available at natural foods stores and by mail order (see page 378).

In my opinion, kamut flour makes the best pita bread. It has a full flavor and toothsome texture. If you prefer a lighter taste, substitute 2 2/3 cups white unbleached all-purpose or bread flour.

Combine the yeast and water in a medium mixing bowl and let stand for about 5 minutes, or until softened. Stir 1 cup of the flour into the yeast mixture, cover with plastic wrap, and let rise for 30 minutes or until mixture is bubbly.

Add the salt and gradually work in enough of the remaining flour, about 1 cup, to make a soft, sticky dough. Turn out onto a lightly floured work surface. Knead for 10 minutes. To help the gluten develop, vigorously punch the dough a few times with your fist or slam the dough on the surface. The dough should be dense and slightly sticky.

Place the dough in a bowl and cover with plastic wrap. Place in a warm draftfree spot and let rise for 1 to 2 hours, or until dough has risen about 1 inch. The dough should be springy and soft. (The dough can be refrigerated overnight at this point until you are ready to use it.)

About 30 minutes before baking, place oven tiles on the floor of the oven and preheat to 550°F.

Divide dough into 6 pieces. Flatten 1 piece of dough. Roll out to form a 6-inch circle. Repeat with remaining balls. Let rest, protected from drafts, for 10 minutes. Slide breads onto the tiles and bake for 3 to 4 minutes, or until they are puffed and the bottoms are a little browned. The inside will be moist but not wet.

Line a bowl with a dry tea towel and wrap the baked breads as soon as you remove them from the oven. Pita is at its best fresh from the oven, but if necessary, the breads can be reheated in foil.

Holiday Breads

For many peoples, bread is sacred, and it is always blessed and held dear. Should a crumb drop to the floor it is picked up and eaten, for nothing divinely given should be wasted. Throughout the western world there is almost no ritualistic gathering, whether of joy or sadness, that is without a symbolic bread, be it funeral breads, challah, Easter egg bread, or even the wafer at communion.

Traditional holiday breads often contain extravagant ingredients and are formed into fanciful shapes. In pre-Christian times, the winter solstice was a celebration of the sun's birthday, and so people shaped loaves into golden orbs to honor the sun god. They believed that eating this loaf was a way of incorporating the god's power. In the Christian tradition, a babe in swaddling clothes is lovingly fashioned from bread. In Ecuador this bread, called *huahua* ("baby" in Quechua), is made in sizes ranging from tiny to larger than life. For the Sabbath, Jewish challah bread is a long braided loaf, but for Rosh Hashanah, the Jewish New Year, it is made round or in a spiral to symbolize the circle of life.

A symbolic three-kings bread for Epiphany is not uncommon. In many European countries, a raw bean is baked in the bread. Whoever gets the piece with the bean is crowned king or queen for the day. In Mexico a tiny porcelain doll is baked in the bread. The one who gets the doll has to host a party on February 2. Every January 6, I invite friends over and bake two breads—one with a doll for the children and one with a bean for the grown-ups. We get the promise of another party, and one of the children wears a handmade, foil-covered crown, with a robe, and rules for the rest of the day with a wooden-spoon scepter.

Harvest Loaf

Makes 16 x 12-inch sheaf

1 tablespoon active dry yeast

5 cups warm water (110°F.)

4 tablespoons (¹/₂ stick) unsalted butter, grated

4 teaspoons sea salt

7 cups whole wheat flour

5 cups bread flour

1 large egg

3 tablespoons sesame seeds

My harvest loaf is a hand-shaped but unadorned whole wheat bread that looks like a sheaf of wheat. One year I tried putting nuts in it, but they made the loaf look too lumpy. I use a minimal amount of yeast. It requires a long proof time and thus lets the bread develop its natural wheaty flavor. I also make it a little richer than usual because it's special and because it stays fresh longer with butter in it.

Combine the yeast and water in a large mixing bowl. Let stand for about 5 minutes, or until bubbly. Stir in the butter and salt. Combine the whole wheat and bread flours and stir in enough to make a soft, sticky dough. Turn out onto a lightly floured work surface and knead in the remaining flour. Knead for about 10 minutes, or until smooth and elastic. Place in a warm bowl. Cover with a damp cloth or plastic wrap and let rise in a warm draft-free spot for 1 ¹/₂ to 2 hours or until doubled in bulk. The dough may be refrigerated for 4 to 8 hours.

Grease a large baking sheet.

Punch the dough down. Shape it into a smooth round, cover, and let rise until doubled in bulk, 45 minutes to 1 hour. Punch the dough down a second time and turn it out onto a lightly floured work surface. Shape it into a smooth round. Cut off 1¹/₂ cups dough for the braided ribbon and set aside. The remaining dough will form the sheaf; divide it into thirds. Using your palms, roll these 3 pieces into smooth ropes, each about 20 inches long. Place the ropes next to one another on the baking sheet, doubling over the top third of each one. This doubled part will be the decorative top of the wheat sheaf and the bottom third will be the base, the stalk. Gently slide the base pieces together.

Divide the remaining piece of dough into 3 equal pieces and

form each into a thin rope about 20 inches long. Braid these together and divide the braid in half. Tuck the end of one braid under the left middle side of the sheaf base and drape it down across the sheaf. Repeat on the right side with the remaining piece of braid. Cover with a damp cloth or plastic wrap and allow to rise for 20 minutes.

Preheat the oven to 425°F.

Uncover the bread and pinch down each strand of dough at the top of the sheaf to represent heads of grain.

Whisk the egg with 1 tablespoon water. Using a pastry brush, generously coat the pinched part of the sheaf with egg wash. Sprinkle with sesame seeds. Bake for 10 minutes. Reduce the heat to 375°F. and continue to bake for 45 minutes more, or until the loaf is browned and sounds hollow when tapped. Remove from the oven and cool on a wire rack. Use the bread as a centerpiece and then pass it around the table, with each person holding it while the next person breaks off a piece.

VARIATION: This recipe can also be used to make a conventional loaf. Grease two 8 ½ × 4 ½ × 2 ½-inch loaf pans. Punch down the dough and divide in half. Form each half into a smooth loaf and place in a pan. Cover and let rise in a warm draft-free spot for about 1 hour, or until the dough has risen to the top of the pan.

Preheat the oven to 350°F.

Using a sharp knife, slash the loaves with 3 parallel, shallow, ½-inch-deep cuts along the surface. Bake for 50 minutes, or until light brown and crusty. Tap out of the pans. Cool on a wire rack.

NATIVE EUROPEAN GRAINS

Rye

Oats

Rye

M Y PANTRY IS FILLED with gallon jars and even fifty-pound bags of grains. Of them, I have used rye (*Secale cereale*) the least. My family does not care for sour bread and since that was my association with rye, I did not often experiment with it. Until, that is, I began to think about this book. I had to give it a fair try if I was going to tell others about it. My children still resist sour bread, but we have found so many other ways to cook with this aromatic grain of the north that I have become a rye enthusiast.

The other reason I wanted to experiment with rye is because the late Belgian-born Jacques de Langre was such a great inspiration. When I first met him in 1970, I don't know which captivated me more, Jacques's Old World charm or his unsurpassed rye bread. I had flown to Los Angeles to give a series of cooking classes. Jacques picked me up at the airport and took me back home. The house was filled with children, guests, his beautiful wife, Yvette—and bread. Loaf upon loaf of sweet-smelling homemade rye bread. According to Jacques, for whom rye bread was near a religion, rye is good for diseases of the circulatory system, will strengthen the digestive system, and, in fact, will cure just about anything that ails you.

For Jacques, the ultimate bread was an all-rye, naturally leavened one, though he did admit to its trickiness. In his book, *The New Bread's Biological Transmutations* (published by the Grain and Salt Society), he observed that if your first attempts at baking an all-rye bread fail "and what you take out of the oven appears inedible, take heart and allow the sticky mass to age and acquire a reputation. With patience and a few days, [it] will either magically change into a delicious cake-like bread, or turn into a gaudy green and pink mildewed stone.... Either way you will have acquired notoriety for your artistry, since black bread supplies a dark and suitable backdrop for the wondrous colors of nature developing from moldy spores." Jacques's Pain de Méteil (see page 305), a mixed rye and wheat loaf, is, however, less problematical.

Rye is a scrappy survivor that is able to sustain itself in all climates. It appears to have come into the world of cultivated crops quite abruptly. In fact, we come closer to understanding the history of rye than that of any other major cereal crop. Unknown before the Iron Age, it originated as a grain field weed in Asia Minor. The ability of the kernel to mature under much less exacting conditions than required by wheat and barley led it to win out over those crops in mountainous regions and on the northern edge of the wheat belts. Rye became the most productive crop in northern soils and those that had been depleted by annual crops of wheat. Its reign in western Europe did not last much past the Middle Ages but from eastern Europe across the Russian plains vast fields of rye still flourish.

Rye seed grows and germinates at temperatures barely above freezing and survives through winter in a dormant phase in sub-zero temperatures. Its soil requirements are almost nil. It is a hardy crop suited to the cold and wet climates and varying soils of those regions, where it remains the peasants' "black wheat."

The early pioneers from Scandinavia, Belgium, and eastern Europe introduced rye to America. Today, the United States produces only about 2 percent of the world's rye total. Most of it is used to make rye whiskey.

Nutritionally, rye is quite similar to wheat. Of all the common grains, it has the highest percentage of the amino acid lysine. It contains eleven B vitamins, vitamin E, protein, and iron as well as various minerals and trace elements. Because of these nutrients, rye has a reputation for building muscle and promoting energy and endurance. But rye also contains phytic acid, which binds with and prevents the absorption of certain minerals. Fermentation, soaking, and sprouting break down the phytates. Infants and toddlers eating whole rye products on a regular basis should eat only soaked or fermented rye.

To make a successful rye bread, it helps to understand three of rye's unusual properties. First, rye tends to ferment easily. The tangy flavor of rye bread has more to do with lactic acid fermentation rather than with the actual taste of rye which, though it has a bit of a tang, is quite sweet. Rye bread starters sour more easily than others, and they give off an intense flavor as the bread rises and then bakes. To retard rye's fermentation, use tepid rather than warm water when making bread and allow the dough to rise at room temperature rather than in a warm spot.

Second, rye has a high water-binding capacity. This means that rye bread retains moisture, producing a moist and heavy bread. This water-binding property is especially noticeable in rye crackers, which give the sensation of fullness as they swell in the stomach. To keep a rye dough from becoming sticky, underknead it.

Third, rye flour has more fragile gluten, compared to wheat. It is usually combined with high-gluten flours for baked goods. To avoid tearing the gluten, handle rye doughs carefully.

With rye, you always know that you are eating something extraordinary. My guests often assume they are supping on some exotic new grain. Then I tell them that it is only that old survivor, rye, and that they can get their ration from any natural foods market.

Rye
Selection and Storage

Dark potent rye berries, unknown in most American kitchens, have claimed a niche in mine. When I want to heighten the character and aroma of a baked dish or cereal, I often use rye.

Whole Rye Berries

Similar in appearance to whole oats or slender wheat but with a curious blue-gray-green tint that turns russet brown when cooked. Your natural foods store will probably have only one variety of whole rye berries. Store, tightly covered, in a cool, dark, and dry area.

Cracked Rye

Whole berries that have been coarsely broken. It can be made at home in a mill or blender or purchased in a natural foods store. Use it as a hot cereal or add it to breads. Store, tightly covered, in the refrigerator or freezer.

Rye Flakes

Whole grain that has been processed with steam rollers in the same manner as oatmeal. Use the flakes as a hot breakfast cereal, in granola, and for baking. Since rye flakes are not a high-volume product with a rapid turnover, they may be stale, so if rye flakes are going to figure in your diet, search out a fresh supply. Store, tightly covered, in the refrigerator or freezer.

Steamed Rye Berries

I would never sit down to a bowl of plain rye berries, unless, that is, they were first pan-toasted. Then they can serve as a filling start to the day.

I don't cook rye berries with salt as it seems to toughen them, but I do season the dish with a sprinkle of Gomasio (page 361) when ready to serve. You can add cooked rye berries to a salad or casserole.

Makes about 3 cups

1 cup rye berries

2 cups water or Vegetable Stock (page 364)

Sea salt, to taste

1 tablespoon unrefined sesame oil or unsalted butter (optional)

Heat a saucepan or wok over high heat until hot. Add the rye berries and toast, stirring constantly, for 4 to 5 minutes, or until the berries have turned a shade darker. Remove from the heat. Pour into a strainer and rinse under running water for 5 seconds or so. Drain the rye, put in a medium saucepan, add the water, and let soak for 1 hour or overnight. Bring rye, soaking water, salt, and oil, if using, to a boil over high heat. Lower the heat and simmer, covered, for 45 minutes, or until tender. Serve hot. Put any leftover rye in a glass bowl, loosely cover with a cotton cloth, and leave out at room temperature for up to 24 hours. Within a few hours of cooking, the rye may be used in salad; thereafter, use in a stir-fry, stuffing, casserole, or stew.

Canapés

❧

A canapé, in culinary terms, is a small piece of bread, toast, or pastry or a cracker with a tasty tidbit on top. Literally, though, the French word canapé *means "couch." To me, there is no tastier couch to sit a piquant bit of food on than homemade rye or pumpernickel bread (see pages 302, 306). Canapé toppings can be made with almost anything, even a bit of butter simply seasoned as with cocktail onions, olives, or scallions and dried herbs and spices such as curry or chili powder or lemon pepper. Once you have the homemade bread, you can have the party!*

Trim the crusts from sliced bread and then cut it into four triangles or use biscuit or cookie cutters to create fancier shapes. Lightly toast the bread if you like in a preheated 300°F. oven for about ten minutes or under a preheated broiler for about two minutes after cutting the shapes.

Some toppings that go particularly well on rye or pumpernickel are:

- Roasted peppers   Roast (see page 353), peel, seed, and chop 1 large red or yellow bell pepper. Combine with 1 minced clove garlic and season with sea salt, freshly ground black pepper, and lime juice to taste. Or process the pepper and garlic to a chunky puree in a food processor and season to taste.
- Savory cream cheese   Blend with a 3-ounce package of cream cheese 4 tablespoons ($^{1}/_{2}$ stick) unsalted butter, 3 tablespoons minced summer savory, 1 teaspoon fresh lemon juice, and a dash of Tabasco Sauce.
- Crab horseradish   Blend 1 cup finely flaked cooked crabmeat with 2 tablespoons heavy cream and 1 tablespoon prepared horseradish.

Each of these toppings will make enough to cover at least 24 canapés. Garnish the tops with minced fresh parsley or other herbs or sieved hard-boiled egg yolk.

Spring Salad of Rye Berries, Fennel, and Green Peas

Make this salad in spring when fresh peas are in season. With plenty of rye berries, it's filling enough to be a light lunch.

Whisk together the olive oil, lemon zest, lemon juice, garlic, salt, pepper, and fennel seeds. Set aside.

Trim the fennel bulb, reserving several sprigs of leaves for garnish. Finely chop the bulb, stalks, and remaining leaves. Combine with the rye berries, peas, and parsley. Pour the dressing over all and toss to combine. Line a shallow bowl with lettuce leaves. Mound salad upon the lettuce, garnish with the reserved fennel leaves, and serve.

Serves 4

6 tablespoons extra virgin olive oil

1 teaspoon freshly grated lemon zest

2 1/2 tablespoons fresh lemon juice

1 clove garlic, minced

1/4 teaspoon sea salt

1/4 teaspoon cracked black pepper

1/8 teaspoon fennel seeds, toasted

1 fennel bulb

4 cups Steamed Rye Berries
  (page 291), cooled

1 1/2 cups fresh green peas
  (1 pound well-filled pods)

1 tablespoon minced fresh Italian
  parsley

5 to 6 leaves red leaf lettuce, washed
  and dried

Warm Red Cabbage and Rye Berry Salad

❦

This salad is like a pilaf with great color. Serve it as a first course or as a side dish with broiled fish. Be sure to peel the apple if not organic.

Serves 4 to 6

2 teaspoons unrefined walnut oil

1 cup walnuts

1 teaspoon freshly grated orange zest

3 tablespoons extra virgin olive oil

1 red onion, diced

1 clove garlic, minced

4 cups coarsely shredded red cabbage

3 tablespoons balsamic vinegar

Sea salt and freshly ground black pepper, to taste

2 cups Steamed Rye Berries (page 291)

1 cup shredded tart apple

½ cup crumbled chèvre, Gruyère, or Tilsit

1 tablespoon minced fresh parsley

1 teaspoon minced fresh chervil

Heat the walnut oil in a small sauté pan over medium-low heat. Add the walnuts and orange zest and sauté for 5 minutes, or until the walnuts are toasted and very aromatic. Remove from the heat. Let cool, coarsely chop, and set aside.

Heat the olive oil in a large sauté pan over medium heat. Add the onion and garlic and sauté for 3 minutes, or just until soft. Stir in the cabbage. Add the vinegar, salt, and pepper and sauté for about 3 minutes, or just until the cabbage begins to lose some color and soften. Remove from the heat and scrape into a large bowl. Add the walnuts, rye berries, apple, chèvre, parsley, and chervil and toss to combine. Taste and adjust seasoning with balsamic vinegar and salt, if necessary. Serve warm.

Tourtière in Rye Crust

A tourtière is a traditional French Canadian Christmas pie that's especially welcome during the longest and coldest time of year. You can use any ground poultry, meat, or game; my favorite is venison. When I use a poultry stuffing, we call it "Four-and-Twenty Blackbirds Baked in a Rye." Why the rye crust? Its delicious flavor. Handle the crust with a delicate touch.

Combine the rye and all-purpose flours, caraway seeds, and ¹/₂ teaspoon of the salt. Cut the butter into the flour to make pea-size crumbs. Add the water, 1 tablespoon at a time, stirring with a fork after each addition. Halfway through water additions, pinch the dough. If it holds together and feels soft and pliable, it is ready. If it is dry, keep adding water, a few drops at a time.

Gather up the dough into 2 balls, one slightly larger than the other. Flatten each into a disk and wrap in plastic wrap. Chill for 30 minutes. Place the larger disk on a lightly floured work surface and roll out into a 12-inch circle about ¹/₈ inch thick. Carefully fit into a 9-inch pie plate. Roll out the remaining disk to a 10-inch circle about ¹/₈ inch thick.

Preheat the oven to 450°F.

Combine the venison, potato, leek, parsley, pepper, cumin, cloves, marjoram, and salt and pepper to taste.

Lightly pack the mixture into the pie shell. Cover with the remaining dough circle. Press the edges together, trim off any excess dough, and flute the edges by pressing with your thumb and forefinger. Prick with a fork to allow steam to escape. Bake for 15 minutes. Lower the heat to 350°F. and bake for 45 minutes, or until the top is browned and the filling has cooked. Cool on a wire rack for 10 minutes before cutting into wedges to serve.

Serves 6

1 cup whole grain rye flour

1 cup unbleached all-purpose flour

1 ¹/₂ teaspoons caraway seeds, toasted

1 ¹/₂ teaspoons sea salt, or to taste

8 tablespoons (1 stick) unsalted butter

About ¹/₃ cup ice water

1 pound ground venison, lean meat, or poultry

1 red potato, peeled and coarsely grated

1 leek, thoroughly washed and finely chopped

3 tablespoons minced fresh parsley

¹/₄ teaspoon ground cumin

¹/₄ teaspoon ground cloves

¹/₄ teaspoon dried marjoram

Sea salt and freshly ground black pepper, to taste

Cauliflower Rye Casserole

Serves 4

*About 5 slices Easy Rye Bread
(page 302) or good-quality rye bread*

2 tablespoons unsalted butter

1 teaspoon caraway seeds

1 leek, thoroughly washed and sliced

*1 head cauliflower, cut into bite-size
pieces*

*2 cups grated sharp white Cheddar
cheese (6 ounces)*

4 large eggs

*1 cup flat microbrewed or other
additive-free ale*

1 teaspoon dry mustard

*Sea salt and freshly ground black
pepper, to taste*

*Here's an old farmhouse recipe from Finland, where cauliflower is the most
popular vegetable and rye the most popular bread. The rye croutons show up
as tender, dark brown morsels in the mélange of cauliflower, egg, and cheese.*

Preheat the oven to 325°F. Butter a 2-quart casserole and set
aside.

Cut the bread into bite-size cubes. You should have 3
cups. Place on a jelly-roll pan and bake for about 10 minutes, or until
dry and crisp. Do not toast. Set aside.

Heat the butter in a large sauté pan over medium heat. Add the
caraway seeds and sauté for 2 minutes, or until aromatic. Add the
leek and sauté for 4 to 5 minutes, or until it softens. Add the cauliflower and sauté for about 4 minutes, or until the cauliflower is just
beginning to be tender. Remove from the heat. Stir in the bread
cubes and cheese and toss to combine. Scrape into the casserole.
Raise the oven heat to 350°F.

Whisk together the eggs, beer, mustard, salt, and pepper and
pour over the cauliflower mixture. Bake for 25 to 30 minutes, or until
the center is set and the casserole is puffed up and golden.

Serve immediately.

That Corn Dish

To me, this was a rye and corn dish until my son, Asa, renamed it by asking repeatedly for "that corn dish." Prepare more than you need because the leftovers make a refreshing salad when combined with diced cucumbers, red bell pepper, and scallions.

Heat the sesame oil in a heavy sauté pan over medium heat. Add the juniper berries and sage and sauté for 1 minute, or until aromatic. Add the shallots and sauté for 4 minutes, or until soft. Add the green beans and sauté for about 3 minutes, or until their color changes. Add the corn and sauté for about 3 minutes, or until its color changes. Carefully stir in the tofu, rye berries, salt, and pepper. Cover and cook for 5 minutes, or just until the tofu and rye berries are hot. Garnish with parsley and serve hot.

VARIATION: Use browned or grilled tofu.

Serve 4

2 tablespoons unrefined sesame oil

8 juniper berries, seeded and, if necessary, crushed

½ teaspoon rubbed sage

3 shallots, minced

1 cup julienned green beans

3 ears fresh corn, husked and kernels removed (see page 32)

8 ounces firm white tofu, packed in water, cubed

1 ½ cups Steamed Rye Berries (page 291)

1 tablespoon chopped fresh parsley or cilantro

Sea salt and freshly ground black pepper, to taste

Rye Dumplings with Sauerkraut

❧

Serves 4

1 cup whole grain rye flour

1/2 teaspoon baking soda

1 teaspoon caraway seeds, toasted

1 teaspoon juniper berries, ground

1/4 teaspoon sea salt

*1/3 cup buttermilk or Clabbered
Soy Milk (see 371)*

1 large egg

1 tablespoon minced fresh thyme

*3 cups sauerkraut, storebought or
homemade (see page 362)*

*1 cup sauerkraut liquid or
Vegetable Stock (page 364) or
Chicken Stock (page 366)*

*A dumpling cooked on a bed of vegetables, rather than in broth, is like a
steamed biscuit. This fragrant side dish takes but minutes to prepare and cook.*

Combine the rye flour, baking soda, caraway seeds, juniper
berries, and salt in a small mixing bowl. In another bowl or
measuring cup, whisk together the buttermilk, egg, and
thyme. Using a fork, mix the egg mixture into the dry ingredients.
Stir to combine.

Put the sauerkraut and liquid in a heavy-bottomed nonreactive
saucepan over medium-high heat and bring to a boil. Lower the heat
to a simmer. Drop the dough by the heaping tablespoonful onto the
sauerkraut. You should have enough for 8 dumplings. Tightly cover
and simmer for 7 minutes, or until the dumplings are cooked. Serve
immediately.

Rye Bread Stuffing
with Apples and Sauerkraut

❦

This aromatic and mouth-watering stuffing, a pleasing blend of sweet and sour flavors, enhances any bird. It's also delicious baked in a casserole dish.

Preheat the oven to 350°F.

Toast the bread in a toaster or the oven until it is crisp and well toasted. Cut it into bite-size cubes. You should have 7½ cups. Set aside.

Heat the butter in a large sauté pan over medium heat. Add the caraway and sauté for 1 minute, or until aromatic. Add the onions and celery and sauté for about 5 minutes, or until soft. Scrape into a large mixing bowl. Add the apple and sauerkraut and stir to combine. (If using storebought sauerkraut, drain well and reserve the juice.) Add the toasted bread cubes and gently toss to combine. If the mixture seems to be dry, add water or reserved sauerkraut juice, 1 tablespoon at a time, just until moist. Taste and add salt and pepper.

Use the mixture when cooled to stuff a turkey (or goose) or place in a buttered 4-quart casserole. Dot with butter and tightly cover. Bake for 25 minutes. Uncover and bake for 10 minutes more, or until the top is crusty. Serve hot from the casserole or remove the stuffing from the bird, place it in a serving dish, and serve hot.

Makes enough for one 12-pound turkey or 1 large goose

10 slices rye bread, such as Easy Rye Bread (page 302) or Jacques de Langre's Pain de Méteil (page 305)

4 tablespoons (½ stick) unsalted butter

1 teaspoon caraway seeds

2 onions, chopped

3 stalks celery with leaves, chopped

2 tart apples, such as Granny Smith or Newton Pippin, diced

3 cups sauerkraut, storebought or homemade (see page 362)

Sea salt and freshly ground black pepper, to taste

1 small (12-pound) turkey or 1 large goose

2 tablespoons unsalted butter, cut into small pieces (optional)

Rye Snaps

✤

Makes about 40 cookies

2 cups whole grain rye flour

⅓ cup unbleached all-purpose flour

1 ½ teaspoons baking soda

2 ½ teaspoons ground ginger

2 teaspoons ground cinnamon

½ teaspoon ground cloves

½ teaspoon ground allspice

¼ teaspoon sea salt

8 tablespoons (1 stick) unsalted butter, softened

½ cup Sucanat or packed light brown sugar

½ cup unsulfured molasses

1 large egg

1 teaspoon pure vanilla extract

About ¼ cup granulated sugar

If you enjoy the flavor and crispness of a ginger snap but not its tough texture, try these crisp-but-meltingly-tender cookies. The spices mask the rye's flavor, but it is the rye that gives the great texture.

Sift together the rye and all-purpose flour, the baking soda, ginger, cinnamon, cloves, allspice, and salt. Set aside. Beat the butter, Sucanat, and molasses together until light and fluffy. Add the egg and vanilla and stir to combine. Add the dry ingredients and beat until smooth. Scrape from the bowl. Tightly wrap the dough with plastic wrap. Refrigerate for at least 2 hours or up to 5 days.

Preheat the oven to 350°F. Grease at least 2 baking sheets and set aside.

Remove one half of the dough from the refrigerator. Pick off pieces of dough large enough to make 1-inch balls. Roll into balls and place on the cookie sheets, at least 1½ inches apart. Grease the bottom of a drinking glass and dip it into the granulated sugar. Push the sugared glass bottom onto the balls to flatten and lightly coat them with sugar, re-sugaring the glass after each press. Repeat with second half of dough.

Place the baking sheets, one at a time, in the oven and bake for 10 minutes, or until edges are lightly browned and cookies are just about firm. Let the cookies rest on the baking sheet for about 90 seconds. Use a spatula to move cookies to a wire rack to finish cooling and crisping. Store in an airtight container at room temperature for up to 2 weeks.

Crybabies

Like gingerbread only better, these moist cookies have the right degree of chewiness and an altogether winning flavor. They are great keepers, but when they get a bit stale, they are terrific dunkers. Try one of these rye babies, and you'll be a crybaby for more.

Cream the butter and Sucanat until light and fluffy. Beat in the molasses and coffee. Stir together the rye and barley flours, the baking soda, salt, cinnamon, and ginger and add to the batter. Stir in the raisins and nuts. Smooth the top of the dough, cover with plastic wrap, and refrigerate for 30 minutes, or until the dough is chilled. It may be refrigerated for up to 5 days.

Preheat the oven to 350°F. Lightly grease at least 2 baking sheets.

Drop the dough by the teaspoonful onto the baking sheets, 1 to 1½ inches apart. Bake for 10 to 12 minutes, or until lightly browned. Remove to a wire rack to cool. Store cookies layered between sheets of wax paper in an airtight container at room temperature for up to 10 days.

Makes about 50 cookies

8 tablespoons (1 stick) unsalted butter, softened

½ cup Sucanat or packed light brown sugar

½ cup unsulfured molasses

½ cup coffee, not hot

¾ cup whole grain rye flour

¾ cup barley flour (see page 212) or whole wheat pastry flour

1 teaspoon baking soda

¼ teaspoon sea salt

1 teaspoon ground cinnamon

¼ teaspoon ground ginger

½ cup raisins

½ cup chopped walnuts

Easy Rye Bread

Makes one 8x4-inch loaf

2 teaspoons active dry yeast

¹/₂ cup tepid water (100°F.)

1 cup flat beer, preferably microbrew- ery beer, at room temperature

2 tablespoons unsulfured molasses

2 tablespoons unsalted butter, softened

1 teaspoon sea salt

1 tablespoon caraway seeds

1 teaspoon freshly grated orange zest

2 cups bread or whole wheat flour

2 cups whole rye flour

This dense rye bread is quick to make—and quick to disappear in sandwiches or toast spread with sweet butter and marmalade. It has a good dark color. For the deepest color and best flavor I favor a microbrewery beer. For the ulti- mate in rye-beer bread, I use a rye beer, such as a Russian kvass or a Ger- man Roggenbier, that I get from a friend.

Combine the yeast and water in a large bowl. Let stand for about 5 minutes, or until the yeast is softened. Add the beer, molasses, butter, salt, caraway seeds, orange zest, and wheat flour. Beat until well combined. Add 1 cup of the rye flour, beating vigorously with a wooden spoon, and mix well. Scrape dough onto a floured surface. Add the remaining rye flour and knead until the dough is smooth, about 10 minutes. The dough will not be as stiff as for an all-wheat loaf. Place in an ungreased bowl, cover with plastic wrap or a damp cloth, and let rise at room temperature in a draft-free spot for about 1 hour, or until almost doubled in bulk.

Preheat the oven to 375°F. Grease an 8 × 4¹/₂-inch loaf pan.

Punch down the dough and turn out onto a lightly floured surface. Knead briefly and shape into an oblong. Place in the pan, cover with a damp cloth or plastic wrap, and let rise in a warm draft-free place for about 20 minutes, or until the dough reaches the top of the pan.

With a sharp knife, make several parallel diagonal slashes about 3 inches long in the dough. Bake for 45 minutes, or until golden brown and crusty. Remove from the pan. Cool on a wire rack.

The bread slices better the second day.

Boston Brown Bread

I recall my mother occasionally making this old-fashioned bread. Its cylindrical shape and moist, almost cakelike texture delighted me then as it does now. Baked beans is the classic side dish, and one that's hard to beat. Coffee or large juice cans with one end removed make the traditional shape. However, because the lead their seams are soldered with finds its way into the bread, I bake mine in a covered casserole or in an Oshawa pot (see page xix).

Combine the rye and wheat flours, cornmeal, baking soda, and salt. Whisk together the buttermilk, molasses, and currants. Add to the flour mixture and stir until well blended.

Grease a 1 1/2-quart casserole or Oshawa pot. Scrape in the batter, cover with the lid, and place the container on a wire rack in a deep large pot. Add enough water to come up 2 inches around the bowl. Cover and bring to a boil over medium-high heat. Lower the heat and simmer for 2 1/2 hours, adding additional hot water as needed, or until a cake tester inserted into the center comes out clean. Remove, take off the lid, and let cool on a wire rack for 15 minutes before tapping the bread out of the container. Serve warm or allow to finish cooling on a wire rack.

Makes 1 loaf

1 cup whole grain rye flour

1 cup whole wheat flour

1 cup stone-ground yellow cornmeal

3/4 teaspoon baking soda

3/4 teaspoon sea salt

2 cups buttermilk or Clabbered Soy Milk (page 371)

3/4 cups unsulfured molasses or sorghum molasses

1 cup currants

Jacques de Langre's Pain de Méteil

Jacques de Langre was born in Belgium to, as he put it, "a family of rye specialists. Every farm, ours included, ground their own whole rye flour. My job was to turn the big handle on the wall-mounted mill." At the end of World War II, Jacques and his wife moved to Los Angeles. Yvette's first trip to the supermarket ended in tears as she found nothing there that she knew as bread. "No problem, my love," said Jacques. "We made it through the war on our rye bread. Let's just consider this a war zone, and I'll make the bread." Jacques made eight loaves a week. And assisted bakers throughout the world through books and videos produced by the Grain and Salt Society.

Sitting on my bread board are two fifty-fifty rye-wheat breads. The ingredients are identical except for the leavening. One I made with yeast and the other with sourdough as per Jacques's directions. I'm astounded at the difference. The yeasted bread is stodgy and unappetizing; passed over by guests and family alike, it will soon feed the chickens. The sweet-smelling natural-leaven Pain de Méteil is full fla-vored, substantial, and has a satisfying earthy tang. The surface cracks naturally to form a true hearth loaf. It's the kind of bread I feel that I too could survive on.

Jacques insisted on using crystal, i.e., unground, sea salt and making sure that every particle of flour be moistened—and therefore inoculated—with the leaven before the salt is added because salt deters the leavening action. Since the salt crystals take a while to dissolve, this gives the leavening action a jump-start. This bread should rest for twenty minutes before kneading because, according to Jacques, "Time is more effective than a hard knead."

I've made Pain de Méteil carefully following Jacques's precise time directions, and I've made it in my own bread-making style—mix the ingredients and then finish a household task, and while the bread rises I may run an errand or you may catch me napping. I find this recipe has ample flex and I don't obsess over watching the clock. Too long a resting period, however, will change the flavor to sour. We have both found that kamut brings rich flavor, color, and texture to the bread.

Jacques de Langre's Pain de Méteil

Until modern strains of wheat were introduced to northern Europe in the 1700s, it was a gamble to plant wheat in the cold, damp climate. Therefore, wheat and rye were sown in the same field, harvested, ground, and baked together. When the wheat failed to produce, there at least would be rye to eat. The French term for a mixed crop of wheat and rye is méteil.

Mix the flours together and set aside. Place the leaven in the bottom of a large mixing bowl. Float the water on top to trap the gas bubbles; this will enhance the leavening action. Mix in the flour a third at a time. Stir in the salt and let the dough rest for 20 minutes. Cover with a cotton cloth. Scrape the dough onto a clean surface. Work with a quick touch with dry hands and knead in earnest for 12 to 14 minutes. Expect a sticky, unwieldly loaf. If the dough sticks to your hands, lightly moisten your hands with water to knead. Cover the dough with the inverted mixing bowl and let it rise for 2 hours, or until it almost doubles in bulk.

Dust a cloth-lined proofing basket or bowl with flour. Punch down the dough, shape into a smooth ball, and place the rounded loaf, smooth side down, into the basket or bowl. Fold the cloth over the bread. Let rise at room temperature in a draft-free spot for 20 minutes, or until it almost doubles in bulk.

Place a baking stone in the oven and preheat to 425°F.

Unfold the cloth and invert the basket or bowl onto a bread peel, if you have one. Remove the basket and slide the bread onto the baking stone. Bake for 10 minutes. Reduce the heat to 375°F. and bake for 35 to 40 minutes, or until done. It should be a rich caramel color, and if you thump the bottom with your fingertips it should sound hollow. Remove from the oven and cool on a wire rack. The bread will be better the next day.

Makes 1 loaf

2 ½ cups whole grain rye flour

2 ½ cups spelt or whole wheat flour or 2 ⅓ cups kamut flour

2 cups wheat or rye sourdough starter (see Note)

2 cups tepid water (100°F.)

1 ½ teaspoons coarse sea salt

Note: Sourdough starters are available from King Arthur and Sourdoughs International (see page 377). You can also use your own (see page 272).

Pumpernickel Bread
with Currants and Walnuts

✹

I believe in the old German and Scandinavian custom of giving as a house-warming gift the most basic of staples—a loaf of home-baked rye bread and a supply of salt.

Makes 2 loaves

1 cup currants

2 cups water

1 tablespoon active dry yeast

1 cup brewed strong coffee or grain coffee, at room temperature

¹/₄ cup 100% barley malt or unsulfured molasses

2 tablespoons unsweetened cocoa powder or carob powder

2 teaspoons sea salt

3 cups whole grain rye flour

2 cups whole wheat flour

2 cups unbleached all-purpose flour

About ¹/₄ cup cornmeal

1 ¹/₂ cups walnuts, toasted and coarsely chopped

1 large egg

2 tablespoons milk or soy milk

Combine the currants and water in a small saucepan, bring to a boil, remove from heat, and let stand for 10 minutes. Set a sieve over a large mixing bowl and strain. Set the currants aside. Let the currant water cool to 110°F. When cooled, add the yeast. Let stand for 5 minutes, or until the yeast is dissolved. Stir in the coffee, barley malt, cocoa powder, and salt. When well combined, stir in the rye and whole wheat flours and as much of the white flour as you can work in before the dough gets too stiff to stir. Turn out onto a lightly floured work surface and let rest for 5 minutes. Begin kneading in the remaining flour. Knead for at least 10 minutes, or until the dough starts to get sticky.

Place in a greased bowl. Cover and let rise at room temperature in a draft-free spot for about 2 hours, or until doubled in bulk.

Grease 2 baking sheets and dust each with 2 tablespoons cornmeal or enough to generously cover. Set aside.

Punch down the dough and pull it out to a wide circle. Add the walnuts and currants and knead for about 4 minutes, or until well incorporated. Divide the dough in half. Shape each half into a ball, molding the sides under and smoothing any edges together. Place 1 loaf on each baking sheet. Cover and let rise in a warm draft-free spot for about 1 hour, or until doubled in bulk.

Preheat the oven to 350°F. Slash the top of each loaf in several places. Whisk together the egg and milk. Generously brush the top surface of each loaf with egg wash. Bake for 1 hour, or until deep brown and crusty and it sounds hollow when thumped on the bottom. Remove from the oven and cool on a wire rack.

Coarse-Grain Sourdough Rye

Here's a clever sourdough rye, clever because it uses cracked rye and rye starter for the hearty rye flavor but relies primarily upon wheat flour for easy kneading and shaping. The sour flavor is understated and the pungent caraway at its best. This loaf is inspired by Daniel Leader, baker and co-author with Judith Blahnik of Bread Alone.

Heat a wok or saucepan over high heat, add the rye berries, and toast, stirring constantly, for 4 to 5 minutes or until the berries are aromatic and have turned a shade darker. Set aside to cool. Place the caraway seeds in the heated pan and toast, stirring constantly, for 1 to 2 minutes, or until they are aromatic and turn a shade darker. Set aside.

When the rye and caraway are cool, combine and grind to a coarse meal in a flour mill, coffee mill, nut or spice grinder, or a blender or food processor. Grind until the rye is reduced to pieces no larger than $1/8$ inch. Set aside 2 tablespoons of the coarse rye mixture.

Put the remaining rye mixture, the starter, and water in a large bowl and stir until thoroughly mixed. Stir in 1 cup flour and salt. Add just enough of the remaining flour to make a thick mass that is difficult to stir. Turn out onto a well-floured surface and knead, adding remaining flour as needed, until dough is soft and smooth, about 15 minutes. The dough should remain slightly sticky. Be careful not to add too much flour when kneading. The dough is ready when you poke it with your finger and it springs back. Shape the dough into a ball and place it in a lightly oiled bowl. Cover with plastic wrap and let rise in a moderately warm draft-free spot for 2 to 3 hours, or until doubled in bulk.

Deflate the dough by punching down in the center and pulling up on the sides. Transfer to a lightly floured work surface and cut

Makes 2 loaves

$1 1/4$ cups rye berries

$1/4$ cup caraway seeds

2 cups rye sourdough starter
(see Note)

3 cups spring water

7 to $7 1/2$ cups whole wheat bread flour,
spelt flour, or kamut flour

1 tablespoon sea salt

Note: Rye sourdough starters are available from King Arthur (see page 377). You can also use your own (see page 272).

into 2 equal pieces. Knead each briefly, then flatten each with the heel of your hand. Shape each piece into a tight ball. Sprinkle the top of each with the remaining cracked rye mixture and gently pat the rye into the dough.

Line 2 bowls or baskets about 8 inches in diameter and 3 inches deep with well-floured cotton cloths. Place the loaves seam side up in the prepared bowls, cover with a clean damp towel or plastic wrap, and put in a moderately warm draft-free place until almost doubled in bulk, or until a slight indentation remains when the dough is pressed with a fingertip.

Place a baking stone on the center rack of the oven and preheat the oven to 450°F.

Gently invert the loaves from the baskets onto a floured peel so that they are right side up. Score the loaves with a sharp knife by making several quick slashes along the surface. Using the peel, slide the loaves onto the stone. Quickly spray the inner walls and floor of the oven with cold water from a spritzer bottle. If there's an electric light bulb in the oven, avoid spraying it directly or it might burst. Spray for several seconds until the oven is steamy. Quickly close the door to trap the steam and bake 5 minutes. Spray again in the same way. Bake until the loaves begin to color, about 20 minutes. Reduce the heat to 400°F., and bake until loaves are a rich caramel color and the crust is firm, 15 to 20 minutes longer.

Remove and hold the loaves upside down. Rap the bottoms firmly with your fingers. If the sound is hollow, the breads are done. Cool completely on a wire rack.

Rye Flour

Whole grain rye flour is a shade darker than whole wheat flour and is available in natural foods stores. Flour made from whole rye contains more flavor and nutrients, and more of the pentosan gums that cause dough to be sticky. Store whole-grain rye flour, tightly wrapped, in the refrigerator for several months or in the freezer for up to 6 months.

The rye flour you find in a supermarket, labeled dark, medium, or light rye flour, is degermed, with the dark flour containing more bran.

Pumpernickel flour is a dark brown, coarsely ground rye meal, which contains coloring and flavoring agents. There is no industry standard for pumpernickel flour.

I prefer making pumpernickel bread with whole-grain rye flour and my own choice of quality coloring and seasoning agents.

Store these flours, tightly wrapped, in a cool, dry cupboard.

Oats

IN 1973, I SPENT A WINTER in Dublin, Ireland, staying with Susan and Anthony Harnett and teaching cooking classes. Anthony was the proprietor of Dublin's first natural foods store, Green Acres. It was great fun introducing unknown cooking methods and natural products to a tiny but eager market. I, in an attempt to balance the trade, developed an appreciation for Guinness stout and tried using oats in every conceivable way.

Our efforts were ahead of their time, and while our enthusiasm was great, our audience remained small. I moved to Kenilworth, England, to study Oriental medicine, and the Harnetts emigrated to Massachusetts, where they opened the trend-setting Bread & Circus store in Brookline Village. It has grown into a large natural foods supermarket chain, respected for the quality of its merchandise as well as for its strong public stand on environmental issues.

Many years later, I can close my eyes and see the soft green country and smell the acrid peat fires of Ireland. I can still taste my first bowl of Irish oatmeal. How I loved its rich, nutty taste. It was only when I traveled on to Scotland, though, that I realized the significance of this cereal in the lands of the Celts. Bannock, broonie, atholl brose, farl, skirlie, sowans, haver, hodgils, and kaaks are the magical names given to some of the many oat dishes of Scotland. In drinks to cakes, oats have nourished generations of Scotsmen. In his famous English dictionary, Samuel Johnson defined oats as "food for men in Scotland, horses in England," to which a Scotsman replied, "England is noted for the excellence of her horses; Scotland for the excellence of her men."

It was long believed that oats originated as a weed, a belief that kept them off the table and in the stable for thousands of years. Recent cytological and genetic studies have thrown that theory to the wind. Cultivated oats (*Avena sativa*) are diploids whereas almost all wild oats are polyploids. This means that the crop could have given rise to the weeds, but not the weeds to the crop.

Oats thrive best in a cold climate. They were probably well established in central Asia and Russia long before they were introduced into Europe around A.D. 100. Through the centuries, oats have remained livestock feed throughout the world. In fact, about 90 percent of all oats grown in the United States is used for feed. It was mainly through the public relations campaign for oat bran that oats captured the attention of health conscious Americans. In the 1980s, they turned to oat bran, hoping to cleanse their arteries and lower their cholesterol. Subsequent data revealed that other brans were equally effective in reducing cholesterol.

The really exciting news goes beyond the brans. It's the revolutionary—or is it old-fashioned?—act of eating the whole grain. Studies have found that rolled oats (oatmeal) have less water soluble fiber than oat bran but share the same ability to reduce cholesterol.

Research also indicates that oats contain an alkaloid that apparently enhances vitality, especially for men. As acknowledged by folk wisdom in such sayings as "feeling your oats" and "sowing wild oats," this simple food is a male aphrodisiac. Controlled studies performed by the Institute for Advanced Study of Human Sexuality in San Francisco support these old observations. Dr. Ted McIlvenna reported that exsativa, an oat extract, increases sexual capacity, provides more intense sensation, and prolongs sexual pleasure in men, but apparently not in women.

If this isn't enough to make you want to start your day with a bowl of oatmeal, there are many other health promoting attributes to recommend it. Science has found that oats help regulate blood sugar. They also contain compounds that prevent cancer in animals, combat inflammation of the skin, and act as a laxative. Folk remedies support the clinical data that oats are an adaptogen that reduces the craving for cigarettes and other addictions, strengthens the nerves, soothes the stomach, and cures a hangover. And, of course, any reader of Victorian novels knows that oats mixed with rosewater and used as a facial scrub will create the glowing skin of a virgin bride. Although I agree that oatmeal should be included in our diet, I also know that it is not a cure-all. Good eating habits that include oats are the true miracle of good health.

Chewy but moist, oats are sweeter and nuttier than other grains because of their higher lipid profile. They're also good sources of B vitamins, calcium, protein, unsaturated fat, and fiber. Oats can easily be incorporated into all types of recipes, not just the morning porridge. I'm constantly amazed at the new ways I find to use all the different kinds of oats I have in my kitchen.

Oats
Selection and Storage

Oats, the slenderest of all the grains, are the only whole-grain cereal that many people eat on a regular basis. Indeed, a bowl of oats can be very soothing and satisfying. As with other grains, I recommend purchasing oats and oat products from a well-stocked natural foods store or by mail order.

Oat Groats

The untreated whole grain with only the two inedible outer chaffs removed, also known as whole oats. Groats offer complete nutritional value. Store airtight in a cool dark place for up to 1 year.

Steel Cut Oats

Whole groats that have been cut into two or three pieces also known as Irish or Scottish oats. They are the type most often used in Irish and Scottish porridges and other traditional dishes. Store airtight in the refrigerator for 3 months or in the freezer for up to 6 months.

Rolled Oats

Oat groats that have been steamed, to soften them, and then rolled, are what we know as oatmeal or old-fashioned oats.

Some natural foods companies flash-toast their rolled oats to enhance flavor. Store airtight in a cool spot for up to 2 months. For longer storage, freeze.

Oat Flour

Ground whole groats. When used for baking, it produces a sweet cakelike crumb that retains its freshness far longer than wheat flour products. Since oats contain very little gluten, oat flour must be combined with wheat in leavened breads. Oat flour is available in natural food stores, but it is better freshly ground. I grind oat groats in a grain mill. Small quantities of coarse oat flour made from the rolled oats may also be made in a spice or coffee grinder or blender. For 1 cup oat flour, use $2/3$ cup oat groats or $1^1/2$ cups oatmeal. It's best to grind oat flour as you need it. Store extra oat flour in an airtight container in the freezer for up to 4 months.

Oat Bran

The outer layer of oats, which looks like a coarse flour. As an ingredient used in baking, it is valued for its cholesterol-lowering benefits. Because it does not contain the germ, oat bran has an indefinite shelf life. Store, tightly covered, in a cool area.

Steamed Oat Groats

❧

Oat groats are almost meaty in taste, with a satisfying moist but chewy texture. They make a great breakfast and, just like brown rice, can be used as a grain entree or in salads, soups, or stuffings. With whole oats you will occasionally bite into an oat hull. This bit of fiber is a reminder that you're eating a minimally processed, very rustic grain. For this we give thanks.

Makes 3 cups

1 cup whole oat groats

1 ¾ cups water or Vegetable Stock (page 364)

¼ teaspoon sea salt, or to taste

1 tablespoon unsalted butter or sesame oil (optional)

Gomasio (page 361)

Toast the groats in a saucepan or wok over medium-high heat, stirring constantly, for about 4 minutes, or until the oats are aromatic and a shade darker.

Combine the water, salt, and butter, if using, in a small saucepan over high heat and bring to a boil. Add the oats, lower the heat, and simmer, covered, 45 minutes, or until the liquid is absorbed and the oats are tender. Remove from the heat and let stand for 10 minutes with the lid on. Fluff with a fork and serve hot with gomasio or another topping. Place leftover groats in a glass bowl, cover with a cotton cloth, and leave at room temperature for 24 hours. Within 4 hours, the cooked groats may be used in a salad; after that, use in a casserole, croquettes, soup, or stir-fry.

VARIATIONS: Instead of toasting, sauté the oat groats in 1 teaspoon ghee (page 359) or butter before cooking.

Cook oats in 1 cup stock and ¾ cup beer.

Add to the stock 1 or 2 minced garlic cloves and/or 1 teaspoon minced rosemary or any herb of choice.

Add ¼ cup chopped toasted nuts or seeds. Add them with the oats if you want a soft texture, or when you fluff the cooked oats if you want the nuts to retain their chewiness.

For a creamy breakfast cereal, add groats to cold water. Bring to a boil, reduce the heat, and simmer, covered, for 45 minutes, or until the liquid is absorbed and the oats are tender.

Steamed Steel Cut Oats

Whole oat groats cut it into two or three pieces are called steel cut oats or Irish or Scottish oats. The advantage of cut oats is that they cook quickly, ten to twelve minutes cooking time compared to forty-five minutes for groats. I use steel cut oats in salads and pilafs. They are also good as a breakfast cereal.

H eat a saucepan or wok over medium-high heat until warm. Add the oats. After 1 minute, reduce the heat to medium and toast, stirring constantly, for about 3 minutes, or until the oats are aromatic and a shade darker.

Combine the water and salt in a medium saucepan over high heat and bring to a boil. Add the oats, lower the heat, and simmer, covered, for 12 minutes, or until the liquid is absorbed and the oats are tender. Remove from the heat and let stand for 10 minutes with the lid on. Fluff with a fork and serve hot.

VARIATIONS: For a creamy breakfast cereal, increase the water to 2 cups, add the oats to cold water, and cook for 25 to 30 minutes.

Instead of toasting, sauté the oats in 2 teaspoons Ghee (page 359) or butter.

Add 1 or 2 minced garlic cloves and/or 1 teaspoon minced rosemary or any herb of choice to the stock.

Add ¼ cup chopped toasted nuts or seeds, such as walnuts, pecans, almonds, hazelnuts, or sunflower or pumpkin seeds.

Makes 2 ¹/₂ cups

1 cup steel cut oats

1 ¹/₂ cups water or Vegetable Stock (page 364) or Chicken Stock (page 366)

Sea salt, to taste

Slow Cooker
Creamy Whole Oat Porridge

✺

This no-fuss breakfast cereal is more warming and hearty than oatmeal because it's made from oat groats. Put up the porridge before you go to bed and waken to its welcoming aroma. See the list of toppings at the end of the recipe. You can use any leftover oats as a thickener for soups.

Serves 4

1 cup oat groats

1 piece (3 inches) cinnamon stick

Pinch of sea salt

4 cups water

Place all the ingredients in a slow cooker. Set on high heat, cover, and simmer overnight.

VARIATIONS: Honey and toasted piñon (pine nuts) or any other toasted nut.

Sliced bananas and maple syrup.

Any fresh fruit, sliced and sautéed in unsalted butter and sugar with a bit of fresh lemon juice.

Molasses and warm poached dried fruits.

Sliced peaches or nectarines macerated in fresh orange juice.

Note: You can also cook the oats in a saucepan. Bring the oats to a boil in an ovenproof pan with a lid. Place in the oven at the lowest temperature and let cook, covered, overnight. Serve hot.

Proper Pot of Porridge

I was taught to make porridge by a farm wife in a cozy kitchen in Scotland, where cooking oatmeal is an art. Proper oatmeal is made with a spurtle, a fat wooden potstick that may be simple in design or elaborately carved. Medium or thick rolled oats work best. You can substitute the handle of a wooden spoon—or even a chopstick—for the spurtle.

Start with 2 cups of water bubbling fast as galloping. Add a pinch of sea salt and with one hand lightly sprinkle 1 cup of oatmeal on top of the water so that each grain falls separately and is instantly sealed. This enables it to become pleasingly plump and not mushy. Never add so much oatmeal that the water stops boiling—and never stop stirring with the spurtle. Simmer, uncovered, for 15 minutes, stirring as necessary. Serve hot with a bowl of milk or cream on the side and dip your porridge into it, one spoonful at a time. This serves 2.

Smoked Chicken, Celery Root, and Oat Groats in Phyllo

2 tablespoons extra virgin olive oil

2 teaspoons celery seeds

2 cloves garlic, minced

1 teaspoon minced fresh ginger

1 small onion, diced

1 cup chopped oyster or other
   mushrooms

1 cup julienned celery root

1 1/2 cups Steamed Oat Groats
   (page 314)

1 cup diced smoked chicken

1/2 cup chopped walnuts

1 red bell pepper, roasted (page 353),
   peeled, seeded, and chopped, or
   1 bottled pimiento, chopped

1/2 cup grated mozzarella

1/4 cup chopped fresh cilantro or Italian
   flat-leaf parsley

1/4 cup chopped scallions

1 tablespoon rice wine vinegar

Sea salt and freshly ground black
   pepper, to taste

16 sheets frozen phyllo dough, thawed

8 tablespoons (1 stick) unsalted
   butter, melted

This party dish can be easily transformed into a pilaf for the family by omitting the phyllo, stirring the oats, chicken, and remaining flavorings into the vegetables, and cooking until warmed through.

Heat the oil in a medium sauté pan over medium heat until warm. Add the celery seeds and sauté until aromatic. Add the garlic and ginger and sauté until aromatic. Do not allow the garlic to brown. Add the onion and sauté for 5 minutes, or until translucent. Add the mushrooms and sauté for 4 minutes, or until soft. Add the celery root, and sauté for about 4 minutes, or until soft. Remove from the heat. Stir in the oat groats, chicken, walnuts, red pepper, mozzarella, cilantro, scallions, and vinegar. Season with salt and pepper. Let filling cool before rolling in phyllo.

Preheat the oven to 325°F.

Place 1 sheet of phyllo on a clean dry surface. Brush with melted butter. Continue to layer and brush with 3 more sheets. (Keep other phyllo sheets well covered to prevent them from drying out.) Cut lengthwise in half. Place 1 rounded cup of filling 1 inch from the end of the phyllo strip, leaving a 1/2-inch edge on each side. Starting at the 1-inch unfilled end, begin rolling to enclose filling. Once filling is enclosed, fold in 1/2 inch of the sides. Continue rolling to make a neat packet. Place, seam side down, on an ungreased baking sheet. Continue layering, cutting, filling, and rolling until all the phyllo and filling are used. Brush the finished packets with remaining butter. Bake for 15 minutes, or until golden. Serve warm or at room temperature.

VARIATIONS: Substitute rice for the oats.

Substitute roasted lamb, chicken, or tempeh for the smoked chicken.

Oat and Roasted Root Vegetable Soup

Welsh, Irish, and Scottish cookbooks abound with oat soups made simply with a seasonal vegetable, stock, and oats. Oat flakes provide a rustic thickener for the stoutly flavored roasted vegetables in this soup. To make it into a meal-in-one, add a cup of cooked beans—baby limas or great white northerns would be good—and serve with whole grain crackers or breadsticks.

Preheat the oven to 350°F.

Wash and trim the leek. Cut lengthwise in half and cut into ½-inch slices. Place leek, root vegetables, and garlic in a roasting pan and toss with sesame oil or butter. Season with salt and pepper. Roast vegetables for 25 to 30 minutes, or until they are a deep golden brown. Set aside.

Toast the oatmeal in a large soup pan for 3 minutes, or until it gives off an oaty fragrance and turns a shade darker. Add the vegetables, stock, ginger juice, and vinegar. Bring to a boil and simmer for 10 minutes, or until all the vegetables are soft. Season with soy sauce. Serve hot.

Serves 4

1 medium leek

3 cups root vegetables, such as carrot, potato, turnip, rutabaga, burdock, daikon, celery root, or parsnip, cut into ½-inch dice

10 cloves garlic

1 tablespoon unrefined sesame oil or unsalted butter

Sea salt and freshly ground black pepper, to taste.

½ cup oatmeal

4 cups Vegetable Stock (page 364) or Shiitake Dashi Stock (page 368)

1 teaspoon Ginger Juice (page 360)

1 tablespoon rice wine vinegar

Tamari soy sauce, to taste

Cream of Shiitake
and Broccoli Soup

❦

Serves 4 to 6

2 stalks broccoli

1 teaspoon unrefined roasted sesame oil

¾ teaspoon ground coriander

1 small onion, diced

3 shiitake mushrooms, trimmed and chopped

5 tablespoons oatmeal

6 cups Vegetable Stock (page 364)

6 tablespoons white or yellow miso (see page 220)

2 tablespoons chopped fresh thyme

Freshly ground black pepper, to taste

Fresh lemon juice

By using oats rather than a dairy product to cream this soup, you turn an ordinary recipe into one with a healthy twist and a light, clean taste.

Separate broccoli into small florets. Chop the stems. Set aside separately.

Heat the oil in a soup pot over medium heat. Add the coriander and sauté for 1 minute, or until aromatic. Add the onion and sauté for 3 to 4 minutes, or until slightly softened. Add the shiitake and sauté for 3 to 4 minutes, or until slightly softened. Add the broccoli stems and the oats and sauté for 3 to 4 minutes, or until the broccoli slightly softens. Add just enough stock to cover the vegetables and bring to a boil. Reduce the heat, cover, and simmer for 15 minutes, or until the broccoli is very tender.

Put the miso in a small bowl, add ⅔ cup of the remaining stock, and puree with a fork. Set aside.

Pour the soup into a blender and puree. Return to the pot. Add the remaining stock, broccoli florets, thyme, and pepper. Bring to a simmer over medium-high heat. Lower the heat and simmer for 5 minutes, or until the florets are just cooked. Stir in the miso puree and a dash of lemon juice. Simmer for 1 minute. Taste and adjust seasoning. Serve hot.

Irish Tabbouleh

If you're as tired of bulgur tabbouleh as I am, my Irish tabbouleh made of steel cut oats will be a welcome change. Oats have a higher lipid content than wheat, so they give the dish a rounder, smoother taste while retaining the satisfying crunch of bulgur.

Put the tomatoes in a fine sieve and let them drain until ready to use. Combine the oats, tomatoes, cucumber, scallions, parsley, and mint in a bowl. Mix together the olive oil, lemon juice, salt, and cayenne, if using. Pour over the oats and vegetables and toss to combine. Cover and refrigerate for at least 1 hour. Serve as is or with chopped lettuce, if desired.

Serves 4

2 medium tomatoes, peeled, cored, seeded (see page 370), and diced

1 cucumber, peeled, cut in half lengthwise, seeded, and diced

2 cups Steamed Steel Cut Oats (page 315), cooled to room temperature

4 scallions, minced

½ cup minced fresh Italian flat-leaf parsley

2 tablespoons minced fresh mint

⅓ cup extra virgin olive oil

⅓ cup fresh lemon juice

Sea salt, to taste

⅛ teaspoon cayenne (optional)

4 romaine lettuce leaves, chopped (optional)

Onion and Sun-dried Tomato Tart in Oat Crust

❧

I don't know why, but oats and onion have an affinity for each other. That's one reason I add oats to the crust of the traditional French onion tart, pissaladière. I also add black cumin seed for its color and mild peppery flavor. If black cumin is not available, substitute plain cumin seeds.

Serves 6

¹/₂ *cup oatmeal*

1 cup unbleached all-purpose white flour

¹/₂ *teaspoon sea salt*

5 tablespoons cold unsalted butter, cut into small pieces

1 tablespoon dried chives

1 large egg

About 1 tablespoon ice water

1 cup sun-dried tomatoes

1 cup boiling water

2 tablespoons extra virgin olive oil

1 teaspoon black cumin seeds

6 cups chopped onion

4 cloves garlic, minced

¹/₂ *teaspoon sea salt*

1 tablespoon minced fresh parsley

¹/₂ *tablespoon minced fresh thyme*

Freshly ground black pepper, to taste

¹/₂ *cup Mediterranean black olives, pitted*

Put the oatmeal in a food processor and process until medium fine, 3 minutes. Add the flour, salt, butter, and chives and process for 2 or 3 pulses. Add the egg and water and pulse 3 or 4 times, just to combine. Remove from the processor and, with damp hands, form a ball. Wrap in plastic wrap and refrigerate for 1 hour before rolling out.

Preheat the oven to 400°F.

Roll out the dough into a 12-inch circle and line a 10-inch tart pan with a removable bottom. Trim off any excess dough. Prick the bottom with a fork and bake for 20 minutes, or until the dough is set but not brown. Remove from the oven and set aside.

Place the sun-dried tomatoes in boiling water. Soak for 5 minutes, or until softened. Drain well, reserving the soaking water for another use. Cut the tomatoes into thin strips and set aside.

Heat the oil in a large heavy saucepan over medium heat. Add the cumin and sauté for 1 minute. Add the onions and garlic, lower the heat, and cook, stirring frequently, for 10 minutes, or until the onions are translucent. Add the salt, cover, and cook, stirring as necessary, for 10 minutes, or until the onions are meltingly tender but not browned. Stir in the parsley, thyme, and pepper and remove from heat.

Preheat the oven to 375°F.

Scrape the onion mixture over the tart shell and spread out evenly. Arrange the sun-dried tomatoes and olives in a decorative pattern. Bake for 15 minutes. Let stand for 10 minutes before serving.

Sesame Oat Fillet of Flounder

Oats and sesame seeds make a crunchy coating for any fish. Here a little turmeric, our most potent source of healthful beta carotenes, gives the flounder a golden glow.

Combine the oat flour, sesame seeds, cilantro, rosemary, pepper, turmeric, and salt in a shallow dish. Dredge the fish in the oat mixture, pressing to coat well.

Heat half of the oil in a heavy skillet over medium-high heat until hot. Add half the fish and fry for about 3 minutes on each side, or until golden and crisp. Remove from the pan and drain on paper towels. Repeat with the remaining oil and fish. Serve immediately with fresh lime wedges.

Serves 4

½ cup oat flour (see page 313)

3 tablespoons sesame seeds

1 tablespoon minced fresh cilantro

1 teaspoon minced fresh rosemary

½ teaspoon freshly ground white pepper

¼ teaspoon turmeric

Sea salt, to taste

4 flounder fillets

⅓ cup unrefined sesame oil

4 lime wedges

Better Than Fried Chicken

Serves 4

1 (3 ½ pounds) chicken or assorted
   chicken parts

1 teaspoon ground cinnamon

1 teaspoon freshly grated nutmeg

1 teaspoon ground cumin

2 tablespoons fresh lemon juice

1 tablespoon minced fresh mint

1 teaspoon unsalted butter

1 cup oatmeal

½ cup unbleached all-purpose flour

Sea salt and freshly ground black
   pepper, to taste

You can reduce the fat by removing the chicken skin. The toasty oats and aromatic blend of spices add so much flavor that you won't miss it.

Rinse the chicken and cut it into serving pieces if necessary. Pat dry. Remove the skin, if desired. Place the chicken in a single layer in a shallow dish. Combine the cinnamon, nutmeg, and cumin and set 2 teaspoons of this mixture aside. Combine the remaining spice mixture with the lemon juice and mint. Rub into the chicken and marinate, refrigerated, for at least 1 hour or up to 1 day.

Preheat the oven to 375°F. Butter a baking sheet.

Combine the oatmeal, flour, salt, pepper, and reserved spice blend in a plastic bag. Shake to combine. Place the chicken pieces, one at a time, in the oatmeal mixture. Shake to coat well.

Place the chicken on the baking sheet, leaving space between the pieces. Bake for about 50 minutes, or until chicken is cooked through and golden. Serve warm, at room temperature, or cold.

Steel Cut Oat Pilaf

Steel cut oats make a particularly delicious pilaf since their nutty texture and flavor contrast so nicely with quickly cooked vegetables. It's a welcome change from a prosaic rice pilaf.

Heat the oil in a heavy saucepan over medium heat. Add the oats and sauté until aromatic and lightly browned. Add the garlic, parsley, thyme, and marjoram and sauté for 2 minutes, or until aromatic. Add the stock, onion, celery, carrot, soy sauce, salt and pepper and bring to a boil. Lower the heat, and simmer, covered, for 20 minutes, or until the stock has been absorbed and the oats are just tender. Remove from the heat and let steam, covered, for 10 minutes. Fluff with a fork. Serve a small dish of gomasio alongside the pilaf and let your guests garnish the pilaf to their own taste.

Serves 4 to 6

3 tablespoons extra virgin olive oil

1 cup steel cut oats

2 cloves garlic, minced

1 tablespoon minced fresh parsley

1 teaspoon minced fresh thyme

$^1/_2$ teaspoon minced fresh marjoram

1 $^3/_4$ cups Vegetable Stock (page 364) or Chicken Stock (page 366), hot

1 small onion, finely diced

1 stalk celery with some leaves, minced

1 small carrot, diced

1 tablespoon tamari soy sauce

Sea salt and freshly ground black pepper, to taste

Gomasio (page 361)

Easy Oat Risotto with Piñon

Serves 4 to 6

2 cups steel cut oats

2 tablespoons unsalted butter

¼ cup minced shallots

2 cloves garlic, minced

½ cup piñon (pine nuts)

½ teaspoon sea salt

4 cups Vegetable Stock (page 364) or
    Shiitake Dashi Stock (page 368), hot

2 tablespoons minced fresh parsley

1 tablespoon fresh lemon juice

½ cup grated pecorino

Freshly ground pepper, to taste

I used to call this Irish risotto. But then I served it to Italians, who found its chewy creaminess very reminiscent of the traditional Arborio-based risotto. Decidedly not rice, oat risotto is equally satisfying and easier to prepare since the cut oat groats cook in a speedy twenty minutes.

Put the oats in a saucepan or wok over medium-high heat and toast, stirring constantly, for 2 to 3 minutes, or until aromatic and lightly browned. Set aside.

Melt the butter in a heavy saucepan over medium-high heat. Add the shallots and garlic and sauté for 3 minutes. Stir in the oats, piñon, and salt and sauté for about 5 minutes, or until the oats are glistening. Begin adding the hot stock, ½ cup at a time, stirring constantly, until each ½ cup is absorbed. When the oats have a rich, creamy texture with a bit of bite left, remove from the heat. Stir in the parsley, lemon juice, pecorino, and pepper. Serve hot.

Plum-Peach Crisp

❧

Here's a homey American dish that offers a pie's great taste but with a fraction of the fuss and half the fat. I use whatever seasonal fruits are on hand. I especially like the purple and gold of plums and peaches.

Preheat the oven to 375°F. Butter a 9-inch pie pan.

Scald the plums and peaches in boiling water for about 15 seconds. Pour into a colander, rinse with cold water, and slip off the skins. Cut in half and remove the pits. Place the plums on the bottom of the pie pan. Arrange peach halves over the plums. Combine the maple syrup, 1 tablespoon flour, liqueur, and orange zest in a small bowl. Pour over the fruit.

Mix the oatmeal, flour, Sucanat, and salt in a food processor or bowl. Add the butter. Process or cut in the butter with 2 knives until crumbly. Stir in the pecans. Sprinkle the topping over the fruit. Bake for 35 to 40 minutes, or until the crust is golden. Let cool for 10 minutes, to allow the top to become crisp. Serve warm, garnished with dollops of whipped cream, if desired.

Serves 6

4 ripe Italian prune plums

4 ripe peaches

1/4 cup maple syrup

1 tablespoon unbleached all-purpose flour

1 tablespoon orange liqueur

1 tablespoon finely slivered orange zest

3/4 cup oatmeal

1/2 cup unbleached all-purpose flour

1/2 cup Sucanat or packed light brown sugar

Pinch of sea salt

4 tablespoons (1/2 stick) cold unsalted butter, cut into small pieces

1/2 cup pecans, toasted

Whipped cream (optional)

Classic Oatmeal Cookies

❦

Makes about 24

8 tablespoons (1 stick) unsalted
   butter

¾ cup Sucanat or packed light brown
   sugar

1 large egg

1 ½ teaspoons pure vanilla extract

1 cup whole wheat pastry flour

¾ teaspoon baking powder

1 cup oatmeal

½ teaspoon sea salt

½ teaspoon ground cinnamon

¾ cup currants

¾ cup chopped walnuts

I'm always amazed at the popularity of these old-fashioned cookies. They're very tender and therefore a little more crumbly when warm than the commercial varieties, but this lends to their homespun richness.

Preheat the oven to 350°F.

Cream the butter and Sucanat. Stir in the egg and vanilla. Combine the dry ingredients and stir into the batter. Stir in the currants and nuts. Drop by the spoonful 2 inches apart onto ungreased baking sheets. Bake for 10 to 12 minutes, or until light brown. Cool on wire racks.

VARIATIONS: Substitute rye or kamut flakes for the oatmeal. Substitute shredded unsweetened coconut for the currants.

Scottish Lace Wafers

Here's one of those great classic recipes that is perfection in its utter simplicity. The butter and sugar lightly coat the oat mixture and turn into both chewy butterscotch and a crisp glaze. As the name suggests, the oats form a lacy filigree.

Preheat the oven to 350°F. Butter 2 baking sheets and set aside. Combine the oatmeal, Sucanat, coconut, flour, nutmeg, and salt in a medium bowl. Combine the butter, egg, and vanilla and mix into the dry ingredients. Immediately drop from a teaspoon in rounds, about 2 inches apart, on the baking sheets. Flatten with a fork. Bake for 8 to 10 minutes or until browned. Let cookies cool on the baking sheet for 2 minutes, to become firm. Remove to a wire rack and cool.

Makes about 24

1 ¼ cups oatmeal

½ cup Sucanat or packed light brown sugar

¼ cup unsweetened shredded coconut

1 tablespoon unbleached all-purpose flour or barley flour (see page 212)

½ teaspoon grated nutmeg or ground mace

¼ teaspoon sea salt

4 tablespoons (½ stick) unsalted butter, melted

1 large egg, beaten

¾ teaspoon pure vanilla extract

Oat and Seed Candy Bar

Makes 15 bars

2 cups oatmeal

½ cup raw pumpkin seeds

½ cup raw sunflower seeds

2 tablespoons chia or flax seeds

½ cup honey or maple syrup

2 tablespoons unsalted butter or tahini

This sweet, chewy, and satisfying energy bar is great for backpacking. It can be made with other flakes, such as rye or kamut, or any other seed or nut you like.

Preheat the oven to 325°F. Butter an 8-inch square baking pan.

Spread the oatmeal and seeds on a baking sheet. Bake for 20 minutes, stirring twice to assure uniform toasting. Transfer to a medium bowl. Set aside.

Pour the honey into a small saucepan and bring to a boil. Reduce the heat to low and simmer for 7 minutes, or until the honey reaches 275°F. on a candy thermometer. (At first the honey will expand and bubble up the sides of the pot. When it starts to condense and thicken it is ready.) Stir in the butter. Pour the hot syrup over the oat mixture, stirring to combine evenly. Transfer the mixture to the baking pan. Let cool for 2 minutes, then press firmly with buttered or lightly moistened hands. Let cool for 10 minutes more. Use a moistened knife to cut into 2 × 1 ½-inch bars. Tightly wrap in plastic wrap or wax paper and store in a cool dry spot.

Sharp Cheddar
Bannock with Fennel Seeds

❦

A bannock is a round Scottish oatcake cooked on a griddle. In a climate too cold and damp for wheat, this simple flatbread was the daily bread for many people. Cheese and fennel turn this bannock into something quite different from the traditional all-grain biscuit. The bits of cheese brown and provide a beautiful color and delicious flavor while the oats impart a pleasant chewiness. My daughter Elizabeth calls the baked ones "no-potato hash browns" and when I make them into "tortillas" (see variation) she packs them for school lunch.

Preheat the oven to 400°F. Lightly grease a baking sheet. Place 1 cup of the oatmeal in a food processor and process for about 2 minutes, or long enough to make a coarse meal. Add the remaining oatmeal, the cheese, butter, salt, and fennel seeds and pulse 4 to 5 times to mix. Add the water and pulse 3 or 4 times to form a dough. Remove from the processor and knead on a lightly floured surface. Roll out ¼ inch thick.

Cut circles with a 2½-inch round cookie cutter. Place on the baking sheet. Bake for 20 minutes, or until golden. Cool on a wire rack.

VARIATION: Roll the dough into ten 1½-inch balls and cook on the stovetop in a hot well-seasoned skillet or griddle for about 3 minutes on each side, or until golden. Or, following manufacturer's directions, shape and cook in an electric tortilla cooker.

Makes 16

2 cups oatmeal

1 cup grated sharp white Cheddar

1 tablespoon unsalted butter, softened

¼ teaspoon sea salt

2 teaspoons fennel seeds

⅓ cup water

Oat Farls

(page 358)

Makes 8

1 cup oatmeal

¹/₄ cup whole wheat flour

1 tablespoon unsalted butter, softened

¹/₄ teaspoon sea salt

¹/₂ cup boiling water

Farls are what Irish and Scottish folk call their traditional oat flatbreads, which are cut into four wedges or "farls." Farls are good with soup, yet when served with butter and jam, they make a homey dessert. This recipe, typical of the Scottish lowlands, uses wheat and rolled oats. In the northern highlands, where wheat doesn't grow, an all-oat farl was traditional.

Process the oatmeal in a food processor for about 1 minute, or just long enough to make a coarse meal. Add the whole wheat flour, butter, and sea salt and process for 5 seconds. With the machine running, add boiling water and process for 2 or 3 seconds more. With moistened hands, form a ball. Expect a sticky dough. Divide the dough in half and, between moistened hands, press into 2 circles 4 inches in diameter.

Heat a skillet over medium heat until hot. Add a dough round. With moistened fingers, immediately flatten the round until it is about 6 inches in diameter. Cut each round into quarters and cook for about 4 minutes on each side, or until the farl is lightly browned and crisp and the edges have begun to curl. Repeat with the remaining round.

VARIATIONS: Add 1 teaspoon Garam Masala (page 358) or curry powder with the whole wheat flour.

For a wheatfree farl, increase the amount of oatmeal to 1¹/₄ cups and reduce it to a finer meal in the food processor.

Substitute quinoa, barley, or oat flour for the wheat flour.

Orange and
Coconut Drop Biscuits

❧

These not-too-sweet biscuits have a rustic enough texture for them to fit into any menu. And unlike most quick breads, these biscuits remain flavorful and moist the next day because of the oats and coconut. If possible, grind cardamom fresh to fully appreciate how its lemony flavor marries well with the coconut, orange, and oats.

Preheat the oven to 425°F. Butter a baking sheet. Sift the flour, baking powder, baking soda, Sucanat, cardamom, and salt into a bowl. Rub in butter to make a meal. Stir in the oatmeal and coconut. In a separate bowl, lightly beat the egg and stir in the buttermilk and orange zest. Quickly combine with the dry ingredients to form a soft, sticky dough. Do not overmix. Drop the dough, by the rounded tablespoon, onto the baking sheet. Place on the middle shelf of the oven and bake for 12 to 15 minutes, or until pale golden. Remove from oven and serve hot with butter and/or honey.

VARIATIONS: Substitute with barley flour for all or some of the flour.
Substitute Clabbered Soy Milk (page 371) for the buttermilk.

Makes 12

1 ½ cups unbleached all-purpose flour or whole wheat pastry flour

1 teaspoon baking powder

¼ teaspoon baking soda

3 tablespoons Sucanat or light brown sugar

1 teaspoon ground cardamom

½ teaspoon sea salt

3 tablespoons unsalted butter, softened

¾ cup oatmeal

¾ cup unsweetened shredded coconut

1 large egg

½ cup buttermilk

2 teaspoons freshly grated orange zest

Oat Groat Pancakes

✦

Makes about 15

²/₃ cup oat groats

¹/₃ cup buckwheat groats, toasted

1 ¹/₄ cups milk or soy milk

3 large eggs

2 tablespoons unsalted butter, melted

¹/₄ teaspoon sea salt

2 tablespoons Sucanat or light brown sugar

1 teaspoon baking powder

¹/₂ teaspoon grated nutmeg

Many people have asked me for this no-fuss recipe. It makes the most moist, tender, and flavorful pancake imaginable. I learned the secret, soaking the whole grains overnight, from Diana Scesny Greene. When soaked, grain flavors blossom and deepen—and not just a little. What's more, soaked grains are easier to assimilate, making these pancakes filling and substantial but not at all heavy. I like this ratio of oats to buckwheat, but feel free to experiment with your own ratio. You can also substitute millet for the buckwheat.

Combine the oats, buckwheat, and milk in a blender container. Cover and let soak refrigerated overnight or for 8 hours. Blend until smooth. Add the remaining ingredients and process to combine. Preheat a griddle. Drop the batter by the ladleful onto the griddle and bake for about 2 minutes on each side, or until golden. Serve hot with the usual pancake accompaniments.

Granola

For those hooked on cold breakfast cereals, the advantage of granola or muesli (unroasted granola) is that the whole grain helps regulate blood sugar and sustain energy through the morning so one can effortlessly bypass a mid-morning snack.

I learned this sweetening trick from food writer Dana Jacobi: For clumpy granola, use all honey; for a less moist and less intensely sweet granola, use half maple syrup and half honey. You can add and subtract different dried fruits, nuts, and seeds, just as you might add or subtract flowers when arranging a floral bouquet. I think granola tastes best with moist dried fruits such as dates, prunes, and raisins.

This is one of the few baked foods in which I use a richly flavored unrefined vegetable oil. Heating at temperatures above 325°F. denatures the delicate unsaturated fatty acids in vegetable oils. When baking at higher temperatures, I use butter since its saturated fatty acids are more stable.

Serve the granola with milk for breakfast or snacks or sprinkle it on yogurt or hot breakfast cereal. Use it as a base for pie crusts and cookies.

Makes 6 cups

1 1/2 cups nutmeats, such as almonds, walnuts, pecans, cashews, or hazelnuts, or a combination

3 cups rolled oats

1/2 cup sunflower seeds

1/2 cup unsweetened shredded coconut

1/4 cup honey

1/4 cup maple syrup

1/4 cup unrefined sesame oil

1/2 teaspoon sea salt

1 teaspoon pure vanilla extract

1/2 teaspoon ground cinnamon

1/2 teaspoon ground cardamom

1 cup chopped dried fruit, such as prunes, raisins, dates, peaches, nectarines, or apples, or a combination

Preheat the oven to 320°F.

Break or cut the nuts into halves. Combine the nuts, oats, sunflower seeds, and coconut in a bowl. Mix together the honey, maple syrup, oil, sea salt, vanilla, cinnamon, and cardamom. Pour over the grain mixture, stirring to combine. Spread the mixture out on a 17 × 11-inch jelly-roll pan and bake for 25 to 30 minutes. After 7 minutes, stir and spread the mixture out again in an even layer. Repeat after 7 minutes. Stir every 5 minutes, or until the oats are crisp and brown, but not burned. Remove from the oven and pour into a large wooden bowl or onto another jelly-roll pan to stop the cooking. Add the dried fruits. Let cool thoroughly. Store in an airtight container in a cool dry spot.

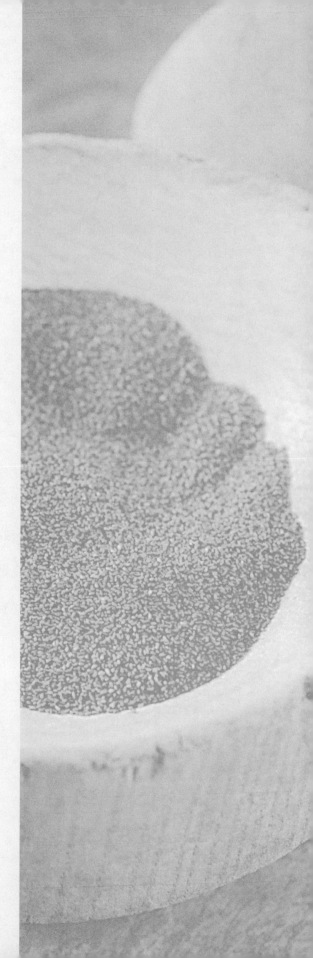

NATIVE AFRICAN GRAINS

Sorghum

Tef

Sorghum

SORGHUM IS AS DELICIOUS a grain as I have ever eaten. Nutty sweet with a pleasing, ricelike texture, it would be one of my staples, if only it were readily available. Not available? What about the miles and miles of sorghum one passes when driving through the midwestern United States? The bulk of the domestic crop is grown for livestock feed and the little remaining is designated for sorghum molasses production; neither of those varieties work well as a table grain. How unfortunate that sorghum for people (*Sorghum bicolor*) is not grown in this country.

Sorghum is a sturdy and genetically diverse member of the grass family that ranks fifth in the world's major cereal crop production. Initially it was probably cultivated in central Africa with subsequent distribution throughout the world. Since it thrives where temperatures soar and rain rarely falls, since both people and animals eat it, and since its yields per acre are generous, it is a precious commodity. Most sorghum is consumed in the area where it is grown, making it a critical food source for many people in the arid regions of Africa and India.

Throughout the world, sorghum is generally made into porridge, flatbread, beverages, and snack foods. There are literally hundreds of names for and variations of the same product, depending on where it is made. In many regions of Africa, sorghum is also eaten as a fresh vegetable much as we eat corn on the cob in the United States.

Traditional milling of sorghum is done by hand with a wooden mortar and pestle. In Africa, it can take two women about one and a half hours to mill the daily portion of sorghum for a family of four. The nutritional profile of sorghum differs from variety to variety, but it is similar to maize, though a little higher in protein.

Sorghum
Selection and Storage

I've seen sorghum for sale in markets specializing in international foods, but, quite frankly, it was such poor quality that I would not purchase it. I hope you have better luck than I. Until table sorghum is available for sale in the United States, it can be easily grown in a home garden.

Store sorghum airtight in a cool, dark, and dry place.

Sorghum Flour

Sorghum flour can be milled in a home grain mill or in a coffee or spice grinder. Use it in combination with wheat in flatbreads and other baked goods. Store airtight in the freezer for up to 4 months.

Steamed Sorghum

I sometimes use sorghum as an alternative to rice or quinoa in pilafs, soups, and casseroles. It is also delicious unto itself.

Heat a saucepan or wok over medium-high heat until warm. Add the sorghum and toast, stirring constantly, for about 4 minutes, or until the sorghum is lightly aromatic and a shade darker. Pour into a strainer and rinse under running water. Put in a medium saucepan, add the water, and let soak for 1 hour or up to 8 hours, if desired. Add the salt and bring to a boil. Reduce the heat and simmer, covered, for 40 minutes, or until the water is absorbed. Remove from the heat and let steam for 5 to 10 minutes. Serve warm, drizzled with olive oil, if desired.

Makes 3 cups

1 cup sorghum

2 cups water

Sea salt, to taste

1 tablespoon extra virgin olive oil (optional)

Tef

IN THE RUGGED WINDSWEPT Simien mountains at the source of the Blue Nile grows a tiny cereal grain, tef (*Eragrostis abyssinica*). The fierce and proud Ethiopians attribute their prowess to tef. Other grains that are easier to cultivate and harvest thrive in Abyssinia, but for millennia tef has remained the premier crop. Tasting almost like hazelnuts, tef is inextricably intertwined with the cultural identity of the people who inhabit these mountains.

Tef is tiny. One hundred fifty grains weigh as much as a single kernel of wheat. One grain is twice the size of the period ending this sentence. As is typical of other heirloom plants, tef is not monochromatic and a seed can be white, red-purple, or brown. It is a superb garden ornamental with silvery stocks and brightly colored heads.

Tef was virtually unknown outside its land of origin until this century. This nutritionally superior grain was a well-kept agricultural secret for several reasons. For one, it is a labor-intensive crop. Its small size makes harvest difficult, and at maturity the seeds fall rather than remain on the stalk. The Amharic word *tef* means "lost" because it is easily lost in the field and during handling. Also, as the seeds mature, the thin stalks do not support their weight, and the crop lies down in random piles. This is called lodging. When other cereals lodge, the crop is lost because the bent stalks impede nutrient flow and prevent ripening. A heaped crop also renders conventional harvesting impossible. Tef, however, grows and matures in lodged piles.

The other reason that tef remained secret concerns the Abyssinians themselves. Until late in the nineteenth century, these people were culturally isolated. At the time of King Haile Selassie's overthrow in 1974, they accepted as historical fact that their dynasty had divine origins and an unbroken three-thousand-year history. This gave the Ethiopians a sense of superiority, which made them resistant to cultural exchange with others. Therefore, tef, like other cultural artifacts, was not traded with others. Unlike other African peoples, they are predominantly Coptic Christians. This, plus the rugged highland geography, helped ensure their isolation.

The Ethiopian government now discourages tef cultivation. Aid organizations provide high-yield seed of other crops which have economic value in the world market. Subsidized wheat makes regional crops costly. This undermines the local culture and economy by forcing subsistence farmers into the agribusiness system, effectively destroying their independence and self-sufficiency. These destructive political practices have caused the irretrievable loss of many valuable tef varieties as well.

Thanks to the efforts of one person, some strains of this ancient grain have been saved. Wayne Carlson, a personable native Californian, is singularly responsible for introducing tef into the United States. He also gives tef seed stock to displaced Ethiopians who have lost their precious seed supply. In 1973 Carlson traveled to rural Ethiopia on a medical research project. "I was living in a small village and eating the available food. I soon developed a taste for injera [tef flatbread] and the spicy Ethiopian foods," Carlson told me. "I learned some Amharic, and I got to know the farmers, and their crops." Later Carlson worked for the Red Cross distributing animal feed–grade surplus corn and wheat to starving Ethiopians. He was glad to be handing out calories, but he wished that it could have been tef. "I dreamed of introducing tef to the United States and of how this would also help the Ethiopians." Back in the States, Carlson and his wife, Elizabeth, have been able to realize this dream from their Caldwell, Idaho, farm.

Tef
Selection and Storage

Tef is available in natural foods stores, Ethiopian markets, or directly from Wayne Carlson (see page 378). Brown tef, the most commonly available variety in the United States, is also the most flavorful. Red and ivory varieties are also available.

Store tef in a cool dark place for 1 year or more.

Tef Flour

Tef grains are too small to be ground in a blender or a small grinder. Use a flour mill or purchase tef flour from your natural foods store. Refrigerate or freeze tef flour for up to 4 months.

Steamed Tef

❧

I've found no historical precedent for using tef whole rather than as flour, but that doesn't stop me from cooking whole tef. I wouldn't serve it to people with conventional palates, who might not know what to make of its minuscule size, but grain connoisseurs love its potent flavor.

Toast the tef in a hot wok or skillet, stirring quickly, for 2 minutes, or until the sound of popping grains is at its height. Pour the tef into a saucepan with boiling liquid, reduce the heat to a simmer, and cook, covered, for 7 minutes, or until the liquid is absorbed. Remove from the heat and let stand for 5 minutes. Serve with gomasio.

Serves 2

1 cup tef
1 cup boiling water or stock
Pinch of sea salt
Gomasio (page 361)

Cream of Tef Breakfast Cereal

‡

Serves 2

¾ cup tef flour

2 cups water

Pinch of sea salt

Begin your day with this energizing hot cereal. It is similar in texture to Cream of Wheat but has a rich, nutty flavor and a beautiful chocolate color. Serve it with maple syrup and milk or soy milk.

Put the tef in a saucepan or wok over medium heat. Toast, stirring constantly, for 2 to 3 minutes, or until it emits a fragrant aroma. Transfer to a small saucepan and stir in water and salt. Bring to a boil, stirring constantly. Reduce the heat and simmer, covered, for 5 minutes, stirring occasionally to prevent sticking. Serve hot.

Corn Quiche in a Tef Crust

✿

Tef's chocolate-colored crust gives dramatic flair to this sunny-colored quiche. The crust holds together easily and slices neatly. While not flaky, it is richly flavored with a light dry texture.

Preheat the oven to 350°F.

Put the tef and whole wheat pastry flours and salt in a food processor and pulse once or twice to mix. Cut the butter into chunks. Add to the flour mixture and pulse to form a crumbly meal. Season water with Tabasco and pulse into flour mixture to make a pliable dough. With your hands, form dough into a flat disk. Let rest for 10 to 15 minutes, no longer. Roll out between 2 sheets of wax paper to an 11-inch circle. Line a 9-inch pie plate.

Combine the corn and milk in a blender and blend until smooth. Add the eggs, more Tabasco, and more salt and blend just to mix. Sprinkle all but 2 tablespoons of cheese on the pie crust. Pour in the corn mixture. Sprinkle scallions, green bell pepper, and remaining cheese over surface. Cut tomatoes into thin slices and arrange around the edge of the filling. Bake for 35 minutes, or until a knife inserted in the center comes out clean.

VARIATIONS: Substitute 2 tablespoons chopped fresh basil or tarragon for the scallions or bell pepper.

Substitute Gouda, Lappi, Monterey Jack, or your favorite cheese for the Swiss.

Serves 6

¾ cup tef flour

¾ cup whole wheat pastry or unbleached all-purpose flour

¼ teaspoon sea salt

4 tablespoons (½ stick) unsalted butter

¼ cup water

Tabasco Sauce, to taste

2 cups fresh corn kernels

1 cup milk or soy milk

4 large eggs

¼ teaspoon sea salt

½ cup shredded Swiss cheese

2 scallions, chopped

½ cup minced green bell pepper

2 cherry tomatoes

Traditional Ethiopian Injera

✣

Makes four 6-inch breads

2 cups tef flour

4 cups spring water

1 teaspoon yeast (optional)

Injera is a flatbread with a unique sour flavor and spongy texture. The best injera is made of tef. When you order injera in an Ethiopian restaurant, be sure to ask for tef injera; otherwise you're apt to be served a less delicious one made of wheat and millet. The national food of Ethiopia, this large flatbread is used as a plate with other foods placed on top. Another injera is served on the side and torn into pieces to scoop up the food. The bread is served cold accompanied with spicy-hot bean, vegetable, and meat dishes.

The traditional way of making injera requires starting the mixture three days in advance, but even so it remains an easy-to-make bread with an incomparable flavor and light texture. If you grind your flour fresh, omit the yeast. Tef's symbiotic yeast provides ample leavening.

Combine the flour, 3 cups of the water, and the yeast, if using, in a 2-quart ceramic or glass bowl. Cover with a bamboo sushi mat or a clean cloth. Leave out on the counter for 2 days in a warm kitchen or 3 days in a cool kitchen, or until the sponge has a strong and distinctively sour aroma. Water will rise to the top. Slowly and carefully pour off this surface water.

Bring 1 cup of spring water to a boil in a small saucepan. Stir ½ cup of the tef mixture into the boiling water. Reduce the heat to medium and cook, stirring, for 1 to 2 minutes, or until the mixture thickens slightly and is smooth. Remove from the heat and let cool to room temperature. Stir this mixture into the soured batter. Add more water, if necessary, to make a thin batter as for pancakes. Cover and let rest for 1 or 2 hours or until the mixture rises.

Heat a 9-inch crêpe pan or skillet that has a tight-fitting lid over high heat until a drop of water bounces on the pan's surface. If using an electric skillet, heat to 420°F. Slowly pour ⅓ cup of the batter into the pan in a thin stream, moving in a spiral from the outer edge toward the center of the pan. Then tilt the pan so the batter can flow over and cover any gaps. Cover and cook over medium-low heat for 2 to 3 minutes, or until the edges of the injera begin to curl away from the pan. Remove immediately and place on a clean cloth to cool. When cooled, wrap to keep moist. Stir the batter well, then cook the remaining breads in the same way.

Note: The temperature and humidity of your kitchen play a role in fermentation time. If after combining the cooked and raw batters, you will not be able to cook the breads within 2 hours, refrigerate the batter for up to 4 hours, or until it rises. If you are unable to cook the batter when it's ready, stir in $1/2$ teaspoon sea salt and refrigerate the batter for up to 24 hours.

Quick Injera

❧

Makes four 6-inch breads

1 cup tef flour

2 cups spring water

2 tablespoons sourdough starter (see page 272)

¼ teaspoon sea salt

Here's an overnight injera. It's comparable to the three-day injera but less spongy and light. This sourdough method is how Wayne and Elizabeth Carlson, the folks who introduced tef to the United States, make their flatbreads.

Mix the tef flour, water, and sourdough starter. Cover loosely and let stand at room temperature for 8 hours, or until the batter bulges upward due to fermentation. The liquid that rises to the batter's surface will prevent the batter from drying out. Slowly pour off surface liquid. Stir in the salt.

Heat a 9-inch crêpe pan or skillet that has a tight-fitting lid over high heat until a drop of water bounces on the pan's surface. If using an electric skillet, heat to 420°F. Slowly pour ⅓ cup of the batter into the pan in a thin stream, moving in a spiral from the edge toward the center of the pan. Then tilt the pan so the batter can flow over and cover any gaps. Cover and cook over medium-low heat for 2 to 3 minutes, or until the edges of the injera begin to curl away from the pan. Remove immediately and place on a clean cloth to cool. When cooled, wrap to keep moist. Stir the batter well, then cook the remaining breads in the same way.

VARIATION: Bake the batter in a waffle iron.

Note: If you are unable to cook the batter when it is ready, pour off any surface liquid and refrigerate the batter for up to 24 hours.

Great Gingerbread

Tef takes gingerbread to new heights. Whereas molasses gives conventional gingerbread its chocolate color and strong flavor, tef colors the cake and lets the pungent flavor of fresh ginger really sparkle. I like to serve it with a bit of vanilla ice cream and sliced peaches, but it is also delicious plain.

Preheat the oven to 425°F. Grease a 9-inch square cake pan. Sift the dry ingredients together. Whisk together the egg, melted butter, milk, and ginger juice. Combine with the dry ingredients in a few rapid strokes. Pour the batter into the pan. Bake for 50 minutes, or until a toothpick inserted into the center comes out clean. Serve hot or cold.

VARIATION: To bake on top of the stove, pour the batter into a greased and heated 8 ^{1}/$_2$ -inch skillet. Place on a Flame Tamer on low heat and cook for 30 minutes, or until the cake pulls away from the sides of the pan and a toothpick inserted in the center comes out clean.

Serves 9

1 ^{1}/$_4$ cups tef flour

^{3}/$_4$ cup whole wheat pastry flour

1 teaspoon baking powder

^{1}/$_2$ cup Sucanat or packed light brown sugar

1 teaspoon ground cinnamon

^{1}/$_2$ teaspoon sea salt

^{1}/$_2$ teaspoon grated nutmeg

^{1}/$_2$ teaspoon ground allspice

^{1}/$_8$ teaspoon ground cloves

1 egg

4 tablespoons (^{1}/$_2$ stick) unsalted butter, melted

1 cup milk or soy milk

2 teaspoons Ginger Juice (page 360)

Tef Waffles

Makes 6 waffles

2 cups tef flour

1 teaspoon baking powder

½ teaspoon ground cinnamon

¼ teaspoon sea salt

2 large eggs, beaten

3 tablespoons unsalted butter, melted

2 cups milk or soy milk

For my family, tef was made for waffles. Almost chocolate in color, this mellow waffle has a satisfying nutty flavor. One taste and you may never again settle for a wheat waffle.

Sift the flour, baking powder, cinnamon, and salt into a mixing bowl. With a few quick strokes, stir in the eggs, butter, and milk. Pour into a heated waffle iron and cook according to manufacturer's directions. Serve with your choice of toppings.

Basics

How to Roast Chilies and Peppers

❧

Indian summer in the Southwest is chili roasting time and the smoky aroma of roasting chilies pervades the air. It comes from backyards, where many people fire up the grill and do it themselves, and from roadside stands and even supermarket lots, where thirty-five pounds at a clip are roasted over large gas-fired lattice barrels, a contraption that has a grid rotating over the fire so that the chilies tumble as they roast. People often buy several bags full and freeze them.

To roast chilies, place them over coals or a gas burner or under the broiler. Roast, turning frequently, for about 10 minutes, or until the skin is blistered and blackened all over. Place in a bowl, cover, and let steam for 10 to 15 minutes. When the skin has loosened and the chilies are cool enough to handle, push and/or rub skin off. Pull out the core. Cut in half and remove the membranes and seeds.

To freeze roasted chilies, pack cooled whole unpeeled chilies in a freezer bag and freeze. Break off one or two from the frozen clump as needed. Thaw by briefly soaking the chilies in warm water or by letting them stand at room temperature for 15 minutes or so. Remove the skin, core, seeds, and membranes and cut as desired.

Coconut Milk

❧

Makes about 3 cups

1 whole coconut

Canned organic coconut milk is available in natural foods stores. If you buy it at a market carrying Asian, Indian, or Caribbean foodstuffs, make sure that you get unsweetened coconut milk, not coconut cream. Of course, the best is what you make at home.

Pierce 2 of the 3 black "eyes" of a coconut. Enlarge 1 hole to allow the liquid to pour out easily. The other hole will let the air circulate. Drain the liquid into a container. Chill and serve the coconut water as a refreshing beverage.

Place the coconut on a cement walk or other hard surface. Hit it with a hammer to crack it open and to break it into 6 to 10 pieces. Using a table knife or screwdriver, pry the white nut meat away from the shell. Peel off and discard the brown skin.

Grate the coconut meat in a food processor. Measure and transfer to a bowl. For every packed cup of grated coconut, add 1 cup boiling water. Let the mixture rest for 20 to 30 minutes. Pour into a blender and puree.

Strain through a double layer of cheesecloth, twisting and squeezing out as much milk as possible. (May be stored, covered, in the refrigerator for up to 5 days.)

Crème Fraîche

Crème fraîche can be used as a dessert topping, with fresh fruits and vegetables, and in sauces and soups. It is easy to make and is also available, though expensive, in some natural foods stores and specialty food markets.

Combine the cream and buttermilk in a glass jar with a lid. Cover tightly and shake for 1 minute. Let stand at room temperature for 8 hours, or until very thick. (May be stored, covered, in the refrigerator for up to 6 weeks.)

Makes 2 cups

2 cups heavy cream
2 tablespoons buttermilk

Dilled Vegetable Pickles

❧

*I always have some kind of pickle on hand, partly because they aid in the diges-
tion of whole grains. Anyone tasting these pickles assumes they are made with
a vinegar solution, but it is just a simple brine of the kind our grandmothers
used to use to make dill pickles. When I have cucumbers from the garden, I
quadruple this recipe and pickle them in gallon jars. Unfortunately, waxed
supermarket cucumbers cannot be pickled, so the rest of the year I use an
assortment of other vegetables (though not potatoes, burdock, or green beans).*

Makes 4 cups

2 cups water

1 ½ tablespoons sea salt

About 4 cups firm vegetables, such as
   carrots, broccoli, cauliflower, turnips,
   rutabaga, daikon, radishes (see Note)

1 small onion, sliced

1 tablespoon dillseed

1 clove garlic

1 bay leaf

Black peppercorns, to taste

Crushed red pepper flakes, to taste

Note: For all the vegetables to pickle in the
same length of time, leave red radishes
whole, cut a medium turnip into 8 wedges,
cut a medium carrot into 4 long diagonal
pieces, and cut broccoli florets into about
the same size. Pickle small summer
squash, such as zucchini, or Kirby cucumbers whole. Home gardeners may also
pickle the following: peeled young lettuce
stalks, purslane stems, cauliflower stalks,
and pods of turnip and nasturtium seeds.

Combine the water and salt in a saucepan over high heat and
bring to a boil. Remove from heat and let cool.

Cut the vegetables into chunks. Put in a widemouthed
quart jar. Add the onion, dill seed, garlic, bay leaf, peppercorns, and
red pepper flakes. Cover with cooled brine. Place a weight, such as a
rock or a small water-filled jar, on the vegetables to keep them submerged. Place the quart jar on a plate to catch any overflow that takes
place as the the weight sinks when the vegetables ferment. Pickling
takes from 3 to 5 days, depending on room temperature, and the density and size of the vegetables. Remove the weight, wash the sides of
the jar, cover, and refrigerate when the color has changed, the pickles
look cooked, and they have enough tang to suit your taste. (May be
stored, covered, in the refrigerator for up to 4 weeks.)

Flavored Butters

Flavored butter adds zest to grilled vegetables or roast poultry and quickly changes the taste of a piece of toast or a fresh muffin. You can make it from almost anything. The master recipe is for anchovy butter; see the variations at the end of the recipe for herb butter, strawberry butter, and chocolate-pecan butter.

Combine the softened butter with the other ingredients. Beat with a wooden spoon until blended. Or process in a food processor. Cover and let stand for 30 minutes to allow flavors to incorporate. Serve at room temperature or chill slightly, form into logs, wrap in plastic wrap, and refrigerate until firm. Cut into pats, if desired. (May be stored in the refrigerator for several days or in the freezer for 2 months.)

VARIATIONS: For herb butter, use 1 tablespoon *each* minced fresh parsley, chives, and tarragon and 1 teaspoon Dijon mustard.

For strawberry butter, use ¼ cup fresh strawberry puree, 1 tablespoon honey, and ½ teaspoon freshly grated orange zest.

For chocolate pecan butter, use ¼ cup chopped toasted pecans, 1 ounce bittersweet chocolate, melted, and 1 teaspoon Sucanat or light brown sugar.

Makes about 1 cup

12 tablespoons (1 ½ sticks) unsalted butter, softened

4 anchovy fillets, minced

1 tablespoon capers, rinsed, drained, and minced

1 teaspoon fresh lemon juice

1 teaspoon minced chives

Garam Masala

✦

Garam Masala imbues any dish with the aromas of Indian cuisine. Valued in ayurvedic medicine, it also helps generate internal body heat and thus aids digestion. The blend is usually added toward the end of cooking, but it may also be used as a table condiment or as a popcorn seasoning.

Makes about 1 1/2 cups

1 cup cumin seeds

1/2 cup coriander seeds

1/4 cup fennel seeds

1 cinnamon stick (3 inches), broken into pieces

2 tablespoons black cardamom seeds

2 tablespoons black peppercorns

2 tablespoons whole cloves

Toast the spices in a heavy skillet over low heat, stirring occasionally, for 15 minutes, or until they begin to release their aroma. Cool thoroughly. Transfer the spices to a coffee mill ,or spice grinder and grind to a fine powder. Sift through a fine sieve. (May be stored in a tightly covered container in a cool, dark spot for up to 6 months.)

VARIATION: Add one or more of the following ingredients, to taste: dried whole chili, mace, mustard seeds, fenugreek, or sesame seeds.

Ghee

❦

Ghee is just clarified butter, but it has a heavenly aroma and a caramel-like flavor. Making ghee is easy—the only tricky part is to remove it from the heat at the proper time. Commercial ghee is exorbitantly expensive and may have been cut with an inexpensive refined oil. It is also frequently rancid. Take a few minutes and make your own. And do use organic butter—it's most delicious and healthful.

Put the butter in a medium saucepan over medium-high heat and bring to a boil. Reduce the heat to maintain a soft, rolling boil. As it boils, the butter will foam, crackle, and bubble. After 10 to 15 minutes, when the bubbling and foaming almost cease and the sound changes to a sizzling frying-oil sound, it is done. Immediately remove from the heat or the ghee might burn. (If it burns, it will begin to foam again and turn brown instead of golden.) Cool slightly. Pour through a dampened piece of cheesecloth or a fine metal strainer into a glass or ceramic container. The sediment in the bottom of the pan may be used creatively in or on any food. (May be stored, covered, at room temperature for 4 or more months.)

Make ³/₄ cup

¹/₂ pound (2 sticks) unsalted, cultured organic butter

Note: Ghee can be made only from unsalted, cultured butter. To make cultured butter, sweet cream is allowed to ripen for several days before being churned into butter.

Ginger Juice

❦

I wouldn't be without a piece of fresh ginger in my refrigerator, and I often use the juice for its pungent fragrance and slightly sweet, hot taste. When buying ginger, pick a piece that is plump and thin skinned. Store it with a paper towel in a tightly sealed plastic bag. Replace the towel as it becomes moist.

Makes 1 teaspoon

2 tablespoons finely grated fresh ginger

Place the grated ginger in the palm of your hand and squeeze to extract its juice.

Note: An old piece of ginger or coarsely grated ginger will yield less juice.

Gomasio

❧

This lightly salted condiment is sprinkled over whole grains to provide savor. Ready-made gomasio is often stale and can't compare in flavor to the home-made. I always add a toasted sea vegetable for the flavor and extra nutrients.

An old salt cellar would make a nice container, but it should be pretty enough to leave on the table. Saltshakers don't work because the holes are too small.

I keep gomasio in a beautiful little stone bowl that my mother gave to me. I'm still waiting to find a tiny silver spoon that will fit inside the bowl. In the meantime, the only spoon that fits is a tiny pink plastic one used to sample ice cream.

P reheat the oven to 350°F.
 Place the dulse on a baking sheet and bake for 10 minutes, or until it starts to brown and gives off an aroma. Let cool. Place in a blender and blend for 15 seconds, or until nearly pulverized.

Wash the sesame seeds and drain well. Place in a saucepan or wok over medium-high heat and cook, stirring constantly, until the seeds start to pop, 2 to 4 minutes. Reduce the heat and continue to stir and toast for another minute, or just until the seeds turn a shade darker. Let cool. Add the seeds and salt to the ground dulse and grind in several on-off pulses. Stop grinding when about 80 percent of the seeds are ground, being careful to not grind into a paste. Cool thoroughly. Place in a small covered container. (May be stored, covered, at room temperature for 3 to 4 months.)

Makes about 1 cup

¹/₄ ounce dulse or wakame (see Note)

³/₄ cup whole sesame seeds (not hulled)

1 tablespoon sea salt

Note: Dulse and wakame are available in Asian markets and natural foods stores. You may replace the seaweed with an equal volume of ground toasted cumin, fennel, cardamom, or any spice that you favor.

Sauerkraut

❦

Makes about 3 1/2 cups

*1 large head cabbage, green or
  purple*

1 tablespoon sea salt

1 tablespoon caraway seeds (optional)

1 to 2 cloves garlic (optional)

My homemade sauerkraut has a delicious refreshing taste. It's a completely different experience from the overly salted, pasteurized sauerkraut from the supermarket. I often make a batch of purple and a batch of green kraut. Having two colors opens up lots of serving options.

Remove any coarse or dry outer cabbage leaves. Cut the cabbage lengthwise into sections. Grate on the small holes of a hand grater or with the small grater blade of a food processor. Mix the cabbage with the salt and caraway seeds and garlic, if using. Pack firmly in a widemouthed quart jar, filling it almost to the brim.

Use a pint jar small enough to fit inside the wide-mouth jar as a weight. Fill the small jar with water and cover tightly. Place on top of the grated cabbage. Set the jars on a plate to collect any overflow that might occur. A brine will form and rise to the surface within 24 hours. The water-filled jar will keep the cabbage submerged in the brine.

The kraut will be ready in 3 to 5 days, or when it has a pleasant and tangy fermented flavor and each piece is translucent rather than opaque. Remove the small jar. Wash the sides of the widemouthed jar and cover. (May be stored, tightly covered, in the refrigerator, for 3 to 4 weeks.)

Note: One-quarter-inch grater holes are ideal. Larger cabbage shreds yield inconsistent results with this pickling technique.

Miso-Walnut Topping

Place all the ingredients in a food processor and process until chunky.

1 cup walnuts, roasted and cooled

1 tablespoon amber-colored miso

½ teaspoon rice wine vinegar

1 teaspoon mirin or sweet wine

Vegetable Stock

❦

Makes about 5 cups

2 onions

3 carrots, scrubbed

7 sprigs of parsley

½ cup dried white beans

2 stalks celery or fennel, washed and
  rinsed

2 bay leaves

3 dried shiitake mushrooms

1 (2 to 4 inches) of strip kombu

8 sprigs of fresh thyme

Assorted vegetable trimmings and
  scraps 8 cups water

Rather than composting good vegetable trimmings and scraps, I pop them into a bag in the freezer. When the bag is full, I use the vegetables to make a rich stock. As a rule, I avoid freezing foods because it diminishes their flavor and nutritional value, but vegetable scraps for stock are an exception. Some of the scraps that I save for stock include: onion skins (just a few to give it a golden color; too many make it bitter); celery trimmings; carrots tops; green bean tips; corn cobs; parsley, cilantro, or other herb stems; broccoli stalks; pea pods; and mushroom parings. I use only organic vegetables for all types of stock, as added chemicals, particularly when concentrated, lessen the flavor and the healthfulness of a stock.

I always add a strip of kombu to stock. It contains a natural glutamic acid and, like monosodium glutamate, acts as a tenderizer and a flavor enhancer but, unlike MSG, does so healthfully.

Whenever the oven is on, I pop in a couple of onions, skin and all, and other whole root vegetables, such as carrots, turnips, rutabagas, or burdock. I bake them for an hour or even a little more. I hold them in the fridge for a day or two if I'm not immediately making stock.

I have used the pressure cooker occasionally for a quick stock, but my favorite method is to simmer gently, uncovered, for a long period until the water is reduced by one quarter. In winter I put the stockpot on the back of the wood stove, the cooler part, and let its aroma perfume the house for hours. I once tested a vegetable stock, tasting it every hour for up to eight hours. The richest, mellowest stock was the six-hour stock. After that the vegetables no longer had flavor.

Preheat the oven to 375°F.

Place the onions and carrots on a baking sheet and roast for 1 hour and 15 minutes. Remove from the oven and cut lengthwise in half. Put in a stockpot with the remaining ingredients, place over high heat, and bring to a boil. Lower the heat to a bare simmer. Simmer for at least 2 hours or up to 6 hours. Strain through a fine sieve or double thickness of cheesecloth. (May be stored, tightly covered, in the refrigerator for up to 2 days or in the freezer for up to 2 months. Freeze in 1-cup containers for easy use.)

Note: To flavor a clear stock, simmer it with a fresh bouquet garni. Stuff a leek leaf or fill a celery or fennel stalk with sprigs of parsley, thyme, and other fresh herbs. Tie with cotton thread or string, leaving a long tail for easy removal, and submerge the bouquet. Remove before serving.

Chicken Stock

✹

Makes about 5 cups

*2 pounds chicken carcasses, necks,
 and/or wings*

1 recipe Vegetable Stock (page 364)

Parsley, for lining the pot

*When making chicken, meat, or fish stock, I always layer the bottom of the
stockpot with parsley, which acts as a sieve to trap sediment.*

Roast the chicken with the onion and carrot. Drain off any
fat. Line the stockpot with parsley. Add the roasted chicken
and vegetables and the remaining ingredients, as listed in
the recipe for Vegetable Stock. Simmer as directed in the recipe for
Vegetable Stock. Strain all but the last ½ cup or so of liquid. Refrigerate for at least 4 hours, or until the fat has risen to the top. Remove
the fat and store the stock as directed in the recipe for Vegetable
Stock.

Fish Stock

Use any lean mild-flavored fish for this. Throw in shrimp shells if you have them. (Like the vegetable scraps, the shells can be frozen until ready to use.) Do not use any strongly flavored vegetables in this stock.

Line the stockpot with parsley. Add the fish and stock ingredients, as listed in the recipe for Vegetable Stock. Simmer, uncovered, for 15 minutes. Strain all but the last ¹/₂ cup or so of liquid. Store the stock as directed in the recipe for Vegetable Stock.

Makes about 5 cups

Parsley, for lining the pot
2 pounds whitefish bones with heads
1 recipe Vegetable Stock (page 364)

Shiitake Dashi Stock

✿

Makes 6 cups

1 strip (6 inches) kombu
3 dried shiitake mushrooms
6½ cups water

The traditional Japanese dashi is made of kombu and hana-katsuo, or fish flakes. I enjoy it the traditional way on occasion but usually substitute shiitake mushrooms for the fish for a flavor that is more pleasing to Western palates.

Soak the kombu and shiitakes in the water for at least 30 minutes or, preferably, for several hours or overnight. Remove the shiitakes, cut off and discard the stems, and thinly slice the caps. Return the caps to the water and heat, uncovered, over medium heat. Remove the kombu just before the water boils. Reduce the heat and simmer for 5 minutes. Remove the mushrooms from the broth. Reserve the kombu and shiitake for another use. (May be stored, tightly covered, in the refrigerator for up to 3 days.)

Tofu Mayonnaise

I learned how to make this mayonnaise from the remarkable couple William Shurtleff and Akiko Aoyagi in the late 1970s, when they were on a cross-country tour introducing soy products.

Hold the tofu over a colander to catch any bits that might fall off and squeeze in both hands to press out extra water. Combine the tofu, lemon juice, oil, salt, pepper, mustard, and cayenne in a food processor and process for 10 seconds, or until smooth. Let stand for 30 minutes before serving. (May be stored, covered, in the refrigerator for 2 to 3 days.)

VARIATIONS: Substitute ½ cup soy milk for the tofu and increase the oil to ½ cup.

Add 2 tablespoons minced fresh herbs, such as parsley, chives and/or cilantro, after the mayonnaise is blended. Pulse in the herbs and let stand for 30 minutes.

Makes about 1 cup

6 ounces firm tofu, packed in water

2 tablespoons fresh lemon juice or white vinegar

2 tablespoons extra virgin olive oil

½ teaspoon sea salt, or 2 teaspoons soy sauce, or 1 tablespoon red miso (see Note)

Dash of ground white pepper

¼ to ½ teaspoon dry mustard

Pinch of cayenne

Note: Top-quality soy sauce and miso are available in Asian markets and natural foods stores.

How to Peel Tomatoes

❦

In certain dishes, peeled tomatoes give a more elegant result. Peeling is easy to do.

Bring water to a boil in a medium saucepan. Immerse the tomato in the water for 1 minute. Remove with a slotted spoon and plunge into cold water. Drain and peel. To seed, cut in half through the belly and gently squeeze each half over a bowl.

Clabbered Soy Milk

You can clabber soy milk (but not rice milk) to use as a substitute for buttermilk in baked goods. Clabbered soy milk gives a more tender crumb in baking than milk or soy milk.

To make 1 cup clabbered soy milk, add 1 tablespoon lemon juice to 1 cup soy milk and set aside for about 5 minutes, or until it clabbers. For ½ cup clabbered soy milk, use 1 ½ teaspoons lemon juice. For ¾ cup, use 2 teaspoons lemon juice.

Glossary

Arrowroot A clear thickening agent from the root of a tropical plant of the same name. Substitute it measure for measure for cornstarch, a highly refined product. Available in the bulk section of natural foods stores and in the spice section of supermarkets.

Barley miso See Miso.

Brown rice vinegar Handcrafted, organic, unrefined vinegar traditionally fermented from brown rice is the Asian equivalent of balsamic vinegar in terms of subtle complexity of flavor. See page 171 for additional information..

Butter An excellent unrefined fat. Unlike vegetable oils, the essential fatty acids in butter withstand temperatures above 320°F., making butter an ideal choice for baked goods. Unsalted organic butter is available in natural foods stores and specialty markets.

Burdock The taproot of a common weed of the same name. To use burdock, wash it to remove any sand but do not peel. Cook burdock like carrots, for a little more time. It is not used raw. Available in natural foods stores and Asian markets, where it is known as gobo.

Chia seeds (*Salvia columbariae*) Tiny gray-black seeds, as small as poppy seeds and almost as black. They turn mucilaginous when combined with water. Chia seeds were prized by Native American peoples of the Southwest as an endurance food. They are available in natural foods stores.

Daikon A giant white radish a foot or more long. Select daikon that are plump and fresh looking, not withered. Available in natural foods stores, Asian markets, and supermarkets.

Dulse A sea vegetable that grows in frigid zones of the Atlantic and Pacific. Deep red in color with a salty flavor, dulse adds excellent flavor to soups and salads and also may be eaten out of hand. To make dulse flakes, lightly crisp dulse leaves in a 350°F. oven for 10 minutes, or until it starts to brown. Let cool. Tear into pieces and pulverize the leaves in a blender or food processor. Available as dried leaves or in small flakes from natural foods stores.

Flaxseeds Small brown seeds, the size of sesame seeds, with a sweet nutty flavor. The best source of the essential fatty acid Omega 3, flaxseeds are available in natural foods stores.

Ghee Clarified butter used in place of plain butter or oil (see page 357).

Hijiki (*Hizikia fusiforme Okam*) Also called hiziki. An assertively flavored, brown-black marine alga that grows in thin strands several inches long. It is available, dried, in natural foods stores, Asian markets, and by mail order (see page 376).

Koji The Japanese catalyst that ferments amasake, miso, sake, specialty pickles, soy sauce, and tamari soy sauce. It is typically made of steamed rice inoculated with spores of *Aspergillus oryzae*. Koji is available in the refrigerated section of natural foods stores, some Asian markets, and by mail order (see page 376). It is possible, but laborious, to make your own koji with a starter from Gem Cultures (see page 377).

Kombu A versatile sea vegetable that acts as tenderizer and flavor enhancer. The main ingredient of monosodium glutamate (MSG), glutamic acid, was originally synthesized from kombu. Kombu's naturally occurring glutamic acid is remarkably healthful. Kombu is a superior source of minerals. It comes in dried strips that triple in volume when wet. Add a small piece (2 to 3 inches) to grains, beans, soups, stews, and vegetable dishes. Available in natural foods stores and Asian markets.

Lemongrass A common tropical grass with a strong citrus flavor, used to flavor soups and sauces. Trim away the outer dry leaves and bruise or mince the core and bulb or add it whole like a bay leaf and remove it before serving. When I see lemongrass with tight, firm, and fragrant leaves and bulbs, I buy several stalks and store a few in the refrigerator to use within the week and freeze the rest, tightly wrapped, for up to 4 months. If lemongrass is unavailable, substitute lemon zest and a few drops of Ginger Juice (page 360). Available fresh or frozen in Asian markets and increasingly in supermarkets.

Mirin An Asian cooking wine, containing 13 to 14 percent alcohol. It is brewed and fermented from sweet rice, a yeast starter called koji, and water. The quality of mirin available varies widely. I favor one naturally brewed from sweet brown rice. Available in natural foods stores.

Miso A fermented paste of soy, salt, and a grain. Miso varies in color from buff to chocolate brown, depending on the ingredients and length of aging. Each type has its own distinct flavor, ranging from sweet to savory. If you're new to miso, I recommend starting with a light-colored variety. Unpasteurized miso is best. It can be stored in the refrigerator for many months. Available in natural foods stores.

New Mexican chili Also known as Anaheim or Hatch chili, this is the most widely used of the green chilies. Its heat scale runs from mild to hot. The state vegetable of New Mexico, this chili is primarily grown in the Hatch, New Mexico, area.

Nori A sea vegetable ideal for wrapping rice and other tasty morsels. It comes in thin black or, when toasted, greenish-brown sheets. To toast nori, slowly wave it over an open flame or the burner of an electric stove. Or buy toasted nori. Available in Asian markets and natural foods stores.

Nuoc nam A sauce made of fermented fish, salt, and water. Available in Asian markets.

Oil Unrefined oils are preferred because they are full flavored. I favor extra virgin olive oil and unrefined sesame oil, which of all the unrefined oils contain the highest percentage of those natural antioxidants that help extend their shelf life. Refrigerate unrefined oils except olive oil. Unrefined oils are available in natural foods stores.

Rice syrup This mildly sweet syrup, with the consistency of honey, is made of rice fermented with enzymes from sprouted barley. Its flavor is at its best concentrated as for Honey Caramel Corn (page 54) or as a topping for toast and waffles rather than in baked goods. Store it on the shelf, and if it thickens, place the jar in a pot with an inch of water and simmer it until the syrup softens. It is available in natural foods stores and by mail order from GoodEats, Gold Mine, Mountain Ark, or Natural Lifestyle (see page 377).

Sea salt A naturally occurring salt. Be discerning about salt. A pinch of good sea salt in any dish enhances rather than detracts from its flavor. I do not recommend the sea salt found in bulk bins at natural foods stores or the inexpensive "natural" brands. The premiere salt is Celtic salt.

Soy milk Approximation of cow's milk. May be substituted for milk in any recipe, measure for measure. Soy milk may be clabbered (see page 371). There's a wide selection of quality milk substitutes at natural foods stores. I've not sampled the milk substitutes found in supermarkets, but I've read their labels and passed them by. Experiment with several brands until you find one that best suits your palate. Available at natural foods stores, Asian markets, and some supermarkets.

Sucanat A sweetener made from dehydrated organic cane juice. It contains all of the cane's minerals and gives depth and character to foods rather than just the sweet taste of refined white or brown sugar. Note, however, that its amber color tints white or light-colored foods. Available in natural foods stores.

Tamari soy sauce A naturally fermented seasoning made with soy, sea salt, and water. Tamari's high glutamic acid content adds a depth of flavor to cooked foods. Available at natural foods stores and many supermarkets.

Tempeh An Indonesian soy food, made of cooked and fermented soy beans bound together by a dense cottony culture (*Rhizopus* mold) into compact white cakes or patties. Tempeh cakes are about ³/₄ inch thick and are available refrigerated or frozen in natural foods stores. The cakes are usually sliced and fried or grilled until the surface is crisp and golden. Tempeh may also be steamed.

Tofu A traditional Asian food made from the pressed curds of coagulated soy milk. Available in supermarkets and even corner groceries, as well as natural foods stores and Asian markets, tofu is an inexpensive, healthful, and versatile protein source. Refrigerated water-packed tofu (packaged individually, not in bulk) is superior to shelf-stable tofu. Once you open the package, store the remaining tofu in water in a sealed container for up to 1 week.

Umeboshi Immature Japanese plums fermented with salt and shiso (beefsteak leaf); also a seasoning agent made from them. Umeboshi has a potent sour and salty flavor. It comes as whole umeboshi plums with pits, and as paste. Available in natural foods stores.

Ume vinegar A pink liquid that salt draws from fermenting umeboshi. Technically it is not a vinegar since it contains salt, but it may be substituted for vinegar and salt in any recipe. Umeboshi vinegar imparts a light citrus flavor that especially enhances salad dressings and steamed vegetables. Available in natural foods stores.

Wakame A variety of kelp imported from Japan. A popular soup ingredient, it may also be used as a vegetable or in salad. When roasted and crumbled, it makes a tasty condiment. Wakame comes dried in fronds or in flakes. Rehydrate the fronds by soaking in water for 5 minutes, cut out the center stipe, and cut the frond to the desired size. Flaked wakame can be added directly to soups without rehydrating. Alaria, a domestic seaweed, is similar in use and flavor to wakame; the two may be used interchangeably. Available in natural foods stores. Wakame is also available in Asian markets.

Wasabi Often called Japanese horseradish, though not related to horseradish. Wasabi is usually found powdered in foil envelopes or small tins. Commercial-quality powdered wasabi often contains green dye. To reconstitute, stir 1 tablespoon wasabi powder into 2 tablespoons warm water. Let stand at room temperature for 10 minutes before using. Available in natural foods stores.

Zest The grated, thin, colored skin of a lemon or orange, which contains a high concentration of citrus oils and is more flavorful than the citrus juice itself. Finely grated citrus zest is used as a flavoring agent. Use only organic citrus to avoid toxic chemical residues. Grate the peel on the finest-grade grater, removing just the first layer and not the underlying bitter-tasting white pith. One large orange yields about 2 tablespoons of grated zest. One large lemon yields about 1 tablespoon of grated zest.

Mail-Order Sources

Specific Grains and Grain Products

Barley
Western Trails, Inc.
P.O. Box 460
Bozeman, MT 59771
406-587-5489
C. R. "Bud" Clem sells unusual whole barley varieties including bronze, black, and gold. Also sells beans.

Buckwheat
Birkett Mills
163 Main Street
Penn Yan, NY 14527
315-536-3311
FAX 315-536-6740
The buckwheat people. Stoneground flour, buckwheat groats, and varying grades of grits. Free recipes upon request. Price list is available for mail order.

For soba gome, the specialty heirloom buckwheat, see Mountain Ark.

Corn
Col. Sanchez Foods
P.O. Box 5848
Santa Monica, CA 90409
310-313-6769
Organic yellow and blue corn masa, tortilla press, tamales, and cookbook.

John Cope's Food Products
P.O. Box 419
Rheems, PA 17570-0419
717-367-5142
FAX 717-367-7317
Dried sweet corn, a traditional Pennsylvania Dutch product, available from Cope's since 1900.

Orlando A. Casados
Ranch O. Casados
P.O. Box 1149
San Juan Pueblo, NM 87566
505-852-4482
Atole, chaquegue (toasted white corn), blue corn masa, white horno chicos, sweet corn horno, corn husks, and chili products.

Mesquite
ProNatura
Mexican Association for Conservation of Nature
240 East Limberlost
Tucson, AZ 85705
520-887-1188
Mesquite meal available with a membership. Recipe booklet included.

Quinoa
White Mountain Farm, Inc.
8890 Lane 4 North
Mosca, CO 81164
719-378-2436
Organic domestic and black quinoa.

Rice
Lundberg Family Farms
P.O. Box 369
Richvale, CA 95974
916-882-4551
FAX 916-882-4500
Wide assortment of rices, including specialty varieties.

Wheat
Oriental Pastry & Grocery Co.
170-172 Atlantic Avenue
Brooklyn, NY 11201-5604
718-875-7687
FAX 718-875-0776
Specialty Middle Eastern spices and wheat products, including green wheat, couscous, and four grades of bulgur.

Wild Rice
Leech Lake Wild Rice Co.
Route 3, Box 100
Cass Lake, MN 56633
218-335-8317
Organic wild rice that is hand harvested, prepared, and packaged by the Leech Lake Indian Reservation.

Manitok Wild Rice
Box 97
Callaway, MN 56521-0097
800-726-1863
Organic wild rice that is hand harvested, prepared, and packaged by the White Earth Indian Reservation. You may select rice harvested from Squaw Lake, Tamarack Lake, Mitchel Dam, or Rice Lake.

General Grains, Grain Products, and Cookware

Arrowhead Mills
P.O. Box 2059
Hereford, TX 79045-2059
800-749-0730
FAX 806-364-8242
Excellent organic grains and grain products as well as other natural products. Available in supermarkets, natural foods stores, and by mail order.

Gem Cultures
30301 Sherwood Road
Fort Bragg, CA 95437
Starter for making koji.

Gold Mine Natural Food Company
3419 Hancock Street
San Diego, CA 92110-4307
800-475-FOOD
Premier quality organic and heirloom grains, oats rolled fresh to order, mochi, sea salt, and other macrobiotic supplies. The Gold Mine Gazette *(free) includes not only mail-order information for food, books, quality cookware, and grain mills but also timely and informative articles about quality products, visits with growers, and other interesting information.*

GoodEats
5 Louise Drive
Ivyland, PA 18947
800-490-0044
FAX 215-443-7087
Your shop-at-home natural foods store. Specializing in organic grains.

Grain and Salt Society
P.O. Box 1935
Asheville, NC 28815
800-867-7258
Natural stone Samap mills and best quality sea salt. Organic, ground-to-order wheat, rye, and other flours.

King Arthur Flour
   Baker's Catalogue
P.O. Box 876
Norwich, VT 05055-0876
800-827-6836
FAX 800-343-3002
All types of flours and baking accessories. Recently introduced a white whole wheat flour made from hard wheat with the germ, bran, and nutrition of 100 percent whole wheat but the light taste and appearance of white flour.

Kushi Foundation Store
Box 7
Becket, MA 01223
413-623-8827
Organic grains, Japanese pasta, cooking equipment, macrobiotic books, and a rice-hulling machine for home use.

Sourdoughs International, Inc.
P.O. Box 1140
Cascade, ID 83611
800-888-9567
Sourdough starters from around the world.

Macrobiotic Company
   of America
799 Old Leicester Highway
Asheville, NC 28806
800-438-4730
Heirloom grains, including soba gome, unpolished Job's tears (hato mugi), and kibi millet (foxtail millet), and other organic grains, beans, sea salt, sea vegetables, condiments, and quality macrobiotic supplies and cookware. Minimum order: $250. See Mountain Ark for smaller orders.

Mountain Ark Trading Co.
799 Old Leicester Highway
Asheville, NC 28806
800-643-8909
Minimum order: $35. Same items as Macrobiotic Company.

Natural Lifestyle Magazine and
   Mail-Order Market
16 Lookout Drive
Asheville, NC 28804
800-752-2775
Quality common and uncommon grains, staples, and cookware.

Precision Foods
Box 2067 Highway 6 West
Tupelo, MI 38803
800-647-8170
Pickling lime.

Shiloh Farms
P.O. Box 97
Sulphur Springs, AR 72768-0097
501-298-9631
800-362-6832
Organic grains and grain products.

Sourcepoint Organic Seeds
1647 2725 Road
Cedaredge, CO 81413
800-927-2527, ext. 4383
Heirloom grains, mesquite meal, and a mesquite pinole mix. Organic heirloom seeds for gardeners of amaranth, quinoa, canihua (a quinoa relative), buckwheat, finger millet, foxtail millet, hull-less barley, wheat, einkorn, sorghum, and corn varieties. Catalogue available for $2.75.

Sprout House
314 Main Street
Great Barrington, MA 01230
800-777-6887
Organic buckwheat and wheat with a high germination rate suitable for

sprouting. Books on and equipment for sprouting

Walnut Acres
Walnut Acres Road
Penns Creek, PA 17862
800-344-9025
Good organic grains, granola, and cereal blends. Household items and prepared cakes.

Wayne Carlson
The Tef Company
P.O. Box A
Caldwell, Idaho 83606
208-454-3330

Well Spring Natural Food Co.
P.O. Box 2473
Amherst, MA 01004
800-578-5301
Grains, flour, pasta. More than 1,000 macrobiotic, natural, and organic products.

Stoneground Flours and Grits

Brewster River Mill
Mill Street
Jefferson, VT 05464
802-644-2987
Organic products ground into flours and meals at a historic gristmill.

Falls Mills
134 Falls Mill Road
Belvidere, TN 37306
615-469-7161
Corn grits and meal. Buckwheat, rice, wheat, and rye flour. Price list on request.

Kenyon Corn Meal Company
P.O. Box 221
West Kingston, RI 02892-0221
401-783-4054
Yellow, blue, and white cornmeal, barley, oat, buckwheat, whole wheat, spelt, kamut, and graham flour plus miller's bran. Many organic. Price list on request.

Morgan's Mills
168 Payson Road
Union, ME 04862
800-373-2756
Thirteen flours. Almost all organic. Price list available.

New Hope Mills
RFD #2
Moravia, NY 13118
315-497-0783
Variety of wheat flours: bread, pastry, graham, and whole wheat. Cornmeal, oat bran, buckwheat and rye flour. Buckwheat grits.

Old Mill of Guilford
1340 N.C. 68 North
Oak Ridge, NC 27310
910-643-4783
Grist mill ground buckwheat, rye, and whole wheat flour. Cornmeal, corn grits, rolled oats, steel-cut oats, wheat bran, and wheat germ. For price list, send a stamped, self-addressed envelope.

Valencia Flour Mill
74 Mill Road
Box 210
Jarales, NM 87203
505-864-0305
Tortilla flour, whole wheat flour, wheat bran, and wheat germ. Regional flour. The tortilla flour, made from a low-gluten hard red winter wheat flour, makes a soft dough which facilitates rolling and doesn't shrink back on the board during repeated hard rolling actions. Mill is not stone, but this is a fifty-year-old flour mill.

Bibliography

Here are key book titles that I rely upon and recommend.

Alford, Jeffrey, and Naomi Duguid. *Flatbreads and Flavors*. New York: William Morrow, 1995.

Algar, Ayla. *Classical Turkish Cooking: Traditional Turkish Food for the American Kitchen*. New York: HarperCollins, 1991.

Baggett, Nancy. *The International Cookie Cookbook*. New York: Stewart, Tabori & Chang, 1988.

Barron, Rosemary. *Flavors of Greece*. New York: William Morrow, 1991.

Batmanglij, Najmieh. *Food of Life: A Book of Ancient Persian and Modern Iranian Cooking and Ceremonies*. Washington, D.C.: Mage Publishers, 1990.

Bayless, Rick, with Deann Gruen Bayless. *Authentic Mexican: Regional Cooking from the Heart of Mexico*. New York: William Morrow, 1987.

Belleme, Jan and John. *Cooking with Japanese Foods: A Guide to the Traditional Natural Foods of Japan*. Brookline, MA: East West Health Books, 1986.

Child, Julia. *The Way to Cook*. New York: Alfred A. Knopf, 1989.

Colbin, Annemarie. *The Natural Gourmet*. New York: Ballantine Books, 1989.

Devi, Yamuna. *Lord Krishna's Cuisine: The Art of Indian Vegetarian Cooking*. New York: E. P. Dutton, 1987.

Del Conte, Anna. *The Italian Pantry*. New York: Harper & Row, 1990.

DeWitt, Dave, and Nancy Gerlach. *The Whole Chile Pepper Book*. Boston: Little, Brown, 1990.

Duran-Weatherman, Patricia, R. D., and Linda Reineke, R. D. *Food Traditions of New Mexico*. Albuquerque, NM: Video Art Journal Ltd., 1991.

Farley, Marta Pisetska. *Festive Ukrainian Cooking*. Pittsburgh, PA: University of Pittsburgh Press, 1990.

Gelles, Carol. *The Complete Whole Grain Cookbook*. New York: Donald Fine, 1989.

Goldstein, Darra. *The Georgian Feast*. New York: HarperCollins, 1993.

Leader, Daniel, and Judith Blahnik. *Bread Alone: Bold Fresh Loaves from Your Own Hands*. New York: William Morrow, 1993.

Levy, Faye. *Faye Levy's International Jewish Cookbook*. New York: Warner Books, 1991.

London, Sheryl and Mel. *The Versatile Grain and the Elegant Bean*. New York: Simon & Schuster, 1992.

Mesfin, Daniel J. *Exotic Ethiopian Cooking*. Falls Church, VA: Ethiopian Cookbook Enterprises, 1990.

Molokhovets, Elena. *Classic Russian Cooking*. Translated by Joyce Toomre. Bloomington, IN: Indiana University Press, 1992.

Morningstar, Amadea. *Ayurvedic Cooking for Westerners: Familiar Western Foods Prepared with Ayurvedic Principles*. Twin Lakes, WI: Lotus Press, 1995.

Muller, Frederick R. *La Comida: The Foods, Cooking, and Traditions of the Upper Rio Grande*. Boulder, CO: Pruett Publishing Company, 1995.

Pitchford, Paul. *Healing with Whole Foods: Oriental Traditions and Modern Nutrition*. Berkeley, CA: North Atlantic Books, 1993.

Rojas-Lombardi, Felipe. *The Art of South American Cooking*. New York: HarperCollins, 1991.

Sass, Lorna J. *Recipes from an Ecological Kitchen: Healthy Meals for You and the Planet*. New York: William Morrow, 1992.

Simeti, Mary Taylor. *Pomp and Sustenance: Twenty-Five Centuries of Sicilian Food*. New York: Alfred A. Knopf, 1989.

Tsuji, Shizuo. *Japanese Cooking: A Simple Art*. Tokyo: Kodansha International, 1980.

Udesky, James. *The Book of Soba*. Tokyo: Kodansha International, 1988.

Wolfert, Paula. *Couscous and Other Good Food from Morocco*. New York: Harper & Row, 1973.

Wood, Ed. *World Sourdoughs from Antiquity*. Cascade, ID: Sinclair Publishing, 1989.

Young, Kay. *Wild Seasons: Gathering and Cooking Wild Plants of the Great Plains*. Lincoln, NB: University of Nebraska Press, 1993.

Index

❦

Page numbers in **boldface** refer to recipes.

nutritional value of, 203
selection of, 204
steamed, **205**
storage of, 204
Judith Choate's kasha paprikás, **131**
juice, ginger, **360**

kabocha, harvest, **190**
kamut (*Triticum durum*), 237, 239
    angel hair pasta with scorched
        tomato sauce, **257**
    coarse-grain sourdough rye, **307–308**
    cultivation of, 243
    flour, 271
    grilled bitter melon with coconut,
        251–252
    Jacques de Langre's pain de méteil,
        305
    pasta, 246–247
    pita bread, **280**
    salad, Mediterranean, **254**
    steamed, **244**
    stuffed with vegetables and fruit, **259**
    see also wheat
kasha:
    and beet salad, **125**
    croquettes, savory, **130**
    filling, for pirozhki, **121**
    knishes with rosemary, **122**
    paprikás, Judith Choate's, **131**
    steamed, **115**
    stuffing, roast duck with chestnut,
        parsnip and, **127**
    see also buckwheat
kiwi sauce, quinoa tarts with, **105**
knishes, kasha with rosemary, **122**
kuchen, barley, with hazelnut streusel,
    228

lace wafers, Scottish, **329**
ladoos, see alegria
lamb:
    -fennel filling, for pirozhki, **121**
    gingered, and quinoa in phyllo, **87**
leavened breads, 272–273
leavening, sourdough, 272–273
lemon coconut rice salad, **187**
linguine, masa, with lobster, fresh corn,
    and tomato sauce, **46**
loaf:
    buckwheat, **128**
    harvest, 282–283

lobster, masa linguine with fresh corn,
    tomato sauce and, **46**
locro, **223**
long-grain brown rice, feta and mint,
    193
long-grain white rice:
    basmati, steamed, **179**
    soubise, **194**
    steamed, **178**

mâche, quinoa and sweet potato salad
    with, **94**
madeleines, millet, with crème fraîche
    and caviar, **149**
mango and wild rice salad, **13**
marjoram, corn tortillas with, **58–59**
marmalade torte, couscous, **261**
masa, 27, 29
    linguine with lobster, fresh corn, and
        tomato sauce, **46**
masa harina, 27, 29
    and turnip flatbread, griddle-cooked,
        57
mayonnaise, tofu, **369**
measuring homemade freshly ground
    flour, 272
Mediterranean kamut salad, **254**
medium-grind bulgur, **248**
melon, bitter, with coconut kamut,
    grilled, **251–252**
mesquite (*Prosopis veluntina*), 67–69
    nutritional value of, 67
    selection of, 68
    storage of, 68
    Tarahumara pinole mix, **69**
    uses of, 67–68
milk:
    clabbered soy, **371**
    coconut, **354**
millet (*Panicum miliaceum*), 141–165
    apricot breakfast cakes, **164**
    bread, crunchy, **163**
    buckwheat and coconut waffles,
        overnight, **165**
    and butternut squash cakes, grilled,
        158
    cultivation of, 141–143
    flour, 142
    horseshoe cookies, **162**
    madeleines with crème fraîche and
        caviar, **149**
    niçoise, **153**

nutritional value of, 143
onions stuffed with sun-dried
    tomatoes and, **154**
orange-pecan, **160**
original polenta, the, **146**
Persian yogurt soup with garlic and
    mint, **151**
polenta, red radishes, water chestnuts
    and tofu on, **155**
quick-cooking cracked, **145**
quinoa and burdock pilaf, **159**
red sunset soup, **150**
salmon rolls, **148**
selection of, 142
shortcake with hot caramelized
    plums, **161**
steamed, **144**
storage of, 142
stuffed artichokes, Sicilian style, **147**
and sweet potato terrine with garam
    masala–mushroom sauce,
    156–157
watercress salad with gingered poppy
    dressing, **152**
minestrone with spelt (minestrone con
    farro), **253**
mint:
    and feta rice, **193**
    Persian yogurt soup with garlic and,
        151
miso, 220
    -walnut topping, **363**
molletes, thumbprint, **53**
Mom's wild rice stuffing, **17**
muffins:
    buckwheat pumpkin, **139**
    corn quinoa raspberry, **61**
mugicha (iced barley tea), **233**
mush, cornmeal, **34**
mushrooms:
    barley risotto with blue cheese and,
        226
    Christmas hens with spicy barley,
        224
    cold zucchini soup with quinoa and,
        92
    cream of shiitake and broccoli soup,
        320
    –garam masala sauce, **157**
    –garam masala sauce, millet and
        sweet potato terrine with,
        156–157